THE BLISSFUL
ABIDANCE SERIES

THE BLISSFUL ABIDANCE SERIES

AN ANTHOLOGY OF ADVAITA BOOKS

(VOLUME TWO)

by

FLOYD HENDERSON

CONTENTS

BOOK SIX OF SIX IN "THE BLISSFUL ABIDANCE SERIES"

When REALITY Is Overlaid Upon the RELATIVE

A NOTE TO READERS

THIS anthology of six books by Floyd Henderson contains the volumes that make up what has been called "The Blissful Abidance Series" for those seeking Realization via the Advaita teachings.

For those who have studied any of the various types of yoga and who have studied either Traditional Advaita Vedanta, Neo-Advaita, Neo-Vedanta, or Pseudo Advaita: the author of this book is a disciple of Sri Nisargadatta Maharaj so he uses the Direct Path Method of teaching along with the Nisarga (Natural) Yoga, all shared in simple, everyday English.

Also available now is "The Advanced Seekers' Series" (Volume One). Visit www.floydhenderson.com for details or to purchase.

Also, all of his books are available at
FloydHenderson.com
and many are available in eBook format at
amazon.com
or
amazon.co.uk
or
amazon.de

FOREWORD

WHEN I attended a three-day Advaita Retreat at Floyd Henderson's lakeside "loft" in Texas in 2009, it was the culmination of over two decades of seeking. After that, I was no longer a "seeker."

Prior to traveling to Texas, I had already participated in Floyd's on-line Advaita Classes, which entailed reading all of his books, some of which are anthologized in this volume. Of course, being a "good spiritual giant" at the time, I tried to start the Advaita Classes at the advanced stage. Floyd suggested I start at the beginning, which was - of course - the proper manner.

As a "recovering" Baptist with a primary Type Six Personality, I was an unlikely seeker. Floyd's teacher, Sri Nisargadatta Maharaj, said that only one in ten million seekers would ever Realize. Type Sixes and those suffering from religious or spiritual intoxication are the most unlikely to be in that miniscule percentage.

After several years of praying and taking communion in the Methodist Church, I took up fasting, chanting, and meditating in the Asian tradition. When none of that worked, I tried to mix Methodist worship and Zen meditation. That was very weird and the chaos of dualistic existence did not end.

Fortunately, I came across Maharaj's book, "I AM THAT" at the Zen Center during my meditation phase. Something about it resonated, and in the years that followed, as I continued to seek, Maharaj's message was always returning.

I began to search for "western advaita" on-line. I found Floyd Henderson's website and began to follow his Nisarga (or Natural) Yoga pointers. Today, as a result of studying Advaita and Nisarga Yoga with Floyd, my existence is no longer ruled by dual thought, personality, and emotion. The meaning of the statement "I Am That; I Am" is understood.

The understanding brought about by following the pointers shared by Floyd is that we have become separated from our Original Nature by seven degrees or stages. This separation is brought about by the conditioning, programming, acculturation, and domestication that are inherent in coming of age in a culture characterized by duality. We accumulate concepts, ideas, and beliefs, all dual in nature and all untrue; in other words, we fall under the influence of learned ignorance.

Utilizing the Direct Path Method and offering the Nisarga Yoga, Floyd Henderson reverses the process and takes the protégé step-by-step back through the stages of separation, discarding the learned ignorance in the order in which it was received. This ignorance includes false identifications and spiritual concepts and religious dogma. There is no longer any need for prayer, worship, communion, chanting, or meditation (as it is typically understood). If the pointers are followed, the protégé can realize her or his Original Nature and live naturally, quietly, and peacefully without the chaos of dual thoughts or the drama of emotional intoxication.

I'll let Floyd tell you about the stages, degrees of separation, and pointers in detail by way of the content of the books in this anthology. The pointers in this collection (along with the readiness) are all that are needed to begin following the Nisargan pointers. Get on with it. Read these books, and if possible, do as I did and visit the "loft" on Lake Conroe. According to Maharaj's estimates, there are only 670 on the planet today that are Fully Realized. Relative living is most enjoyable if you happen to be one of those.

Andrew C. McMaster

Florissant, MO

WHO IS FLOYD HENDERSON?

THE literary tradition is to preface a book with a biographical snapshot of the author as a person. What can be said then, about the Advaitin Teacher, who has moved beyond personal biography?

To describe the person or the personal (the date of birth, the nationality, the job, the interests, the home, the child, the books read, the path followed) is to describe the attributes that actually take us further away from uncovering the teacher's identity.

The reality is that this "Who Is ..." question itself brings us to deeper and more authentic questions. What is this understanding in which the teacher resides? The state of Realization is not different from teacher to teacher. That Self-Knowledge is unchanging. In this way, there is no difference between a Nisargadatta Maharaj, a Floyd Henderson, or any other Realized teacher.

The Realisation of SELF means the shattering of the shell of separation so that the non-dual nature of Reality is directly known. How can this be different from person to person? Only in the ABSENCE of the person is this nature revealed. In this way, Floyd Henderson invites us to strip away all that is personal, all that is dualistic, all that separates us from this understanding of Oneness – from our True Selves.

The summative statement "I AM THAT; I AM" describes that under-standing of SELF in absolute terms as well as its expression in the relative. Floyd Henderson is THAT – just like all human beings; however, Floyd is fixed unshak-ably in this understanding, so all functioning, relatively speaking, flows directly from this SELF-Knowledge.

In this way, the biographical details (such as, "born" in Louisiana; moved to Texas; worked as a teacher and business owner over several decades before taking early retirement to write; father of a daughter named Ashley; current resident in the community of Walden on Lake Conroe in Texas; years of seeking followed by twenty-five months in the forest dweller stage and experiencing a vision that resulted in the dramatic peripetia or flash of Realization; functioning as a Direct

Path, Nisargan teacher; and author of over forty Advaita books) are the attributes or flavourings which coloured the pure consciousness in the particular shape and form at the relative level.

Yet, these attributes are false ingredients. They cannot provide a true answer to the question "Who is Floyd Henderson?" because he recognizes no who-ness at all ... believes in no "who" that is living "here" at all. He once explained it this way when asked if he was ever bothered by people:

"... How could persons possibly bother Me? They do not have even the slightest clue about where I truly live. Only a few on the entire planet called "earth" have a clue. Some might enter what is called 'floyd's house' or 'floyd's home,' but that is not where I live; in fact, 'where' I live has nothing to do with a 'where' at all.

In this regard, there is actually only the 'how.' 'How' I abide is as the aware-ness, as the Original Nature, as the natural state which has no boundaries, which has no defining traits, and which does not change. 'How' I abide is without conditions or conditioning, without qualifications, and without limitations.

I can seem to be 'here' one second and 'there' the next, but that is about 'how-ness,' not any actual 'here-ness' or 'there-ness.' I am not confined to a space or form; furthermore, I can enter other spaces and forms, and do so regularly (as might happen the instant You read these words).

Abiding beyond consciousness and beyond beingness and beyond non-being-ness, I can span the globe ... I can span the universe ... I have spanned all universes. Yet such 'while manifested' spannings seldom happen anymore, requiring far more energy than is worth the effort, and it most assuredly need not happen with You.

As for Me, abidance will continue to happen in a whole and unadulterated and unambiguous manner until the consciousness unmanifests. Until that happens, then abidance will happen as Reality is overlaid on the relative without exception. When the consciousness unmanifests, then the drop shall enter the ocean of energy from which it came and will span the Absolute; Awareness shall be, but aware of-ness shall not. Later, other universes might be spanned as well, or might not. Yet all of that is stated, so it, too, cannot be the Truth which You know but do not yet know that You know. Tap into the source and know Truth, but even then, do not suppose that You will be able to express Truth in words."

Thus, Floyd describes the AM-ness regarding "floyd" as a "composite unity" of an elemental plant food body that is circulating air and that is temporarily housing the manifested consciousness.

The THAT-ness he sees as a field of energy from which the conscious-energy manifests and to which it will return.

As for identification with any WHO-ness, he discarded that when identification with the Nothingness came, followed eventually by not even identifying with Nothing - or anything else.

Louise Sterling

Cape Town, South Africa

EDITOR'S NOTE

BEFORE I found the Advaita teachings, both my seeking and my life were totally disorganized. I had read over two hundred books during my search which began around the age of eleven or twelve. All of the content of those books was very confusing. Why?

While some presented teachings that seemed in the beginning to be of value, in the end they proved useless because none of the pointers were organized in a way to offer in a step-by-step manner the route that had to be followed to move away from identification with the false "I" and return to My Original Nature.

It became clear that - in my case - I required a teacher that could offer such an explanation and that could be available to answer my many questions along the way.

Though my reading left me a supposed "expert" is subjects dealing with the brain and the mind and psychology and psychiatry, there was no understanding at all of the functioning of the totality.

So my searching continued for many more years, moving from one book to the next and from one religion to the next and from one spiritual movement to the next and from one philosophy to the next. I studied Taoism, Christianity, Hinduism, Buddhism - you name it - I studied it.

It is suspected that many may have traveled as arduous a road as the one I traveled, but few likely traveled a more arduous route than the one I traveled during my years of seeking.

The searching in one venue after another continued until an acquaintance shared certain profound pointers that seemed to resonance deeply within me.I asked what he was talking about ... asked if the pointers he was sharing were associated with any particular philosophy or religion that I could further investigate. He answered, "What I'm sharing is what is called 'a non-dual perspective'."

"What is that?" I asked.

"Basically, the simplest teaching is that everything is one."

That made little sense, but it did seem to reverberate at some spot deep inside me. Eventually, intuition was re-awakened and there was some sort of "psychic consciousness" that began to vibrate when non-duality pointers were being considered.

After being given some labels for further investigation - specifically, "non-duality" and "Advaita" - it soon became clear that I needed to find a capable Advaita teacher.

The irony was that, as I began searching for a teacher, all of the online sites promoting and ranking various teachers were actually reinforcing duality ... ranking this one as "best" and that one as "good" and that other one as "not so adept." Instead of focusing on how we could eliminate our beliefs in hierarchies and separation and judgment, they were promoting all of those.

So I left the listings and began googling "Advaita" and found a blog site where Floyd Henderson was offering daily postings of non-dual pointers.

I began investigating this guy, wondering who he thought he was to be posting pointers about Advaita. He was not even from the Far East. Worse, my investigations uncovered the fact that this guy lived in Texas.

Being yet embroiled in ego, I asked, "Who does this guy living outside of Houston, Texas think he is ... acting like he 'knows it all' about these teachings?" I concluded, "Heck, I live in Texas. I guarantee I already know as much about non-duality as any other person living in Texas. Who from Texas could offer anything about this eastern philosophy?"

Then I clicked the link for the retreats he offered and saw that, of even greater offense, he wanted to charge a fee for retreats where he teaches non-duality. (At the time, it did not register that I was not providing free meals to everyone who entered one of the restaurants in the chain I own.)

[NOTE: What Andy is not revealing here is all of the altruistic and philanthropic projects and charities which he has funded for years, offering assistance to the downtrodden and suffering.]

A year would pass, and more and more searching continued, but at least once a week, the name "Floyd Henderson" came into the forefront of consciousness.

As much as I tried to ignore the name, it would not leave me, so after a year of continued seeking even after having first found his name and websites, I finally went back to his Advaita blog site, looked at the cost of a retreat with him, and concluded, differently this time, "Well, actually it really is only a nominal fee he is charging, and he does have to pay his bills."

So it came to me, "What if this guy just might have what you've been looking for all of your life?" I determined that I might as well spend a few dollars - a small amount really in comparison to the fortune I had already spent during decades of seeking and searching ... all with no permanent results at all.

Right now, it is giving me cold chills just reflecting on that decision and what happened afterwards. I had reached a point where I felt as if I were going to pop right out of my skin from all of the suffering and misery and anxiety and stress that had characterized my existence.

For me, it had to get so bad that I became willing and ready - ready to give up all of the ideas and beliefs that had served me not at all and to seek the Truth that was obviously beyond all of the concepts I had ever taken to be the truth.

Eventually, I went to a retreat at Floyd's home and left three days later having found that I was not only willing to give up all of those concepts but had become willing to give up this fear-based "andy" that had been at the root of my problems.

Now, I look back and laugh. Before the time spent in Floyd's home, I hated to wake up in the morning. Now, I can't wait to get up and enjoy every day.

I was raised to believe that Jesus had the answers that people need. At Floyd's retreat, I found out that in many cases, he did, but the answers were not the ones I was taught in church.

I found that "the later Jesus" who returned to Jerusalem was sharing the non-dual, Advaita teachings - teachings I had heard on occasion when I was younger but that no one in the church could or would explain to me when I asked about those statements.

I went to Floyd's that first time with a considerable fear of death (rooted, I would learn, in body and mind and personality identification). He suggested that if I was so afraid of death that the best thing I could do would be to "go ahead and die now."

Of course that was an anger-invoking, shocking comment to hear, but before I left, I understood that I could not die because I was not born - that what he was saying is that my ego(s) and my egotism must "die."

I understood after that retreat that I cannot truly live until this ego - this illusion - dies. To that point, I was entering Floyd's house one morning through the door he leaves open while he is preparing breakfast for participants.

As I entered, I shouted, "Knock knock ... anybody home?" He yelled back, "No." I got it ... I knew exactly what he meant, and that understanding has remained and I have since enjoyed the freedom every day of knowing I am no body ... nobody.

I came to understood that everything merely cycles and that timelines are a fraud, and Floyd also taught me the meaning of every part of his vision, and I learned by way of the eagle the difference in Subject-Object Witnessing and Pure Witnessing.

Why am I making this second anthology available for all seekers to use now and to be available long after "floyd" and "andy" have taken *mahasamadhi* and are "gone"? First, because the books in this anthology offer the step-by-step process by which Realization can happen; secondly, because the books helped me in that undertaking; and thirdly, because they can show seekers how to live blissfully on a daily basis.

I want to preserve Floyd's vision and his writings for all who are seeking. I decided to support the printing of this anthology to make his teachings and methods available - to all that might be interested - because of what happened with me after sitting with Floyd and receiving the message that came by way of his step-by-step method which I realized was exactly what I had been seeking all of my life.

I am taking the action to help make these books available to interested seekers because I now know beyond a shadow of a doubt that if the understanding offered in these books - and Floyd's other books - could come to me, then the understanding can come to almost anyone.

May you allow the pure consciousness to see and receive the content of the works in this anthology and then also receive as a result the blissful freedom that came to me via the content of these and the other writings by Floyd Henderson.

Andrew Gugar, Jr.

Tyler, TX

FROM THE AUTHOR

THIS anthology contains six books that many seekers have used in order to abide blissfully.

The six-book series offers an opportunity for seekers to:

1. understand what bliss is and what bliss is not; and to

2. understand why one must reach a zero-concept, no-mind state if any degree of peace is to manifest; and to

3. understand how to be liberated from the bliss-negating influence of personality; and to

4. understand how to fixate in the bliss rather than fluctuating constantly between states of happiness and unhappiness; and to

5. understand why freedom is built from a position of emptiness and neutrality; and to

6. find how to overlay Reality on the relative so that the relative can be enjoyed.

A synopsis of the six books follows:

BOOK ONE
What BLISS Is and What BLISS Is Not

How many seekers are frustrated by not having attained bliss?

How many seekers think that they have failed or that their teacher has failed when what they believe to be bliss does not manifest or when they think that bliss comes on occasion but does not remain?

Those are the thoughts and beliefs of seekers who are at what Sri Nisargadatta Maharaj called "the kindergarten level of spirituality." How many feel that their goal to become "perfectly spiritual, and thereby perfectly blissful" is being thwarted at every turn?

Maharaj said, "No ambition is spiritual. All ambitions are for the sake of the 'I am'. The ambitions of the so-called Yogis are preposterous. A man's desire for a woman is innocence itself compared to the lusting for an everlasting personal bliss. The mind is a cheat. The more pious it seems, the worse the betrayal."

In the pages of this book, the author explains what bliss is not and what bliss actually is. To understand that distinction is to provide the opportunity to finally relax and take it easy, to understand what Real Love is, and to understand why Maharaj said that "Love is knowing that You Are everything and wisdom is knowing that You Are nothing."

BOOK TWO
THERE'S NO SUCH THING AS "PEACE OF MIND"
(There Is Only Peace if You're Out of Your Mind)

This book leads to the next level of freedom, allowing seekers to transition beyond the mind. The content explores the history of the human brain, including the fact that for millions of years, human and human-like beings functioned without any mind. The book uncovers the ways that the brain evolved over the ages and developed an ability to store and retrieve memories.

It then shows how the original memories were used constructively but how programming and conditioning changed all that and created a "mind" that most often overrules the brain and generates relative-existence harm and destruction.

Additionally, the book shows the way that personality develops during childhood as a means for survival and adaptation but later becomes a liability when those childhood personality traits continue to drive adult thinking and behavior.

Ultimately, the content of the book shows why Advaitin sages for centuries have correctly identified the "problems of the planet" as being rooted in body-mind-personality identification and offers suggestions for being free of all of that nonsense via Realization.

BOOK THREE
LIBERATION
(Attaining Freedom from Personality via Realization)

This book helps remove the next barrier to Realization after body and mind identification have been discarded, namely, personality.

After being freed from identification with the phenomenal body and phenomenal mind, transitioning into the next step begins the process of being freed from identification with personas (that is, false selves, roles, identities, ego-states, etc.) and from being unconsciously controlled by personality traits.

This book studies the nine most basic persona types as identified in the enneagram method and offers the way to be free of the influences of personality (or, as is more often the case, the influence of multiple personalities).

The first part of that process beginning with an understanding of the way that personality generates desires and fears and the way that personality drives thoughts and words and deeds as a subconscious motivator of all three.

BOOK FOUR
Freedom From Shifting Between States of Happiness and Unhappiness

Almost all persons on the planet are seeking. Some few claim to be seeking Realization or enlightenment or an awakening or awareness, but what most are seeking (even those who do not know it) is happiness ... is inner peace.

Some claim to be happy, but dissociated as they are from their true state, they are unable to touch their own reality, much less Reality.

Others claim that they are "happy most of the time." The fact remains, however, that even those will admit that they are happy at times and most unhappy at other times, denying their true state and trapped in the fluctuations between happiness and unhappiness that mark and mar the relative existence of most persons.

Contrary to what the masses believe and what only a few will ever realize is this: there is a way to stabilize, to avoid the fluctuations, to be free of the chaos that so many face and that so many, in fact, seek out as a means to escape the boredom and tedium and monotony which so many have normalized as "just the way it is."

While it might be the way it is, it need not be that way. There is a means by which freedom from the constant shifting between a state of happiness and a state of unhappiness can end, once and for all.

In this book, the author shares the exchanges that took place during a series of satsang sessions when some admitted that the constant shifts have taken their toll and that they were finally seeking stability.

To that end, the source of fluctuations and chaos are discussed and the means by which they can end - once and for all - is offered in detail.

BOOK FIVE
Why You Must Be Empty If You Would Be Full

The content of this book shares a series of satsang exchanges that were conducted via an internet forum. The first session began with this consideration: Advaitins speak of "the drop dissolving into the ocean." Govinda, however, (influenced by Buddhists, the Gelug-pa sect members, Advaitins, et. al.) spoke of the next step: "the ocean slipping into the drop."

The author notes that most try to take their corrupted "mind" and just add some new ideas and new thoughts and new beliefs to it, filtering out or abandoning some former concepts, thinking they then have a pure "mind," and then believing that they can just add some new concepts to replace the old.

Such efforts will always prove to be futile. The entire contents must be discarded if you would "fill the cup" with that which can bring you something with a taste that can be enjoyed. There is no other way than the way of emptiness first, fullness second … no other way than the way of de-accumulation first.

Then, something with a taste of sweetness can come. When all learned ignorance is tossed, then everything that also accompanies ignorance will go. At that point, You will know that You Are as a drop dissolving into the ocean. You are At One with all.

You will have returned to Your original nature … Your original state … merging into that ocean of awareness without aware-of-ness. Call the effect "bliss" if you like, but that is not a state of bliss. A state of bliss is a state in which the bliss is known … is felt. That can only happen NOW, not "later" … only "here," not "there." At the point when You begin to abide as that original state, then nothing is needed, nothing is desired, and the nothingness is relished. You will have tasted the sweet taste of the nectar of immortality;

You will have been healed via the ultimate medicine; You will have returned to that state prior to consciousness; You will have found the source of the seeds of consciousness; and You will abide as That Which Is What Can Make Stability Possible rather than as the consciousness which guarantees fluctuations and instability, dualistic up's and down's, and, yes, even chaos.

The essence is that which is "the root, the foundation, the timeless and spaceless possibility" of what is called during the manifestation "all experience." What seekers would taste is the sweetness of the essence, but they are trying to taste it indirectly by clinging either to body-mind-personality identification or to religious or spiritual personas or to some elevated notions about the value of consciousness.

Maharaj taught that the natural and original state as understood by the Realized "tastes of the pure, uncaused, undiluted bliss." He pointed out that to know the sweetness, You must taste it. Its sweetness cannot be otherwise understood. In this book, the circumstance is not unlike that of a tour guide taking you to a vineyard for a wine tasting.

In this book, You will be guided to "The Vineyard of the Absolute" where the sweetest tastings take place. Here, if you complete a seven-step "journey," the tour will end with a savoring of the only nectar that is Real. Few can complete the "trip" alone since they are blocked by the obstacles of distortion and delusions and illusions.

The author offers this for consideration: currently, the taste is being ruined by impurities. The cup that You Are must be emptied first if it is ever to be filled with all that provides the taste of sweetness that is possible during the manifestation.

All must be tossed so that the original state of emptiness can return and so that a pleasant fullness can happen. Then being filled with the Realization that brings joy can happen. Empty, the ocean can slip into the drop. This book provides a discussion of the means by which the emptiness can happen so that the fullness can manifest.

BOOK SIX
When Reality Is Overlaid Upon the Relative

The summative statement of the Advaita teachings - "I AM THAT; I AM" - generates much confusion. Post-Realization, am I THAT only? Does everything formerly associated with the relative end? Must I separate and isolate myself from everything relative? Will that happen automatically? Is the relative discounted and does abidance happen in a manner that is totally dissociated from all relative happenings?

Not according to Nisargans. Here, the point is that post-Realization, Reality will be overlaid upon the relative and the understanding that I AM THAT; I AM will continue for the entire manifestation.

The summative statement most assuredly does not imply that the AM-ness must be forfeited or abandoned. What is abandoned is identifying solely with the AM-ness.

Then, there is a return to the original simplicity that marked the relative existence of humans for millions of years ... a relative existence that was a most simple existence prior to efforts by controlling men and women to overlay supernatural concepts onto the previously all-natural existence.

When Reality is not overlaid on the relative, then the most fundamental aspects of the relative existence will guarantee (a) belief in nonsensical dualities; (b) instability rather than steadiness; (c) the restlessness of doingness rather than the freedom of beingness; and (d) dilemmas to deal with rather than detachment.

The content of this book will provide clear markers of what the relative existence will look like when Reality is overlaid upon it, and what it will be like if that overlay does not happen.

It will also make clear how "I AM THAT; I AM" is completely compatible with "advaita" (that is, with "not two").

BOOK ONE OF SIX IN
"THE BLISSFUL ABIDANCE SERIES"

WHAT BLISS IS
AND
WHAT BLISS IS NOT

CHAPTER ONE

HOW many seekers are frustrated by not having attained bliss? How many seekers think that they have failed or that their teacher has failed when what they believe to be bliss does not manifest or when they think that bliss comes on occasion but does not remain?

Those are the thoughts and beliefs of seekers who are at what my teacher called "the kindergarten level of spirituality." How many feel that their goal to become "perfectly spiritual, and thereby perfectly blissful" is being thwarted at every turn?

Sri Nisargadatta Maharaj said, "No ambition is spiritual. All ambitions are for the sake of the 'I am'. The ambitions of the so-called Yogis are preposterous. A man's desire for a woman is innocence itself compared to the lusting for an everlasting personal bliss. The mind is a cheat. The more pious it seems, the worse the betrayal."

Regularly, seekers who come to Advaita retreats with the author and who speak of "the darkness" and of "higher levels of consciousness" are told that there is no darkness and that there are no levels of consciousness.

The so-called "darkness" in which the non-Realized live is not really darkness at all but is merely an absence of light caused by the blockages that have accumulated, and the consciousness is merely consciousness that is either blocked from seeing accurately and blocked from seeing truth or is not. The consciousness is merely a form of energy, and it is what it is. There are no levels of such energy, only energy that can see clearly or energy that has been blocked from seeing clearly by the nonsense placed into "the mind" via programming, conditioning, acculturation, and domestication.

When so many blockages accumulate, then the light cannot penetrate and all seems dark, but that absence of witnessing the light does not mean that the light is not there. It is simply not observable because of a separation from the source of the light - either because the light has been blocked or because there is nothing available to reflect the light.

Consider a day when the sky seems to be covered in clouds. All might seem dark, but in fact the light is very much there. That which lies on the other side of the clouds is the way it has been, the way it is, and the way it shall be, all in spite of the clouds that block any opportunity to witness the light at that moment. So it is with "darkness" and consciousness.

Yet there is a higher level of understanding in regards to this topic: (1) not only is "no ambition spiritual," nothing is spiritual; and (2) not only is "the mind a cheat" but the "mind" is actually as much an illusion as the darkness.

If the seeker would "find bliss," then the seeker must know what bliss is and what bliss is not. If one that is in kindergarten is sent to the store to buy the materials needed to build a "what-cha-ma-call-it," the kindergarten-age-child will not have the slightest clue about what he is seeking and neither will anyone else that he asks to help with finding everything required to build a "what-cha-ma-call-it."

The reason most never "find bliss" is that they are as mistaken about what bliss is and what bliss is not as persons are mistaken about what "the world" is and what it is not or as one would be mistaken if asked to define specifically what a "what-cha-ma-call-it" is.

In order to appreciate the pointers in this book—and in order to end the challenges involved with "occasionally experiencing bliss but not being able to hold on to it" or with "not finding the bliss that others claim they have found" or with "dealing with the frustrations of wanting bliss but not having found it"—the reader is invited to take a few moments to complete the following preparatory exercise:

(A) List all of the ways you would define bliss.
(B) List all of the ways that bliss could be evidenced during the manifestation.
(C) Write a description of what you think the relative existence would look like for you if you were to "attain bliss" once and for all.

Your writings might be used to reveal your prevailing beliefs about bliss and to help distinguish between myth and fact as the discussion continues.

CHAPTER TWO

OVER the years, so many have come to complain about the fact that—after all of their seeking—"permanent bliss still has not come." They were told that they may as well complain, "I have dedicated my life to climbing mountains and searching in the nests of eagles for that one unique case where a fish is living among the birds of prey."

They are searching in the relative for that which will never be found in the relative; furthermore, they could be asked, "And exactly what form of fish do you think can fly into the mountains and live without being in the water and live without consequence among that which would eat the fish?" They are searching in nests for that which is not in nests, which has never been in nests, and which shall never be found in nests.

And it is as if they answer, "Well, my wise teacher has spoken often of such a fish." Then the reply would be, "You cannot differentiate wisdom from ignorance, so rather than search for such a fish out of water, it is suggested that you search for a different teacher."

Those who have been asked to define specifically the "bliss" that they seek will either parrot some words that they have heard but have not understood or will parrot the words that were used by "holy men" or "holy books" in order to program them.

One of the invitations offered earlier was to "list all of the ways you would define bliss." When that exercise is conducted during Advaita retreats here, it is rare that even one of the responses comes close to identifying bliss as it can actually manifest during the relative existence.

Most efforts to define "what bliss is" reveal no evidence at all of what the respondents know or what they have come to realize by having tapped into the inner guru; instead, their words are usually a regurgitation of some of the following concepts (which they have collected from such sources as Hinduism or Buddhism):

"Bliss is what comes at the end of the cycles of reincarnation when desire and suffering both end."

"Bliss is liberation from the effects of karmic rebalancing."

"Bliss is finally being free from rebirths."

"Bliss is freedom from pain and suffering."

So it can be seen that even among those reading Advaitin pointers, many seek not the purest messages that Advaita can offer but are seeking a blend of Advaita and other concepts to which they are yet attached.

The responses to those statements will be an invitation to reach a different understanding … an understanding rooted in logic and reason rather than in concept-filled texts. First, to the statement that "bliss is freedom from pain and suffering."

Freedom from that misperception requires an understanding of the difference in "pain" on the one hand and "suffering" on the other.

Pain is of the body, suffering is of the "mind." Pain is felt because of nerve and brain activity, a process that is usually considered to be an asset to the degree that it can reveal physical problems that might otherwise go undetected or to the degree that it can bring an end to activities that are damaging to the body.

For one person to pick up a hot pan without experiencing pain is to assure that far greater damage will come to that person than to one who can feel pain and would immediately drop a hot pan before any further physical damage occurs. To explain in more detail:

For the body to no longer feel pain, you would have to undergo some degree of paralysis, nerve damage, or brain damage. You would be deprived of one tool that is intended to protect the body for the time that the elements remain together.

For example, if you touch any extremely hot object, pain sends a message to the brain that one should stop touching that object immediately. Without pain, you could continue to grasp the object and would undergo severe physical damage to an appendage.

Do you really desire that your body forfeit all ability to experience pain if the consequences would include damaging the body regularly and severely as a result of having no means for sending signals to the brain to stop behaviors that are damaging the body?

If you must undergo severe nerve damage? If the body must be paralyzed in order to fulfill your desire to feel no pain? If you would have to undergo brain damage in order to fulfill your desire to experience a pain-free relative existence?

One old adage is, "Be careful what you wish for—you might get it." The Advaitin pointer is, "Stop wishing, period, especially if you have no actual clue at all about that for which you are wishing." To wish that one could feel no pain in the relative existence is not only to wish for something that could prove detrimental - relatively speaking - but something that is impossible unless one has undergone severe and major physical damage to the body.

As for suffering, that is of the "mind" wherein beliefs in false personas are stored; thus, elimination of suffering requires neither rebirths nor additional lives. It involves elimination of the "mind" that stores the lies that generate suffering, and that elimination can happen now.

The fact is that it could not possibly happen "later" because any "subsequent lives" would be guaranteed to involve more programming and more "mind"-formation and more persona-adoptions because that pattern—now the pattern being adhered to by all on the planet with the exception of the smallest fraction of a fraction of the population—is the way it is and the way it shall remain.

Undergoing multiple relative lives would assure that a never-ending loop of suffering would result. No, the Ultimate Medicine that can bring about an end to suffering requires no additional manifestations. [For more explanation of that subject, see the eBook at Amazon.com entitled, "The Ultimate Sickness / The Ultimate Medicine."] The understanding that the "mind" is an illusion (as is all of its content) can only happen now; thus, the sickness that causes suffering can only end during this manifestation by use of the Ultimate Medicine, now.

There is no need to wait. There is no need to believe that the end of suffering must involve "future" opportunities. The only opportunity is here and now. If You Realize, then suffering will end at the only time when it can: presently.

Once mahasamadhi is taken, then the conscious-energy will return to that pool of energy from which it came, namely, The Absolute. In that pool of awareness, awareness IS but there is no aware-OF-ness. How could there possibly be any post-manifestation suffering or pleasure? If the composite unity is understood, then it is understood that what the non-Realized refer to as "self" is a three-part composite unity that is really an assortment of elements that forms a temporary plant food body through which air circulates and in which the conscious-energy is temporarily manifested.

Which of those three - elements, air, energy - could possibly feel anything post-manifestation? Some say, "But it is the soul that will experience pain or suffering." Really? The soul is nothing more than a "spiritual persona" - dreamed up by men - and is no more real than any other imaginary persona or role or stage character or ego-state or false identity.

If You can understand that a fire that never occurred cannot possibly re-occur, then You can understand that one that was never born cannot possibly be "re-born." If you do not understand that, then the end of your suffering will be put "on hold" and will never happen.

As for pain, again, there will be no escaping that during the relative existence unless nerve or brain or spinal cord injuries should occur; however, pain can be managed when the consciousness witnesses the pain but knows that it is happening not to ItSelf but is happening to a finite body (which the consciousness is not).

CHAPTER THREE

NOW, to continue with the pointers that are offered to those who define "bliss" in the following ways:

"Bliss is what comes at the end of the cycles of reincarnation when desire and suffering both end."

"Bliss is liberation from the cycles of karmic rebalancing."

"Bliss is finally being free from rebirths."

Review this pointer: "That which was not born cannot be re-born." Few, however, who have been programmed to believe in multiplicities will even attempt to use reason and logic to re-consider the concepts of "birth" and "death" or "multiple births" and "multiple deaths." If I was not born - and I was not - then how could I be re-born?

Most, too, who have been programmed to believe that there is "this life" and then "a future eternal life in heaven or in hell" will be just as unwilling to see the nonsense behind the notion that the elemental components of a rotted or cremated body can re-group with its same mind and same personality and exist forever.

To believe that a speck of consciousness can maintain some version of singularity and continuity and be reincarnated or resurrected is to fail to understand that there is no singularity or continuous speck of consciousness even now, much less "later."

Persons generally eat on a daily basis to replenish upon a daily basis the conscious-energy. Only the illusion of "memories" would drive anyone to think that a single speck of energy has remained manifested for decades. Most fail to understand that there has not even been a continuous body throughout "this existence." Consider skin cells: the cells that were observable 28 days ago are no longer there. All of the skin on a human body is replaced every twenty-eight days. The human body that was last month is not the same human body that is this month.

Many seekers also cite a frequent but totally inaccurate notion that "bliss is constant ecstasy." That belief is most definitely a setup for disappointment and misery.

Yet some seekers do, on occasion, do accurately point toward what "bliss" is (while touching at the same time the facts regarding the "B" question above about how bliss could be evidenced during the relative existence):

"Neutrality, stability, and an absence of desire and fear," wrote one. Those are all within reach and could result when the state of "bliss" is reached. "Bliss would be non-attachment," said another. Also attainable, also an accurate pointer to that which accompanies the bliss state.

But to be free of all of the inaccurate beliefs about bliss (including, "In that state, I will continuously be experiencing rapturous joy for all of the rest of the relative existence") then one can review the most common definitions of bliss that are offered.

To understand those definitions should provide a chance to see bliss in the proper light and to understand what bliss is—and is not—in a reasonable way that includes a chance for it to manifest in a realistic manner (which will never involve the mythical idea about "continuous, rapturous joy during the relative"):

"Bliss" has most often been defined as "blithesomeness" (meaning "light-heartedness"); as "gladness" or "happiness"; as "agreeableness"; as "amiability or compatibility with nature"; as "harmoniousness"; or as "mellowness."

Understand those definitions which are admittedly more narrow than the conceptualized goal of "experiencing continuous, rapturous joy during the relative existence" and then the fruitless search for some earthly "Eldorado" or earthly "Utopia" or earthly "Shangri-La" or earthly "Paradise Regained" can end.

Maharaj explained that "the undisturbed state of being is bliss"; as long as the beingness is, why seek any more than that? It really is all so simple.

If the unachievable pursuit of a utopia-on-earth ends, then what would also come to an end would be the frustrated efforts (and the always-thwarted ambitions) of those seekers who do not understand the means by which Reality can be overlaid upon the relative but who naively want to remake the relative instead.

Then, too, the next level of understanding might manifest and it might become clear that "bliss" has nothing to do with "anything"—and nothing to do with "something"—but has everything to do with nothing itself.

To that end, consider Maharaj's pointer about the ultimate bliss state: "The Ultimate state is that state in which nothing exists, neither I, nor you, nor manifestation."

CHAPTER FOUR

O F the definitions of bliss cited earlier, the ones that are most aligned with the Direct Path, nisarga yoga are "amiability or compatibility with nature" and "harmoniousness."

Being at harmony with nature during the relative can bring happiness and peace, but being compatible (or more accurately, "at one") with Your original, true nature is the way that bliss can manifest.

The bliss myth is the belief among some seekers that they can find some means by which all of the fluctuations of the relative existence can be transcended by undertaking enough "spiritual work" or engaging in enough "spiritual exercises" that they can identify with the consciousness only and expect an eventual replacement of the ebbs and flows of the relative with a condition that involves "constant, rapturous joy."

Yet it is the manifested consciousness that not only makes possible such fluctuations but also guarantees such movement and constant ebbs and flows. Moreover, to expect is to desire, and to desire is to be disappointed. So what could reasonably be "anticipated" in terms of "bliss" without setting oneself up for disappointment?

One visitor remarked, after hearing the pointers offer earlier that he "was not engaged at all in a fruitless search for some earthly 'Eldorado' or earthly 'Utopia' or earthly 'Shangri-La' or earthly 'Paradise Regained'." Then, his subsequent comments revealed that he is seeking a personal "Eldorado" or personal "Utopia" or personal "Shangri-La" or personal "Paradise Regained."

Of that goal, Maharaj said, "Don't say that you are an individual; just stay in the beingness. The whole problem is the sense of being a separate entity. Once that subsides, that is true bliss."

To work toward the "creation" of a perfect existence that is characterized by a constant feeling of ecstasy will be as fruitless and futile and frustrating as the efforts of others to create a perfect relative "world." To want a continuous sense of ecstasy is to guarantee that one will never be "compatible with nature" and that one will be disappointed and unhappy instead.

In nature, ecstasy comes as an occasional "break" from a typically non-ecstatic existence. Ecstatic happenings can only be known dualistically ... when they occur as a diversion in contrast to the more typical stretches of non-ecstatic happenings.

To experience ecstasy constantly would not only be incompatible with nature but would automatically and ironically bring to an end any sense of ecstasy. Why? Because its continuity would end the dualistic component that separates it from the non-ecstatic (which is a required counterpart that would allow the ecstatic to be definable by being distinguishable from the non-ecstatic).

One might as well claim he / she wants to be physically awake constantly and never physically asleep at all. It is a total impossibility, and so is "constant ecstasy." It is just one more example of the many impossible dreams that "the mind" can generate. And WHO would be experiencing such ecstasy if it could exist in the continuous manner desired? Of that, Maharaj taught:

"Sat-chit-ananda" (being-consciousness-bliss) "will, in due course, become the Paramatman" (the so-called Supreme Self, which is merely a term used as a thorn "along the way.") He continued: "Satchitananda" (a.k.a., Satchidananda) "is 'I Amness' and is itself a state of bliss, a state of love."

Then he further clarified: "But it is an experiential state, so long as consciousness is there, and consciousness is there so long as the body is available - it is a time-bound state. You must transcend the sat-chit-ananda state."

Look to nature and see "compatibility with nature" as displayed by the model frequently offered as an example by the author—the deer. The deer roaming about in the yard hear each night are assuredly being; within those spaces the consciousness was assuredly manifest; and their simply being (without any notion of "being this" or "being that") would be, by Maharaj's definition, bliss.

Why would that not be "enough" for humans? To want bliss to be more than that is to reject de-accumulation, which is required for abidance to happen as one's true nature. Therein lies the opportunity for another understanding in regards to bliss, namely, being compatible not only with relative nature but with the true, original nature as well. There is the essence of overlaying Reality upon the relative.

Being mindless, the deer need not "transcend." Such is not the case with humans-cum-minds. Recall two pointers offered by Maharaj: "The mind is a cheat" and "You must transcend the sat-chit-ananda state."

To be happy now and at peace now, belief in the content of the "mind" must go and attachment to the beingness and consciousness and notions about "relative bliss" must go.

WHO (what non-Realized person) thinks that beingness would not be "enough"? WHO is seeking more of the type of bliss that supposedly involves "continuous, rapturous joy"? WHO thinks that nature could sustain such an experience? WHO thinks there is someone personal who could experience that … or anything else?

Consider the key pointer in this exchange where the original, natural state is discussed in opposition to nature as associated with the relative:

Questioner: "Is a Self-realized person always in a state of bliss?"

Maharaj: "One who has transcended the body idea does not need the ananda (bliss). When you didn't have experience of the body, you were in that blissful state."

Again, the nothingness-bliss link. So WHO wants bliss? WHO has not transcended body identification? WHO does not see that the very wanting of bliss—or anything else—is rooted in the fear/desire components of personality?

Furthermore, WHO does not see that personality can never feel "fulfilled" since it is an illusion? And WHO does not see that wanting / desiring anything— including bliss—automatically eliminates any possibility for bliss to manifest?

Understand that and You will understand what Maharaj meant when he said, "Desirelessness is the highest form of bliss." The deer grazing in the yard here each night want nothing. Eating was merely happening spontaneously and mindlessly. Too, there was no evidence at all that they were "unhappy" or had a belief that they were "lacking" something.

CHAPTER FIVE

REVISIT two of the most common definitions of bliss that were offered earlier: "compatibility with nature" and "harmoniousness." Actually, the Advaitin would not even agree with the "harmoniousness" definition to the extent that it implies, dualistically, that (1) there is some "A" that is getting along with some "B" or that (2) there is some sort of congruity of parts with one another as well as with the whole.

Yet there is some relevance to the degree that the term points away from disharmony, which is the style in which the relative typically unfolds in the absence of Realization.

In that absence, all seems to be out of harmony ... all split, if you will. Persons believe that they are split in "time," having a past and a present and, always hopefully and wishfully, a future. They are split into various identities. They suffer splits in "relationships."

Such "divisions" mark the pre-Realization relative existence and disharmony becomes the abnormal norm as everything eventually ends up involving dualities— "this" not being harmonious with "that"; "this one" not getting along with "that one"; "this one" running into "that one"; and then all sorts of constant confronting and all kinds of banging against, of challenging and of being challenged; of tackling; of dealing with; of not dealing with.

One that is Realized recently referred to "this lineage," to this "River of Truth that is continuing to run," and to the river's subsequent "bubbles of dissolution that bring enjoyment," which could be another understanding of "bliss" and how it manifests.

Yet the non-Realized would even see a river as being split into unrelated parts or disparate segments. Such are the distortions that are given credibility by the non-Realized.

Note the way that a sense of being split and being totally incompatible with nature manifests by reviewing the actions taken by the members of one particular family that has been farming in south Texas since their ancestors migrated there from Germany in the mid-1800's:

The father kills all birds that sing outside his window, birds simply singing as birds are prone to do, because they disturb his morning sleep; the daughter demands the killing of chirping crickets and croaking frogs, chirping or croaking as those are prone to do, because their sounds disturb her "peace of mind"; their barn is adorned with a thousand trophy-heads or horn-sets from animals shot; and the son kills the pets of neighbors that stray across property lines, as dogs are prone to do.

This is an entire family that is out of harmony with nature ... that has no "compatibility with nature" and, therefore, has no awareness of Self and most assuredly no awareness of bliss.

Is it any wonder, then, that the family rule is, "We don't hug," a hug being an outward token during the relative existence of an inner awareness of the Oneness? Such disharmony ... such splitness from Self and into "selves." So it is when a nisarga style of functioning does not manifest.

The Realized—compatible with nature as they are—can enjoy birds singing, crickets chirping, and frogs croaking. They are content to witness various species in the wild, not being driven in the least to gun down as many animals or birds or frogs or crickets as possible.

Such compatibility with nature provides an obvious distinction between blissful beingness and relative destruction that ends (with violence) a variety of nature's varied forms of beingness.

By contrast, incompatibility with nature sets the stage for persons to be incompatible with themselves, and with all persons, so it is a small leap from gunning down animals to gunning down each other in their "soured relationships" or in battles between groups or in wars between states or nations. No bliss can be known when dualistic incompatibility ("A" not getting along with "B") becomes a dominant trait among persons on the planet.

That feeling of "split-ness" or "two-ness" or "multiplicity-ness" generates the frustration of never feeling complete. "The experience of the jnani," Maharaj said, "is the same as your state prior to birth. It is a complete state." That sense of completeness, of no-split-ness, is another form of bliss.

In light of the sense of splitness vs. an understanding of the unicity, consider some of the replies to the invitation to write descriptors of the relative existence were bliss to manifest: (1) "Peacefulness; absence of emotional reactivity; delight in what is ordinary and natural; sensory sensitivity": and (2) "Although there is not much self-identity left, there is a sense that the vast no-self spaciousness would be the perpetual view - with no trace of the individual at all." As a follow-up to that, this addendum was shared recently: (3) "Today I would put it this way: There is the final understanding - via a peripetia moment (often described as an accident or grace and unrelated to any spiritual practices). The CONSEQUENCE of this understanding appears to be: bliss, love, joy. So...the relative life revealing its true nature in the absence of the filter of a suffering individual = bliss."

Related to that state marked by the "absence of [belief in] a suffering individual," Maharaj taught: "To know one's Real Self is bliss; to forget is sorrow." He said, "I found that I am conscious and happy absolutely and only by mistake I thought I owed being-consciousness-bliss to the body and the world of bodies. Bliss is more of the nature of a great peace."

Not "continuous, rapturous joy?" No, not at all. In agreement with the pointer that bliss can be considered the absence of individuality or personal attributes—specifically, the "absence of the filter of a suffering individual"—Maharaj also concluded that…

"Bliss is not to be known. One is always bliss, but never blissful. Bliss is not an attribute." Again, WHO would know bliss? WHO would be blissful? WHO could have attributes? Many seekers are being set up for disappointment when erroneous notions about what bliss is are presented as dangling carrots that can never be reached.

When "floyd" was nothing more than a potentiality of unmanifested energy, a non-existing thing, there was no individual and, therefore, no chance for any possibility that a "non-blissful" state could materialize.

The same can happen even as the conscious-energy is manifested if it is understood that "floyd" is nothing more than a phantom, thus allowing abidance to happen as that pre-manifestation, natural, original state. In that regard, Maharaj said,

"First I thought I was the body; then, I experienced that I was not the body but I was the consciousness; then, I got the experience that this consciousness is not really me, and there is no form, no individuality, no nothing.

"That non-existing thing suddenly came into existence. What is the validity of its existence? It is an apparition only … it can't be the truth. That's why I dare talk like this. This is a big hoax, a big fraud, created out of nothingness. Can you create something out of nothing?"

CHAPTER SIX

THE following was part of a reply to a visitor's comments shared during satsang. The pointers are relevant to the on-going discussion:

Yes - some teacher / seeker "relationships" differ not at all from that of a pursuer / pursued "relationship" wherein a man promises a woman the moon, as if that could be delivered.

It is the same with this "bliss" concept. The seeker who is oversold a bill of goods—who is "promised the moon" in terms of "what bliss is"—will be placed in an expectation mode.

And there's the rub: the seeker in such instances is led to expect something (which can never be delivered) rather than understanding that bliss has to do with the Realization of the nothingness and has not one thing at all to do with either the "something-ness" or the "everything-ness."

Having been misled, though, the seeker anticipating far more than that which bliss actually is will be trapped in the search for some pot at the end of a rainbow when both the pot and the rainbow are mere mental illusions.

So, to continue the clarification of what bliss is and what bliss is not, the understanding of the role of the "mind" in blocking any opportunity for bliss to manifest must also be understood.

The manifested consciousness and the brain can function together and bliss can happen. Once the "mind" becomes involved, bliss cannot possibly happen. The "mind" can be cast aside. [For more details, the full discussion of being freed from "the mind" is available in the eBook, There's No Such Thing As "Peace of Mind."]

Maharaj said: "The state of freedom from all thoughts will happen suddenly and by the bliss of it you shall recognise it."

So bliss is also to be understood as freedom from thoughts ... freedom from "the mind." There is no misery or suffering among persons that does not begin with thought(s). The progression among humans is always from thought to word to deed, and most often the sequence involves nonsensical thoughts to nonsensical words to nonsensical actions.

He also explained to visitors to the loft that they should not use the mind to try to find bliss. His advice, instead, was to "do nothing." To seekers far along "the path" he said, "Identify with the nothingness until even that identity fades away."

As for that nothingness, he also said, "The Ultimate state in 'spirituality' is that state where no needs are felt at any time, where nothing is useful for anything." What could be more blissful than needing nothing and fearing nothing?

Since desires and fears are rooted in personality, then the discarding of all identity can set the stage for being free of desires and fears which, in turn, sets the stage for blissful beingness throughout the remainder of the manifestation.

Maharaj also taught in regards to the bliss-nothingness link: "You must thoroughly understand what You are, or what You could be when nothing is. When nothing is, You still are. What is that You?"

CHAPTER SEVEN

CONSIDER again this statement from Maharaj that can be used to provide the final understanding about what bliss is:

"You must thoroughly understand what You are, or what You could be when nothing is. When nothing is, You still are. What is that You?"

Understand that he is not referring to anything dealing with the Absolute or to the awareness that is not aware of or to the Nothingness prior to the Absolute.

Everything which is post-manifestation is beyond beingness and non-beingness, but look at the verbs being used by Maharaj in that quote: "are, could be, is, still are." His point deals with what can manifest, with what can be understood NOW, during the beingness ... not afterwards.

Those verbs make clear that he is pointing to a condition—to an understanding—that happens during the manifestation, not after it; thus, the question "What is that You?" must be answered in terms of the present manifestation.

He is pointing to the last "stage" where bliss can be "known" (which means it must be during the manifestation for nothing can be known post-manifestation since the awareness is not aware of ... since awareness cannot be aware of Self or bliss or anything).

So go back to these two statements: Wisdom is knowing I am nothing and Love is knowing that I AM everything. Understanding You Are nothing is wisdom and understanding that You Are everything is Love.

If all identification has been forfeited (first, "I AM nothing" and then eventually, even the nothingness as an identity falls away), then all that is left during the manifestation that is understood is ... Love. What is that You? Love.

Therefore, bliss is knowing I am everything ... knowing the unicity ... and then not knowing Love but being Love.

In light of that, revisit these pointers from Maharaj that were offered earlier: "Bliss is not to be known. One is always bliss, but never blissful. Bliss is not an attribute," and "The 'I Amness' is itself a state of bliss, a state of Love" after all identity has dissolved.

TO REVIEW:

Now, You are invited to reconsider these pointers offered in the series:

Bliss has to do with the Realization of the nothingness

Bliss is freedom from all thoughts

Bliss is a no-need state, a state where "no needs are felt at any time, where nothing is useful for anything"

Bliss is being free of desires and fears

Bliss is compatibility with nature, observable when freedom from anxiety and tension and discontent are gone and when there is no drive or desire to harm or kill (be it birds or animals or pets or frogs or crickets or humans or entire species or entire races or all of the members of a religion that is not one's own)

Bliss is freedom from the false sense of being split, divided, separated, incomplete

As one visitor wrote: Bliss is what follows having been immersed in this "River of Truth" and having been exposed to the "bubbles of dissolution" that allow for identification with the nothingness until even that identity falls away

Bliss is abiding as that original, natural state without any "trace of an individual"

Bliss is, as one wrote, "the absence of the filter of a suffering individual"

Maharaj taught: "To know one's Real Self is bliss" and "Bliss is more of the nature of a great peace."

Maharaj said, "Don't say that you are an individual; just stay in the beingness. The whole problem is the sense of being a separate entity. Once that subsides, that is true bliss."

Bliss is not continuous, rapturous joy and has nothing to do with "birth and rebirth" or with cycle-after-cycle of "being better" or "getting better" or "being more and more pure."

Bliss is being Love.

Post-manifestation, the awareness will not be aware of anything, so bliss cannot possibly register "later." Bliss and freedom and happiness and compatibility with nature in the nisarga fashion can only happen NOW. This is Your only chance. The invitation is to be bliss now, to be at-one now, to be Love now.

"PLEASURE-PAIN VS. BLISS," Part One

On occasion, others questions have been raised regarding what the teachings have to say about pleasure and pain and bliss. One query addressed the confusion around the Advaita pointer that "pleasure leads to pain" on one hand and comments about "Realization leading to bliss" on the other.

On another occasion, a man promoted abstinence as opposed to the Nisarga / natural style of functioning that is offered here. (Later, he would contradict himself and promote "tantric sex.")

His words exposed (1) debilitating levels of angst and strum und drang and distortion around sexuality in general, (2) much confusion around "his sex and love experiences," and (3) a near-total misunderstanding of what post-Realization, natural living looks like, specifically.

He, too, has failed to grasp the differences in pleasure and bliss, the differences in suffering and misery vs. pain, and the difference in pre-Realization living vs. post-Realization, Nisargan (natural) abidance.

So, to clarify: pain is of the body, that is, it is a sensation which can be experienced by a plant food body. To continue with Maharaj's teachings that science and the Advaita teachings are not only compatible but that science can facilitate the understanding, understand this:

At the nerve endings in the skin, the pain process begins as a neuron sends a signal toward the spinal cord where that signal connects with nearby neurons and eventually connects via a synapse to a second-order neuron that rises to the thalamus. The thalamus forwards the pain signal through fibers that reach the cortex, which results in the brain being conscious of pain.

As long as the consciousness is manifested in a body-cum-consciousness, then pain can be experienced. Nerves and skin and neurons and cords and the brain and fibers and pain are all natural. Conversely, misery and suffering are the product of the "mind," which is totally unnatural.

Here is the distinction: "Consciousness is rooted in the Absolute; the brain is rooted in the elements; the 'mind' is rooted in wrong programming and faulty conditioning and lies and concepts and ideas and superstitions and falsehoods."

To the estimated five million to one-hundred million species on the planet, add in also all of the species that have come and gone, then know this: only one of all of the species that have come and gone, and only one species among the millions that presently exist, has ever developed a "mind."

That fact alone should make clear that the "mind" is most unnatural. What is "natural"? Specifically, that which is natural is defined as "that which exists in, or is in conformity with, nature—which is neither supernatural nor magical."

So pain requires the presence of elemental nerves and an elemental brain and manifest consciousness if it is to be sensed; misery and suffering, conversely, require the presence of a "mind," which is merely the conglomeration of all of the false ideas and beliefs and concepts and attitudes and identities that are taught via programming and conditioning.

Now, to the pleasure-pain conundrum. The teaching is that whatever leads to pleasure can lead to pain and that whatever gives the most pleasure will often produce the most pain. (Consider such pain as that associated with AIDS or other diseases that are transmitted when an elemental body is experiencing physical pleasure and can later experience physical pain).

That all deals with the elemental body and brain and consciousness only. (If unconscious, a doctor can cut open your chest, remove your heart, insert another in its place, and you will feel nothing at all, if not conscious.)

Contrast that with the teaching that whatever leads to pleasure can lead to misery and suffering and that whatever gives the most pleasure will often produce the most misery and suffering.

In that case, considering the earlier pointer that "misery and suffering are the product of the 'mind,' which is totally unnatural," it should be seen that the teaching in the second case refers to the miserable, relative results that can manifest when being driven by the desires and fears generated by the warped content of the "mind."

Thus, pain can be quite natural (unless self-inflicted) whereas misery and suffering and anything that is thought to be "supernatural or magical" are all totally unnatural.

Thus, pain can be natural when it occurs in an elemental body; can be unnatural if self-induced; and can be unnatural if potentially-threatening pleasures are engaged in—in ignorance—after having been warned of the relative dangers or in the ignorance of having no awareness of the relative dangers.

Suffering and misery, on the other hand, are a product of the content of the "mind." As long as the consciousness is manifested, it will register pain on occasion. If suffering and misery are to be eliminated, then the attachment to the content of the "mind" must be eliminated.

Next, the differences in "pleasure" and "bliss" will be discussed along with what is natural about both.

"PLEASURE-PAIN VS. BLISS," Part Two

So, questions and comments have revealed that the Nisargan teachings are misunderstood by some in regards to pleasure, pain, misery, suffering, and bliss as well as in terms of how the natural, post-Realization abidance unfolds.

While bliss has to do with the Realization of the nothingness, pleasure has to do with something … with something in the relative existence. The deer that pause in the front yard here can be seen enjoying the pleasure of grazing; they can be seen enjoying the pleasure of shade and rest during the heat of the afternoon;

they have been witnessed while in a clearing in the woods nearby this house as they enjoy the pleasures of sex. All of that is natural, and to avoid that which is natural is unnatural—even when done in the name of being "religious" or "spiritual" or "supernatural"—and is a part of the sickness that is addressed with the Ultimate Medicine.

Abuse yourself with a mace if you like in your efforts to be more religious or spiritual; accept the distorted view that suffering is an asset rather than something unacceptable that is to be addressed and removed and avoided;

eat your bitter herbs or tasteless roots; dip your food in salt water and vinegar; avoid sexual relations; but here, now that natural living is happening spontaneously, the pleasures of succulent meals will be enjoyed:

tasks that are to happen for sustenance shall happen, but the pleasures of rest will also be enjoyed; deprive yourself of the joys of sex if you want, but here, all natural things will continue to happen and will continue to be enjoyed.

Consider how truly sick and distorted and insane any teachings or beliefs are if they drive persons to abide in a painful, miserable, pleasureless manner.

Functioning in either (A) the unnatural extreme of unfettered hedonism and "self"-indulgence or functioning in (B) a manner at the opposite extreme of the spectrum that involves total deprivation in the name of being "religious" or "spiritual" or "better" or "better than" or "improved" might be (and is) considered supernatural living by many, but such a manner of living will not be considered natural by the sane and sound and stable and Realized.

Unnatural and supernatural living will only be mistakenly seen as a natural means of living by those functioning under the auspices of a warped mind and warped personas that are driven by personality (or personalities) and by the defects and disorders that personality always generates.

Finally, understand that pleasure and pain and misery and suffering and bliss are the "stuff" of NOW only—the "stuff" of the limited period of manifestation during the relative existence—and the relative existence will happen in a natural manner if Reality is overlaid upon it.

To make clear, there will be no post-manifestation pleasure or pain or misery or suffering or bliss. NOW, is the only time that pleasures can be enjoyed in a non-destructive and non-self-destructive fashion among the sane and stable;

NOW is the time that misery and suffering can be eliminated if you take the Ultimate Medicine that dissolves the "mind" but leaves the brain and consciousness and natural instincts intact so that natural, spontaneous abidance can happen;

And NOW is the only time that the bliss can be understood. To that end, here are some pointers offered previously about bliss, which is probably misunderstood more than any of the other teachings:

Bliss is freedom from all thoughts

Bliss is a no-need state, a state where no needs are felt at any time, where nothing is useful for anything (Maharaj)

Bliss is being free of desires and fears though natural drives such as thirst and hunger and sex will continue to happen

Bliss is compatibility with nature, observable when freedom from anxiety and tension and discontentment are gone and when there is no drive or desire to harm or kill (be it birds or animals or pets or frogs or crickets or humans or entire species or entire races or all of the members of a religion that is not one's own)

Bliss is freedom from the false sense of being split, divided, separated, incomplete

As Advaitin Louise Sterling wrote: Bliss is what follows having been immersed in this "River of Truth"; bliss is having been exposed to the "bubbles of dissolution" that allow for identification with the nothingness until even that identity falls away; bliss is "the absence of the filter of a suffering individual"

Bliss is abiding as that original, natural state without any "trace of an individual"

Maharaj taught: "To know one's Real Self is bliss" and "Bliss is more of the nature of a great peace"

Maharaj said, "Don't say that you are an individual; just stay in the beingness.

The whole problem is the sense of being a separate entity. Once that subsides, that is true bliss"

Bliss is not continuous, rapturous joy and has nothing to do with "birth and rebirth" or with cycle-after-cycle or "being better" or "getting better" or "being more and more pure"

Bliss is being Love while also being nothing.

BOOK TWO OF SIX IN
"THE BLISSFUL ABIDANCE SERIES"

THERE'S NO SUCH THING AS "PEACE OF MIND"

(THERE'S ONLY PEACE IF YOU ARE OUT OF YOUR MIND)

A CONSIDERATION

MOST persons will never reach a point where they are awake enough to even ask the questions that indicate they know that they have no "peace of mind." Some will ask one or more of the following: "How can I attain peace of mind?" "Why is my mind constantly in motion?" "Why do I start thinking about one thing and get hung up on that?" "Why does my mind sometimes feel as if there's the chatter of a thousand monkeys going on inside my head?" "How can I purify my mind and get rid of all the troublesome things that fill it all day long?" "Why can't I stop my mind at night and go to sleep and stay asleep until morning?"

The answers will be provided in this book. Best regards on your "journey" as you seek them.

CHAPTER ONE

"MIND" and MEMORIES:

When Nature's "Assets" Become Warped into "Liabilities"

"CONSCIOUSNESS is rooted in the Absolute. The brain is rooted in the elements. The 'mind' is rooted in wrong programming and faulty conditioning and lies and concepts and ideas and superstitions and falsehoods. Personas are rooted in programmed minds and are sustained by the ego-based lies and by the learned ignorance that are being taught in most modern cultures."

At the root of all relative existence problems involving persons is this: that which was one of nature's assets (the formation of a mind after the brain evolved and developed the ability to store memories) has been warped into an unnatural or supernatural liability. While no Advaitins would suggest that seekers must learn science in order to Realize, Maharaj did say that someday science would advance enough to catch up with the Advaita understanding and validate scientifically the philosophical Teachings. He was correct, so please bear with this approach that might resonate with some.

The smaller human brain, in its earlier and simpler stages of development, allowed humans then to live as deer live today: hunt/forage/find food for survival; interact; take actions that are self-defensive and self-constructive; and procreate in order that the species will survive. As more and more humans walked the planet, the simplicity of existence would be lost as the simplicity of the brain was lost.

Complications resulted because of an increase in human interactions (and an increase in both individual as well as tribal interests and agendas). The brain began to evolve in order to compensate, and eventually areas that could store memories came into being. At that point, the mind and the brain worked in tandem and in harmony to contribute to the survival of individuals and the species. The mind came about as "memories" began to be stored. As a part of the defense mechanisms for survival of the species, the mind had its role and played it "properly" (naturally) for thousands of years.

For example, if a caveman remembered that his companion fell from a cliff and died as a result, the caveman might avoid falling from cliffs. The original process was as follows: over a period of evolution, the brain expanded to include a cerebral cortex and a hippocampus. Afterwards, when an event happened (such as a human falling off a cliff) or when someone learned something (such as, "falling off a cliff can kill you"), the brain placed the memory of that event and the related knowledge acquisition in its "memory files." That is all the mind was: a collection of memories filed away in those "newer" parts of the brain.

The memory of both old and new happenings would be processed and stored away in different areas of the cerebral cortex, or the "gray matter" of the brain. The hippocampus would process the memories. (As a side note in that regard, a disease receiving considerable attention nowadays—Alzheimer's—comes about when the hippocampus is damaged, resulting in...what else...memory loss. Is it not interesting that one who might have been a fighter for years and who loved chaos suddenly becomes peaceful when the ability to tap into dualistic memories is lost? Witness the way that the ability to remember dualistic concepts and dogma are now the curse of the planet, relatively speaking.)

Over a period of time, language developed which allowed controlling men with hidden, personal agendas to dream up concepts and teach those ideas to others who could—by that point—remember them. The overabundance of dualistic concepts and beliefs and dogma (which were destructive and separatist in nature) began to outnumber the earlier class of memories that were survival-related.

It was one thing for the caveman to "feel bad" if the fish that was going to feed him and his family that day happened to get away. Such feelings are natural. It is quite another thing when modern persons—as a result of living under the auspices of a warped, dualistic "mind"—truly believe that they should feel "bad" when they do things that are also natural, such as masturbation or fornication. It is one thing for the caveman to feel "good" when he killed a deer for supper. It is quite another thing when a modern person, as a result of a warped, dualistic "mind," feels "good" if he kills another human who has different religious beliefs filed away in the storage areas of the brain.

Now, because of the warped dualistic "mind," persons feel "good" if they beat their "bad" children or if they whip a wife who flashed a bit of ankle in public. As the "mind" formed, it allowed a class of beliefs and concepts to be accumulated that no longer contribute to the survival of the species but that have become a driving factor in the perversion of interactions and the destruction of humans by humans. Dualistic thinking was born, and all of the horrors of the relative existence began. Prior to attachment to dualistic beliefs, early tribal fights might deal with water rights. After the "mind" quit working in tandem and in harmony with the brain, it began to overrule the brain. Thereafter, fighting dealt far less with survival issues and far more with conflicts over differing beliefs and concepts.

Those fights/wars would eventually result in the killing of more humans that anything other than natural causes: political wars; religious wars; holocausts; the invasion of continents and the decimation of native populations; and acts of racial, ethnic and religious genocide. Dual-mindedness had begun, and the persons of the planet are still bound in its grip. It is now at the root of everything called "evil," and the accuracy of the words of the Advaitin teacher of 2000 years ago (who said that "A dual-minded person is unstable in all ways") are proving to be as factual today as in 30 A.D.

CHAPTER TWO

"MIND" and MEMORIES:

When Nature's "Assets" Become Warped into "Liabilities"

SO, it can be seen that the term "the mind" is just a name given to a set of files. Originally those files were stored in the brain (as what would come to be called "memories") so that the file information could be retrieved if needed in order to help humans survive dangerous situations (i.e., "Remember when the fellow in the next cave thought he was picking up a stick and it was a snake. Check more carefully.") It can be seen that now the "mind" has been so distorted that the persons of the planet believe that a rope is a snake.

Those files/memories are so contaminated with distortions, misperceptions, dogma and all other kinds of lies that the "mind" can no longer serve its original purpose. Where it was intended by nature to work with the rest of the brain to avoid destruction, in its present condition, the typical "mind" is generating more destruction and chaos than survival and peace. It is one thing to remember that a snake which looks like a stick can kill you; it is something else to remember dualistic messages that include: "We're better than all others on the planet because we live in the greatest country on earth," or "It's OK to attack or kill those who have been taught the tenets of a religion that is different from your religion," or "People with that skin color are all ignorant and criminal."

It can be seen, therefore, that the current, distorted state of the modern "mind" came about after languages and personal agendas developed which enabled persons to begin teaching dualistic concepts. After that occurred, persons used languages to pass on as fact an entire body of lies, lies that were not based in actual happenings or fact at all (things such as beliefs, ideas, myths, superstitions, dogma, theories, attitudes, "spiritual knowledge," religious "knowledge," concepts, false identities, etc.) It can be seen that the distortions being stored nowadays as remembered lessons/memories are not memories that can be used for survival but are corruptions that are driving conduct that is destructive, self-destructive, and detrimental to both peace and survival.

As a result of the distorted concepts and beliefs that are currently being stored in what is called the "mind," nature's intent has been invalidated. That original storehouse of files in the brain which was intended by nature to work with the rest of the brain to guide the body to behave in a natural fashion, is now resulting in the body being guided by a warped "mind" that generates unnatural "thinking" and conduct and supernatural "thinking" and conduct.

Nowadays, memories are not being retrieved from the mind to avoid dangerous animals or the precarious edges of cliffs but are generating dualistic "thoughts" such as, "They are ignorant…we are smart"; "I am good, but they are bad"; "I deserve reward but they deserve punishment"; "I heard a God in another world tell me to drop bombs on people in this world"; "I am going to destroy you (or "reject you" or "leave you" or "punish you") because you have said things and done things that are different from what I wanted you to say and do"; or, "You can't be good…you're different from me."

Now, a natural mind no longer works with a natural brain to generate natural living. Instead, the content of the typical "mind" today generates a style of living that is more often unnatural (meaning characterized by delusional "thinking") and that is very often supernatural (meaning characterized by magical "thinking"). The "thoughts" behind both of those types of "thinking" are rooted in duality, and dualistic "thinking" is at the core of anything considered a dilemma or problem or crisis in the relative existence.

Whereas the brain is "wired" for self-constructive behavior, the modern "mind" is now "wired" for self-destructive behavior because of the vast pool of learned ignorance that is being passed on to (and accepted as truth by) billions of persons, their level of education or intelligence notwithstanding. Because behavior is now being controlled by the bogus, programmed "mind" more than the brain, the personalized, individualized "mind" is able to inspire persons to destruct and self-destruct in opposition to the self-constructive actions that a normal brain would guide an organism to take.

So a shift in what was typical and "normal" human behavior happened as the brain evolved over thousands of years: the development of the brain's capacity to store memories, and to retrieve memories from storage, was followed by the development of language. The development of language was followed by the teaching of dualistic concepts. Those dualistic teachings have resulted in the contemporary "mind" which is nothing more than a repository of lies. Those lies/false beliefs generate a sense of separation and the judgmental labeling of persons as "bad," "immoral," "wrong," ad infinitum. Now, because of the warped, dualistic "mind," persons truly believe that they are "bad" (or they are labeled as "bad") if they believe in vaginal births but refuse to believe in a virginal birth.

They feel they are "bad" (or they are labeled as "bad") if they are repelled by descriptions of a god who was a mass murderer. Now, because of the warped, dualistic "mind," persons truly believe that they are "bad" (or they are labeled as "bad") if they don't care to participate in a rite of worship called "communion" that reenacts ancient rites of cannibalism and vampirism. They can feel they are "bad" (or at the very least, "not as good as") if they have not been dunked or sprinkled with water that some claim is "holy."

Now, because of the warped, dualistic "mind," persons truly believe that killers are "good" if they kill people whose stored files contain information that differs from the killers' stored files. The insanity that currently dominates the planet (as a result of the warped "mind" that takes duality to be real) is pervasive, and the majority of the dualistic beliefs which have had the most vicious results have been dreamed up and passed down by members of one specific institution over the last 5000 years.

"Brain-washing" is an inaccurate term. "Brain-trashing" is what has been happening for many millennia now, inspiring the call for a complete "brain-flush" now. Why? The institution that has been touting dual-mindedness for thousands of years has been joined by programmed parents and conditioned teachers and acculturated politicians and by various other sources in the global pursuit of training persons to accept as fact the seemingly endless supply of dualistic lies. The concepts that need to be eliminated from the "mind" via a brain-flush should be obvious. The purging of belief in all dualities begins with questioning it all and continues with the discarding of all learned ignorance in order to then be free.

CHAPTER THREE

"MIND" and MEMORIES:

When Nature's "Assets" Become Warped into "Liabilities"

IT is emphasized again that (1) it's all energy at the core, that (2) nowadays natural living can only happen under the auspices of the brain and never while under the influence of the corrupted "mind," and that (3) all learned ignorance—stored as a "mind"—must be tossed if peace is to happen. Note how each step in the following analysis moves from something wrongly-perceived (such as "a human body") down to the most basic "ingredient" of the universe that is common to all in the universe. (Call it "strings," call it "that," call it "sparticles," or point toward it with any term you choose, but there is that single, most basic "whatever" that all is. Differences in appearance are caused by nothing more than a variance of the vibrational rate at which "that" moves when manifested.) Here's how it works, as explained earlier:

1. A human's body mass is mostly water. Carbon, the basic unit of organic molecules, is the second most common element.
2. A "molecule" is a group of atoms in a definite arrangement held together by chemical bonds.
3. In August of 2005, this pointer was offered:

At the core of the sun, four hydrogen nuclei fuse together to form one helium nucleus, and that happens over and over. The part of the energy that process releases as light travels in particle and wave form. Plant photosynthesis sets the stage for another cycling of manifested energy-consciousness.

4. Likewise, the energy drawn into a cycle from the Absolute pool manifests in plants after it "travels" in a particle or wave form; humans consume

the plants (or the animals that ate the plants), triggering a "transfer" of energy; multi-part atoms of energy are at the core of organic molecules, and organic molecules are at the core of the human body. Everything that is considered "body" can be traced back to its most basic ingredient and that ingredient can be seen to be a temporary manifestation of energy from that field of energy called the Absolute.

What does that have to do with clarifying for students the role of the brain, the "mind," and the consciousness in the Teachings? Recall the earlier pointer: "Consciousness is rooted in the Absolute. The brain is rooted in the elements. The 'mind' is rooted in wrong programming and faulty conditioning and lies and concepts and ideas and superstitions and falsehoods."

THE CONSCIOUSNESS: The conscious-energy, temporarily manifested, is "real" to the degree that it is a form of energy with specific levels of functioning that can be measured. (Why "real" in quotes? Because even this manifested consciousness is time-bound, a temporary expression of that which is truly and eternally real.) Among the triad of elements-breath-consciousness that sustains "life," the manifest consciousness is required. The energy cannot be destroyed. It is and will be.

THE BRAIN: The science above shows that the brain, at its most basic level, is elemental and that conscious-energy is temporarily manifested via those elements; therefore, it is "real" to the degree that all is energy. (This differs not at all from what is revealed about a steel beam if it is studied under an electron microscope: what is not real is the beam as it appears; what is real is that swirling mass of energy that is not visible to the naked eye. Such is the case with the body and with parts such as the brain.) Among the triad of elements-breath-consciousness that sustains "life," the elemental brain is required, the modern use of resuscitating equipment to sustain a body notwithstanding. The elements cannot be destroyed. They will be.

THE "MIND": The "mind" is neither elemental nor energy, so it is not real and it will fade away. It is nothing more than a conglomeration of images and memories that are not real, that are fictional and that are misperceptions. Because it is false and is not "real," it can be purged. Pluck out your brain: end of manifestation. Take steps to end the manifest consciousness: end of manifestation. Purge the mind: not the end of the manifestation. (Because it is only temporary, an Advaitin said, "Heaven and earth shall fades away." Meaning? Just as with all images, when the consciousness fades away, so shall the misconceived images stored in the brain. One could as easily say to the ex-husband mourning the loss of his imagined role, "Your wife and family shall fade away someday." They are just misperceived images in the "mind," and those wrongly-perceived images will not last. When "he" "dies," "she" "dies.") Among the triad of elements-breath-consciousness that sustains "life," the "mind" is not included. It has been shown why "the mind" happened: there was originally a natural part that it was to play in the process of natural living. That is no longer the case.

Maharaj revealed much about that fictional conglomeration called "the mind" and about its false character. He pointed out that awareness is the source of (but different from) the personal, individualized consciousness which manifests via the nervous system of an elemental body and which becomes corrupted. The "mind" and memory, he said, are responsible for association with a particular body; awareness (that pool of energy that has the ability to be aware of if pulled into a cycle of manifestation) exists prior to both mind and memory. He said that this world (which is known to be an illusion) is nothing more than a collection of memories. The collection differs in the mind of every individual, so there are as many imaginary worlds as there are persons. "The world" for each is in them, in their "minds."

He spoke of memories as being time-bound and transient, so they cannot be real. He made the point that only that which is free of memories is timeless and therefore real. He said that desires and fears are based in the memory and that the root of desires and fears are the expectations that are born of memory. Persona / personality is just a shadow of the mind, he said, and the mind he identified as nothing more than "the sum total of memories." Imagination based on memories is unreal. He said the understanding of that would free persons of the trap of memory. The light of consciousness passes through the film of memory and throws pictures on your brain, he said. Thus, because of the chaotic and distorted state of that part of the brain where memories are stored, what you perceive is distorted and colored by feelings of "like" and "dislike."

CHAPTER FOUR

"MIND" and MEMORIES:
When Nature's "Assets" Become Warped into "Liabilities"

THE "deficient and distorted" part of the brain that Maharaj referred to is, of course, that part which stores and accesses memories, so all memories are deficient distortions. Nothing is as it appears to you, and nothing that has ever appeared to you was really the way it was perceived. You have been fooled because that which "they" gave you to use for perceiving is an accumulation of foolishness. Since the "mind" is the sum total of memories, and because all memories are distortions, then the "mind" is the sum total of your distortions. Want to be free of distortions and to Realize truth? Be rid of the "mind." Yet you cannot go beyond the "mind" when you are constantly looking at the "mind" (that is, paying attention to "thought"). In order to go beyond the mind, Maharaj said, you must look away from the "mind" and its fictional contents. That means, therefore, that "minds" are nowadays so deficient and distorted that they should be ignored.

If you have not Realized, you do not see things now the way that they truly are, so it would have been totally impossible to have seen them the way they truly were in the past; therefore, the invitation is to Realize, to see that none of the memories that you are clinging to are accurate (including memories about "happenings," memories involving "persons," and all of the things you were taught to believe that are still stored "in your memory").

Next, understand the reason that there is some talk in the teachings about "Now." (By the way, there is no "power of now" since there is no power. Power is just a concept to which persons become addicted). "Time" too is a concept, so why even speak of now? Because anything supposedly recalled from the "past" is a memory, and it has been established that memories are distortions, so there is

no past and there are no accurate memories. In fact, your entire world is in you...
in your "mind," so how could that which is merely in your "mind" and which
you think is "the world" possibly be real?

The most that the I-Amness can ever claim, therefore, is now, but if
Realization has not happened, even perceptions regarding "now" are distortions.

(Eventually, even that speck of now-time measurement will become meaningless, if you Realize.) If Realized—and thereby free of (false) memories—no
action now would be triggered by a memory of something past. That in itself
would be another level of freedom. For example:

MEMORY-DRIVEN DISTORTION LEADING TO EMOTIONAL

INTOXICATION:

"I am upset because we are no longer together and I don't have the love
now that I had back then."

CLEAR PERCEPTION NOW AS A RESULT OF NOT BELIEVING IN A

DISTORTED, ILLUSORY MEMORY:

"What I thought I had back then was not even close to True Love."

For the Realized, only the now is happening and even that is fleeting. The
more significant point is this: focus on "the now" only as long as it takes to allow
all illusions about "the past" to dissolve. "They" spent so much time building
the walls of your prison with "their" concepts. Then, you took over the task by
taking memories of wrongly-perceived events and persons to be real and thereby
increased the content of your "mind." In that process, you have spent far too
much time adding to the walls and strengthening your prison. Focus any effort
only on breaking the wall which your "mind" has built and which blocks clear
witnessing. Bring in the wrecking crew. You and your teacher together form that
crew. It is time to demolish those walls.

See that, because of programming and conditioning and enculturation and
hidden agendas, what nature had intended to be an asset (memory/"mind") has
become a liability as persons began to desire to control other persons, began to
desire power in order to control others and to control events, and then began to
store misperceptions and misconceptions in the brain.

Earlier it was mentioned: See that the distorted memories being stored today are not being used for survival but are driving conduct that is detrimental to survival. A body that nature intended to be guided by a brain is not being guided more often by a "mind," and whereas the brain is "wired" for self-constructive behavior, the "mind" is now "wired" for self-destructive behavior because of the vast pool of learned ignorance that is being passed on to, and accepted as truth by, billions of persons. (The other factor that drives the "mind" to inspire destructive or self-destructive conduct is the accumulation of the distorted memories of which the "mind" is now composed.)

CHAPTER FIVE

"MIND" and MEMORIES:

When Nature's "Assets" Become Warped into "Liabilities"

TO review, the brain (which was intended by nature to function in a "sustain and preserve" capacity) has now been overridden by the "mind" (which is bent toward chaos, destruction, and self-destruction). The parts of the brain that store and retrieve memories are overshadowing and overpowering all of the rest of the brain in determining how persons emote and behave. Historically, humankind in general attempted to take all necessary action to survive. That has changed.

Today, honor is bestowed by some on those who brag, "I'm willing to die for my country." Today, persons are willing to strap on a dynamite vest and blow up their own bodies and the bodies of those whom they dualistically view as "others" simply because those "others" have different beliefs stored in their "minds." The brain would say, "This is stupid. Do not do that." The dualistic beliefs that make up the "mind" say, "Do it anyway. They are different, so they deserve to die." Supernatural (i.e., religious or spiritual) thinking has perverted the "mind's" original role and has produced more dualistic concepts than any other single source. That single source, in turn, has resulted in more relative existence human deaths than all other causes combined (after natural causes).

NOTE: When such pointers are offered, volumes of mail arrive, asking, "Do you hate religions and spiritual movements?" The response is, "What WHO could be present to hate anything?" If the bag containing your household garbage for several days is finally discarded, are you discarding it because you hate it? Or is it just the sane thing to do? As the garbage is sitting there, are you hating it? No. If your neighbors have not taken out their garbage and really want to hang onto their garbage for a few more days, or even forever, do you hate them for clinging to their trash? Of course not. As you are taking the garbage out to the collection site, are you resenting it? No. You are not giving it a single thought. You realize that it is nothing of value which is being cast aside but is, instead, just garbage.

The tossing of the trash happens without emotion or attachment because you can look at it objectively and see clearly that it is garbage. And if a roommate or spouse says, "This trash has been here too long. It's having a negative impact our lives. Would you throw it away when you go out, please?" Would you ask, "Why do you hate the garbage so much? Why do you suggest I get rid of it? I was taught to love the garbage. I am even willing to fight to preserve the garbage. What is wrong with you that you do not love the garbage?" (Actually, the garbage served a purpose for a time, but it cannot serve a purpose for all time. There comes a point in the history of all garbage when the sane thing to do is to cast it aside and move on. Today, most garbage is stored in that part of the brain called the "mind." It's time to discard the garbage. Will that happen? Only among a very small percentage of the earth's population. So it is.)

To continue, here are a couple of current examples of the "mind" overruling the brain, and the subsequent consequences:

1. The brain of one might say, "You people have no right to start a war and to drop bombs on a country that has done nothing to your country." Similarly, the pure consciousness, aware of the Oneness, would never even consider such an act. But a person functioning under the control of a distorted "mind" that has been programmed with dogmatic nonsense can claim that he has talked with a god from another realm and can claim that his god told him that he should drop bombs on a country that has done no harm to his country.

It should be seen that all conduct that is considered harmful or destructive in the relative existence is a result of programmed and conditioned "minds" over-riding the natural aspects of persons' brains. Therefore, all harmful or destructive conduct (relatively speaking) is based in that which is supernatural or in that which is unnatural (all inspired by the content of the warped "mind"). None of that conduct is inspired by the brain or by the pure consciousness.

2. Consider as another example the case of a person who has weak coping

skills. As pressure mounts, that person might begin to abuse alcohol to escape. One night, that person might consume alcohol until consciousness is lost. The next day, the brain registers the physical condition of the body and sends the message, "That hurt…don't do that anymore." The brain-inspired mouth says, "That hurt. I'm not going to do that anymore."

By 6 P.M. the next evening, the body will have processed much of the alcohol out of the system, the person is feeling better physically, the stress has returned, and he/she repeats the same process of alcohol poisoning again. Where the brain would normally have prevented the insane and harmful repetition, the "mind" nowadays overrules the brain. The person over-drinks again because of the influence of the illogical, unnatural "mind" while ignoring the messages being sent by the logical, natural brain.

The "mind," intended by nature to function in coordination with the brain in order to inspire sane, constructive, and self-constructive behavior (relatively speaking) now short-circuits the natural process and drives destructive and/or self-destructive behavior instead. Thus today the unreal, fictional "mind" drives persons more often, not the real brain and not the real (pure) consciousness. The "mind," no longer a register of things perceived properly, has become a storehouse of beliefs and concepts and dogma and lies and distortions and illusions and all other kinds of faulty perceptions. Whereas the "mind" and brain were intended by nature to work in tandem, today the "mind" supersedes the brain, and since the "mind" is false and corrupt, it reinforces continued belief in the false and corrupt.

CHAPTER SIX

"MIND" and MEMORIES:

When Nature's "Assets" Become Warped into "Liabilities"

THUS, memories form the "mind" as they are stored in the file inside the brain. The memories / "mind" generate body identification, "mind" identification, and personality identification, all of which are illusions but which nevertheless generate catastrophic results (relatively speaking). The memories / "mind" have become the source of "the problem" because the "mind" interrupts the ability of the brain and the pure consciousness to function naturally; furthermore, that "mind," and its belief in illusions and lies, blocks awareness of that which is true and real (the Absolute) and which is prior to body, "mind" and memory.

It should be seen, therefore, that neither "the relative problems of the planet" nor "the problem of being out of touch with reality" has anything to do with either the brain or with the pure consciousness. The problems have everything to do with the false, fictitious "mind" which is nothing more than a body of fallacious information and reasoning fallacies and lies and distortions that have been filed away in a part of the brain. That original system of filing facts away in the brain and of compiling a mind (a storehouse of useful information) which once served humanity so well has now become the scourge of the planet, relatively speaking. That which was once totally natural has been warped by supernatural and dualistic teachings which now drive the unnatural behaviors that plague humanity.

So the "mind" overrides the brain and pure consciousness so that the natural functions of the brain and pure consciousness are interrupted. To return to natural functioning (to live naturally and not live unnaturally or supernaturally) the brain-consciousness balance must be restored. For that to happen, the "mind" (all of the learned ignorance, concepts, beliefs and ideas) must go.

Another visitor asked, "Is a teacher always a requirement, and if so, why?" The answer is, "Yes, with rare exceptions." Why? Because "minds" are warped and twisted and usually require assistance in developing an ability to perceive correctly (meaning in a fashion that is usually 180-degrees opposite of the way that programmed persons perceive things). It has been seen that "mind" formation nowadays interrupts the natural process and results in distorted, unnatural, and supernatural thinking. Here's another example to illustrate what happens and why a teacher is usually required:

To understand the metaphor, you must understand a game played by many young males in east Texas, a game that is called "Riding Pines." The game works like this. Boys will go into the woods and find a pine tree with a thin trunk and 30 feet of height. They climb to around the 20 foot mark. Because of the depth of the tap root and the flexibility of the truck of the tree at that point, they can begin shifting their weight back and forth to the right and then the left and cause the tree to begin to swing widely from side to side. (You may have seen circus performers doing something like this on poles.)

As the tree begins to sway more and more, the rider will eventually cause the tree to sway as far as it can in one direction and then as it swings in the opposite direction, he'll hold the thin trunk and toss his body off the limb he was standing on and then ride the tree down to the ground. If he ends up two or three feet off the ground, he drops, but the goal is to ride it down to the point where the feet end up touching the ground lightly at the perfect height for letting go and standing up without movement. The one who ends up hanging the closest to the ground wins.

On release, a tree springs back to no more than a 45-degree angle, but without intervention the trunk will not straighten back up to its natural and normal vertical condition after it has been warped. The tree will never be able to return to its natural state on its own; however, foresters sometimes find trees that have been ridden and they'll use ropes to pull a tree back to its natural, original condition. Now, here's the Advaitin pointer:

In the forest the life cycle of a pine tree begins when a mature pine cone releases its seeds and germination happens. The consciousness manifested in the seed provides all of the awareness that the seed needs to produce a tree. Soon, a pine tree will begin to grow. At some point, young boys come along and ride the tree. The tree becomes twisted and warped. It will try to straighten up on its own, but it cannot. The tip will seek the light, but the majority of the tree will continue to be bent. The natural functioning, the natural process, was interrupted. Only if foresters attach tension ropes to the tree can it eventually be straightened and returned it to its natural, original condition.

Now, compare that with humans. At maturity, a seed can be released and a pregnancy can happen. The consciousness manifested in the seed provides all of the awareness that the seed needs to produce a "child." Soon, the child might begin to grow. At some point, parents and other persons come along and begin teaching the child. The child becomes twisted and warped because it is being taught lies which adults are claiming to be truth. Later, usually when the stress of the relative existence makes the child feel as if the weight of the world is on his shoulder and riding him down, he might try to straighten up on his own, but he cannot.

The warped tree cannot straighten itself, and the warped "mind" cannot straighten itself. Children as adults might seek the light, but the majority will continue to be bent. If their warped mind is pointed out to them, tension often happens. As with the foresters, a great deal of tension can be involved in straightening out that which is bent and crooked and unnatural.

That which is natural has been interrupted and abandoned among persons, and most cultures try to treat that which is warped by encouraging the accumulation of more knowledge. An Advaita teacher might come along and reveal the way to straighten that which has been twisted and distorted and to return it to its natural, original condition by the only method that works: discarding the content of the warped, illusory, fiction-filled "mind."

CHAPTER SEVEN

"MIND" and MEMORIES:

When Nature's "Assets" Become Warped into "Liabilities"

A seeker asked, "How can consciousness be 'warped' or 'corrupted' if it's just energy?"

There are two views on the issue:

(A) consciousness cannot be warped or made impure. The pure consciousness is merely obscured by layers of lies and concepts that form a "mind" and that obstruct the consciousness from seeing reality and truth when obscured. Adherents of this notion say, "Energy is energy."

(B) Others, however, point out that electricity is energy and that it can be distorted (e.g., an electrical disturbance is merely a type of distorted electricity). Thus, some suggest that the consciousness itself can be warped or contaminated. Svami Prabhupada spoke of contaminated consciousness in the introduction to his translation of the Bhagavad-Gita when he wrote:

> "One cannot say anything about the transcendental world without being free from materially contaminated consciousness. Our consciousness, at the present moment...is materially contaminated. The Bhagavad-gita teaches that we have to purify this materially contaminated consciousness. The activities of the devotee or of the Lord are not contaminated by impure consciousness or matter. We should know, however, that at this point our consciousness is contaminated."

Without debating the merits of "A" or "B" above, seekers can move along the path by understanding the more relevant pointer: whether the consciousness is warped or whether the consciousness is blocked, the content of the "mind" must be removed if Full Realization is to happen. That includes removing beliefs, ideas, dogma, theories, attitudes, "spiritual knowledge," "religious knowledge," and concepts. Only then will the discarded content of the "mind" no longer be able to generate false identifications, and only if the "mind" stops generating personality will there be an end to the emotional reactions and the personality defects that are generated by the assignment of, or the adoption of, personas.

Thus, discussion of the problem of the "mind" must include discussion of the problem of "personality" because they are inextricably linked and because the intricate confusion generated by that linkage cannot end until the false "mind" and its false beliefs in personality end. Only then can the "journey" to Full Realization continue. The terms "Total Freedom," "Liberation," "Awakening," "Realization," "Enlightenment," "Abiding as the Absolute," and "Actualization," all refer to the "condition" of being freed from body-mind-personality identification, knowing the Pure Consciousness, and then attaining the Full Understanding.

Thus, freedom from personality cannot happen without freedom from "mind." It can be seen, therefore, why some Advaitins encourage the casting aside of "mind" which triggers the adoption of personas: the "mind" is defective; the "mind" generates personality; therefore, personality is always defective as well.

That means that, contrary to popular belief, personality—which is generated by a defective "mind"—does not have both "liabilities and assets." All "personality traits" are personality defects (a.k.a., "character defects" since a persona is just a role that is being played as if by a character on a stage). How could a false identity, an imaginary role, possibly have "assets"? That concept is just more of the nonsense generated by ego. "Liabilities as opposed to assets" is just more duality. And the longer that persons remain identified with personality—that is, the longer they play their character roles—the more they attach to their false identities and the farther removed they become from reality. Furthermore, the longer that persons identify with their personality or the roles being played, the more their psyches will deteriorate (that is, the more personality defects will manifest).

The cancerous polyps that once formed in this space did not magically appear. Those malignancies formed as a result of accumulated contamination. Similarly, personality is the cancer on the relative existence, and personality does not magically appear. Personality "forms" as a result of the accumulated contamination that is known as "the mind." The best plan that the mainstream medical community could come up with for this space was to perform surgery, two times per year, "forever," ignorantly addressing the symptoms rather than the cause.

Freedom from the cancer came with a non-traditional, holistic approach. The first step of that approach removed the accumulated contamination which was the filthy quagmire in which the cancer flourished. The "mind" is the quagmire in which the relative-existence filth of personality festers. Advaita is the holistic approach that can remove all of the accumulated contamination and thereby treat the cause and not just the symptoms (the symptoms being all of the suffering and misery or all of the nonsense and stupidity that mark the relative existence of persons.)

Why will fewer than 1 in 10,000,000 be freed of the filthy quagmires of mind and personality? Because of the ego's pride in its mind, because of the ego's sense of self-importance that follows the adoption of religious or spiritual personas and which, in turn, prevents the completion of the full "journey" to Realization, and because of the ego's vanity around its accumulation of knowledge (a.k.a., learned ignorance).

CHAPTER EIGHT

"MIND" and PERSONALITY:
What Cultures Consider "Assets" Are Actually "Liabilities"

"MIND" and "personality" cannot be separated since the former gener-ates belief in the latter. The latter, in turn, generates all emotional intoxication. [While the Realized can witness feelings rise and fall, only ego-states—only assumed personas—emote. When personas believe that they are experiencing some slight, hurt, threat or interference, a series of actions and reactions are inspired that trigger emotional intoxication as well as destructive and/or self-destructive behavior.] When persons are trapped in the agendas of their false roles, then emotions will always overwhelm cognitive functioning, so now a new pointer is available:

It has been seen that the "mind" can override the constructive functioning of the brain; now it is seen that persona-generated emotionalism can also subdue the manner in which nature had originally intended that the brain should function. Now the degree of wisdom behind the Advaitin pointer that one must relinquish identification with the "mind" and the personality as well as with the body becomes clear. Review the evolution of the brain in regards to this latest understanding:

Humanity functioned with a mind-less brain for thousands of years. The brain evolved, developing an area for storing memories and an organ that could retrieve memories. Those two areas of the brain were intended to help humanity survive and to behave constructively. No personas were taken to be identities.

As language developed, information being stored in the brain was less and less of the character of things observed and became filled more and more with the remembering of things told. To observe a friend who touched a burning log, to see his pain, to file away that memory, and to recall that memory when next in the presence of a burning log produced behavior that would be considered "sane." To the contrary, to observe crops dying as a result of the lack of rain, and then to be told that the rain is being withheld by an angry god who wants a priest to fornicate with a virgin and who wants the priest to cut out her beating heart with a sharp-edged rock and pass it through the crowd during a commune-with-god service produced behavior that would be considered "insane."

The result of thousands of years of being conditioned to believe in whatever one is told rather than witnessing objectively and believing in that which is observable and provable has resulted in a planet that is populated with masses of sheep-like persons who unquestioning go along with almost anything that they are told by persons who are labeled as "their leaders" or as so-called "experts" in their cultures. After centuries and millennia of such conditioning, the ability among persons to distinguish true from false has been lost. The result is an appearance that the earth's masses are all insane because they have abandoned natural living and are living unnaturally or supernaturally (that is, trapped in magical thinking that tries to explain naturally-occurring events with supernatural explanations that amount to nothing more than fantasies).

In modern cultures, however, such phrases as "Look at that idiot" or "That's guy's insane" are usually off the mark. A more accurate diagnosis would be, "Look at that space that has assumed a persona which is inspiring idiot-like behavior" or "Look at that space that has assumed a persona which is inspiring insane-like behavior." The distinction must be made: the teachings of the Advaita philosophy cannot address mental illness. The teachings address the far more common condition in which persons appear to be suffering a mental illness when in fact they are merely trapped in identification with personas that were assigned by members of a culture or that have been adopted by persons living under the influence of a culture. Thus, an earlier quote can now be expanded:

"Consciousness is rooted in the Absolute. The brain is rooted in the elements. The 'mind' is rooted in wrong programming and faulty conditioning and lies and concepts and ideas and superstitions and falsehoods. Personas are rooted in programmed minds and are sustained by the ego-based lies and by the learned ignorance that are being taught in most modern cultures."

Since mental illnesses cannot be addressed by philosophical teachings, the difference in being truly insane and in merely functioning under the auspices of a warped "mind" (and under the influence of believing that personas are real identities) must be made clear. The pointer is often offered that it certainly appears insane when one does not know Who/What He / She Truly Is. Now the clarification can be offered that, technically, that is not insanity. That is nothing more than evidence of the power of programming. For example, it certainly appeared insane when Pavlov's dogs salivated at the sound of a bell rather than as a result of smelling the aroma of meat. But those dogs were not insane. They were programmed and conditioned.

Such is the case with almost all of humanity today, so while most who do not know Who/What They Truly Are would be considered insane, the "not-knowing" is understandable when it is clear that programming and conditioning and enculturation combine to blind persons and to block them from knowing the True Self. That "not-knowing" of their Real Identity, then, sets persons up to adopt false identities instead.

CHAPTER NINE

"MIND" and PERSONALITY:
What Cultures Consider "Assets" Are Actually "Liabilities"

So to differentiate between behavior that is driven by mental illness as opposed to that which is driven by programming and conditioning and enculturation, it must be understood that taking personas to be actual identities results in personality disorders which only look like insanity to the objective witness; nevertheless, personality disorders do block the cognitive functioning of the brain. Further, personality disorders block the natural and normal functioning of the brain and body far more often than do mental illnesses. The results of a study of global mental illness by the World Health Organization and Harvard Medical School, as reported in The Journal of the American Medical Association, reveal that from 1 to 5 percent of the populations of most of the countries surveyed had serious mental illness.

By contrast, estimates are that 99% of the earth's population suffer from one or more personality disorders; thus, as Advaitin sages have taught for centuries, the relative existence problems of the planet are rooted in personality. Realization offers the opportunity to eliminate most of the problems of the planet since they are rooted in personality, not in mental illness. When diagnosable mental health problems reach a level of seriousness that is labeled "clinical," then a mental illness exists and professional intervention and treatment are indicated. Advaita cannot treat such conditions; however, those mental illnesses are very different from personality disorders, and personality disorders can be addressed and eliminated via the understanding that is attainable by way of the Advaita teachings. Psychiatrists and psychotherapists attempt to treat mental illnesses. Realization offers the treatment for personality disorders.

Since personality disorders are far more common on planet earth than are mental illnesses, then a logical approach would involve this: when insane-type behavior is being observed, look first to determine if personality is inspiring the conduct in an effort to sustain an illusory self. Again, while the effects of personality on behavior often appear to involve some degree of mental illness—with persons certainly seeming to be totally insane at times—mental illness and personality disorders are different.

59% of all women and 41% of all men who are killed in the U.S. will die during a "relationship breakup." Some speak of "temporary insanity" as a persona (such as "husband" or "wife" or "lover") strikes out when a false identity feels threatened. Those crimes appear to be evidence of a mental illness, yet the stage for those murders is always set long before the murders happen. The murders happen as a result of enculturation whereby persons accept a culturally-assigned persona as a true identity, take it to define who they truly are, and are then willing to kill in an effort to protect a fictitious role assigned within their societies. That which is labeled "insanity" or "temporary insanity" in such cases is not actually a mental illness at all. The astronomical murder rate across the planet is a result of personality, not a result of clinical mental illness. Yet most people on the planet dismiss such conduct as "insane" while never being aware of the actual role that personality is playing.

Another reason that personality defects and mental illnesses are mistaken (one for the other) is because the same type of destructive or self-destructive tendencies can be triggered by either. It is true that mental illnesses and personality disorders both call for "treatment," and the call should be an urgent one, but the effective treatments for those two conditions are quite different. Again, psychiatrists and psychotherapists attempt to treat mental illnesses. Realization offers the treatment for personality disorders.

All but the truly insane, the too young, or the brain-damaged can Realize, though the power of faulty programming and conditioning will prevent most persons from ever doing so. Most will remain trapped in personality for the entire period of manifestation. If Realization is to happen, some questions to be asked include, "What personas have you adopted and how powerful is their influence upon your behavior? When angry or hurt, WHO is feeling the anger or hurt? What persona is causing you to be miserable or to suffer or to generate conflict? How is ego, and your assumption of ego-states as identities, driving you throughout each and every day, all day long?"

CHAPTER TEN

"MIND" and PERSONALITY:
What Cultures Consider "Assets" Are Actually "Liabilities"

PLEASE consider: one Advaitin seeker who had prostate cancer reported that, if the passing of blood had not happened, he would have never known the problem so he would never have sought the solution. This book is identifying the root of the widespread problems of the planet in order that persons might (a) better understand the cause of their problems and also know that (b) the Advaita Teachings offer a solution.

While many would dismiss other persons as "insane" if they disagree with them, most behavior that appears to be insane is actually rooted in personality. So that is the problem. Then, knowing the problem, one might be willing to seek the solution, namely, Realization. For some, the direct path approach will "work" for some persons; the traditional path might work for some seekers; and other, newer approaches might work for other seekers. The solution is found when the suitable "path" is followed to its end.

So, the problems of the planet are, for the most part, rooted in "personality conflict." That is a term that is typically used to minimize the reasons that a "relationship" "failed," but the term can be used accurately in light of the statistics shared earlier: while up to 5% of the planet's population was shown by research to have mental illnesses, 99% have personality disorders. As evidence, one estimate is that 99% suffer from the Addictive Personality Disorder, being addicted to substances or food or spending or gambling or sex or money or power, ad infinitum.

Most persons suffer from multiple problems because most have internalized several of the basic personality types and dozens of others. Each type can cause the manifestation of more than one disorder. Are you beginning to understand what persons are "up against" in any effort to be free? Are you beginning to see why some sages have estimated that less than 1% of the planet's population will ever Realize fully and then be free of the effects of programming, enculturation, conditioning and be freed simultaneously from the nonsense and conflict and angst that accompany body-mind-personality identification?

Thus, the major "problem of the planet" is personality and the warped "mind" that generates and supports it; furthermore, the treatment for identification with personality will never be sought simply as a result of being diagnosed with a personality disorder. Most persons will either remain blind to their disorders, will deny their disorders, will discount or dismiss their disorders, or will minimize the relative effects of their disorders. Some will even use their personality type to justify their behavior and dismiss any suggestions that they consider getting free of the effects of personality, claiming, "That's just the way I am." Usually, major consequences are required in order for most persons to be inspired to even try to become free of the impact of personality and the destruction associated with their personality-driven conduct.

While some cultures make exception for those suffering from clinical mental illnesses ("innocent by reason of insanity") most do not understand at all the far more prevalent nonsense and suffering generated by personality. Thus, both the problem (personality) and the solution (Realization) are being identified to allow visitors to know where their problems are likely rooted and to know that the solution is offered via the Advaita teachings and Full Realization.

If no relative existence consequences manifest from the nonsense and stupidity and misery and suffering that are generated by (the always defective) personality, then persons will never exert any effort to become free of personality defects and the relative-existence-effects of those personality flaws. Seekers are those who know "something is wrong in this picture" or who sense that "something is missing" or who at least consider the possibility that "maybe some of my ideas and beliefs and thoughts are contributing to my problems." The non-seekers living under the influence of personality will continue along their destructive path and can eventually become sociopaths who will never seek any change or any alternate perspective. They will fight to defend their false images/personas to the "end."

Three factors cause persons to attach to their false identities, to be driven to fight to defend their false personality / personalities, to descend into the depths of what some professionals term "an unhealthy psyche," and then to suffer the effects of personality disorders. Those three factors are (1) stress, (2) extreme piety or spirituality, and (3) the linking of money / income with a persona. For example?

One who receives money as a result of playing a spiritual role will become far more attached to the role than one playing a spiritual role for ego-gratification only but not receiving money as a result of assuming that role. As another example, a person sitting in a congregation playing the role of "The Super Christian" becomes far more trapped in that role if she/he is subsequently hired to serve on the staff of the church and is paid to work in that position. All three areas will be reviewed.

> STRESS: The enneagram method of "personality classification" and "behavior forecasting" is highly accurate in showing that certain types will disintegrate into behaving like another type when under stress. (No recommendation is being made to become an "expert" in personality functioning. It will only generate another ego-state, it might give credibility to personality rather than help all personality dissolve, and it is certainly not necessary to become an expert in mirages to understand a mirage is a mirage.) The pointer is, persons who are stressed will cling to their personas, will fight to defend their image(s), and will stay absorbed in personality until it drives them into those levels of "an unhealthy psyche."

> INCOME: It should be easily understood why a persona that generates income will drive a person to attach to and defend that persona.

> ASSUMPTION OF "GOOD ROLES": That leaves extreme piety and/or spirituality. Most who play those roles, even including Advaitin seekers following some of the newer paths or the traditional path, haven't a clue that they have merely fixated in another role when the goal is to be role-free. Others will claim that their religion or spiritual program is "getting them in touch with the Great Reality" or "makes then kind and loving" and "does nothing to create anything that separates them from others." Records of the historical conduct of those two personas as well as objective observation of their conduct nowadays attests to the contrary. Those

roles do represent the third of the seven steps to Reality, but to fixate in the playing of those roles will prevent Full Realization.

Now an additional obstacle to Realization can be seen. A basic irony involved in the search for Realization and freedom from personality is that the very reasons that inspire many seekers to undertake the "journey" are also the very reasons that they cannot complete the "journey." Some seekers want to be stress-free and at peace. Some seekers long to be free of all role-playing and to know the True Self and to find the answers to the age-old questions about "the functioning of the Totality." Some want to live in a simpler fashion and to be free of the money games and the accumulation games in which they are trapped.

Yet stress, role-playing "the good roles" of "The Religious One" or "The Spiritual Giant," and co-mingling role-playing with money accumulation are the three buttresses that support the assumption and defense of phony roles...of false identities...of personality. What is the solution?

CHAPTER ELEVEN

"MIND" and PERSONALITY:
What Cultures Consider "Assets" Are Actually "Liabilities"

PART of the solution to being free of the influence of personality is to understand why personality develops and to see how truly bizarre and perverted are its roots. Why did Maharaj teach that the relative problems of adulthood are rooted in the distortions of childhood? Genetic and body chemistry factors aside, personality develops primarily as children attempt to develop a strategy for coping with the circumstances that they face in their families of origin, circumstances that have become increasingly bizarre as the centuries have passed.

Those behavioral patterns developed during childhood (patterns which came about as a result of bizarre circumstances) then drive persons throughout the rest of their childhood and their adulthood as well, a fact which guarantees the continued cycling of lunacy and nonsense. Bizarre circumstances produce a bizarre personality which generates even more bizarre behavior and circumstances during adulthood. Subsequently, those adults will bear children and then another generation will face bizarre circumstances as a result of bizarre-thinking adults and the bizarre programming and conditioning and enculturation that they pass along. Such environments force another generation of children to develop defective personalities in an effort to cope with the defective circumstances presented by adults who are driven by defective minds and defective thoughts and defective personalities.

To understand that adults are being driven by the subconscious strategies of a child within makes clear why so much childish nonsense is being generated among adults. It explains why adults will childishly follow a leader as he guides them into the depths of hell-on-earth; it explains why adults will childishly and unquestioningly believe the most nonsensical claims about "the supernatural," claims that have been dreamed up in the minds of controlling men dominated by their magical thinking; it explains why most of the 6.5 billion persons on the planet behave like children, no matter the chronological age of their bodies; it explains why persons erroneously think they have power and are making choices when they are choosing nothing but are being driven, powerlessly and unconsciously, by the personality/strategies of those remnants of a child within.

That is why the masses are sleepwalking: they are as children, children with warped minds and perverted personalities, who are walking about in adult-age bodies. To see the roots of personality and to see the foolishness that personality generates should inspire any person with any degree of wisdom at all to understand why the Teachings urge seekers to discard the distorted contents of the mind and to reject the influence of the always-defective personality.

The irony is that something that is an illusion (such as the personas that are generated by the circumstances described above) can impact the relative existence. Seekers are invited to realize how even a mirage can affect behavior if the mirage is taken to be real. An example used in the past involves the driver of a car moving along a road when a mirage appears, whereupon the driver jerks the steering wheel quickly (in order to avoid the mirage) and crashes into a tree. Though the mirage is certainly not real, the relative-existence effects of taking a mirage to be real are indisputable.

Eventually, persona-playing will always lead persons to personality disorders, to believing that their images are real, and to believing that they know why they do what they do and believing they know who they are when, in fact, they do not have the slightest clue. Here's the way that novelist John D. MacDonald described that detachment from reality in the life of a man who is typical of all persons:

"...The world is full of reasonably nice guys.... They go through all the motions of home and family, but there is no genuine love or emotion involved. There is an imitation kind. They are unconscious practicing hypocrites. They're stunted in a way that they don't and can't recognize. [They] go around with the unspoken, unrealized conviction that nobody else exists, really, except as ... bits of stage dressing in the life roles that they are playing. So wife and child and job and home are part of the image...but without any deep involvement with anybody but [self]. But don't fault him. He believes he is really in the midst of life and always has been. He doesn't know any better, because he's never known anything else. What a limited man believes is emotional reality is his emotional reality."

Then an exchange between two characters follows that point:

"Doesn't everybody fake a little in their own way?"

"Sure. And you're aware of it when you do it, aren't you?"

"Uncomfortably."

"But he isn't. And that's the difference."

That is the description of the typical relative existence of any person being driven by strategies developed during childhood and accepting the limited identification with the body and the limited identification with "mind"-induced personas as identities. Persons (those identifying with their bodies and minds and personalities) are fakes, yet they haven't a clue that they're fakes. Most are self-absorbed (absorbed in their false selves, their false personalities) but they haven't a clue. Nor do they have the slightest suspicion that they are suffering from "Seven Degrees of Separation From Reality" as a result of taking their false personalities and false beliefs and false concepts and false ideas to be truth.

CHAPTER TWELVE

"MIND" and PERSONALITY:
What Cultures Consider "Assets" Are Actually "Liabilities"

IF one walks into a forest and becomes lost, the surest way out is to retrace one's steps, exactly, in reverse order. Similarly, the "path" to Realization is the exact opposite, step-by-step, of the way one became lost in body-mind-personality identification. This series is showing how the contamination process happened in order to see what must occur for the re-purification of the consciousness to happen. Only if one sees, "Oh, my gosh, yes, that applies to me" might one realize why the "journey" is indicated as the appropriate "treatment" for what ails the earth's human population.

So, see that persons are like that character in MacDonald's novel (as reported in the previous chapter): totally out of touch with reality, living as if actors on a stage, and playing their fake roles and not knowing that they are fakes. They truly believe that their roles define who they are, and that's why those trapped in personality identification appear to be insane and totally out of touch with reality. They developed a set of tools during childhood to use to address one specific set of circumstances. The folly is that they continue to use that same set of tools (their personality and the behaviors that are driven by their personality) in every situation that arises throughout adulthood.

Therefore, the earlier points that "persona-playing will lead persons to personality disorders" and that "adults behave in childish ways" should now be understood. What remains to be understood is what those "bizarre circumstances" are that drive children to develop a specific personality and to behave in the ways that are unique to that personality type. (Note: the egotism of most parents will inspire them to reject any consideration that they created a bizarre environment for their children to be raised in, and the egotism of most children will reject the same consideration. The tendency among persons is to "normalize" their circumstances, no matter how many elephants in the kitchen are being ignored, or to "minimize" their circumstances: "Well, they did the best they could.")

So does the term "bizarre circumstances" include sexual abuse and therefore not apply to the majority who believe they were "pretty darn good parents" or that they had "pretty darn good parents"? No, as bizarre as sexual abuse is, that is not the bizarre environment that most grew up in; however, most children do suffer from physical, mental and emotional abuse as well as abnormal parent-child relations. The most common "bizarre circumstances" that force children to develop personalities for coping with an abnormal environment include families that are overly-restrictive and that impose rigid, puritanical demands; families that offer only conditional love or none at all; families that are overly-indulgent in child-rearing or who create dual imaging (public vs. private) so that family secrets are kept behind closed doors; and families in which neither parent understands their children or in which abandonment issues are fostered.

Also included are families which generate in children a sense of threat or fear more often than they provide a sense of security and well-being; families in which a parent is anal-retentive and overly-critical; families in which one or both parents engage in contests for control with the children, contests which the children often win; and families that spoil the children so badly that as adults those children have no drive or motivation, develop a sense of entitlement, and thus expect to be taken care of by others. These are the most prevalent types of environments that are not healthy and that are bizarre in terms of parent-child relations. Those are the environments that inspire children to develop coping skills/personality in order to deal with abnormal circumstances.

Each of the nine personality types identified by the enneagram, therefore, developed certain traits and behaviors in childhood that "worked" to some degree in those early, unhealthy parent-child relations but that become major obstacles when applied to adult-aged relations (which are most typically marred with the playing of "The Child role" or "The Parent role" in the absence of "Adult"-appropriate conduct). Here are the abnormal home conditions that generate personality and that set children on a destructive course as they apply their childhood strategies to adult-age circumstances (meaning, as they unconsciously allow personality to dictate the ways that they think, emote, and behave):

Often, Type Ones as children were trying to cope with a rigid, judgmental environment in which parents set forth unreasonably excessive moral and ethical demands and expectations, especially involving religious restrictions. Ones become reformers or perfectionists, can become highly self-critical if they don't adhere as adults to the parental expectations that were set forth during childhood, can become judgmental, and will often label others as being "bad" or "evil."

Often, Type Twos as children were trying to cope with an environment in which parents were emotionally unavailable, were offering only a conditional version of love, or wherein a parent (often the father) was in absentia, physically or otherwise. They can spend their entire adulthood is a search for love and will give away far too much in the quest.

Often, Type Threes as children were reacting to an especially indulgent parent (often to the mother). Sometimes, an abusive male parent was present, and the hiding of family secrets set the stage for manufacturing the images that were shown outside the home (which were quite different from the abusive reality that existed inside the home). The stage was set for creating and maintaining positive images while living darker lives behind closed doors. Threes, therefore, can experience a sense of incongruity since their "positive" outside image never matches their "negative" inside reality. Adult Threes can be charming in public venues but can be sadistic behind the closed doors of an office, a home, etc. They become charismatic performers and achievers in public but that is fakery. They usually become vicious as they competitively strive to outdo or even crush all others who do not please them, and they will use a vile tongue to try to diminish the objects of their anger.

Often Type Fours as children were trying to cope with a fear of abandonment and being misunderstood by parents. An internal, fantasy-driven inner life often developed. They become the romantics who are the most likely to engage in the "search for Self," but that often leaves them remote and distant. Fours who do not find Self can eventually isolate; Fours who do find Self can enjoy the solitude without becoming isolationists.

Often, Type Fives as children were trying to cope with a hostile environment wherein their parents generated a sense of threat more often than a sense of security. Some Fives also had an early experience with death. Obsessing over what many take to be "the morbid" can dominate their thoughts and conduct.

Often, Type Sixes as children were trying to cope with a perceived need to develop a relationship with an authority figure (often a male) in order to feel secure. They will spend a lifetime seeking security and following the orders of their political or religious or spiritual leaders (usually males) no matter the degree of nonsense or self-contradiction expounded by those leaders. Fifty percent of all people are Sixes (who often show the personality traits of Type Threes. The planet, therefore, is dominated by those showing Type Three-Six traits.) Sixes, during adulthood, can be dominated by fear and a search for security, which explains their blind loyalty to political and religious leaders whom they think can protect them, both now and "forevermore."

The other types will be discussed tomorrow, but do you understand the role that the warped mind plays as it generates warped personalities as a result of growing up in warped environments? Are you seeing why adults perform so poorly in trying to create healthy relations during their relative existence? Are you seeing why most adults behave childishly and why, short of Full Realization, they will never be able to choose to behave differently...driven as they are by their childhood tool set? Are you seeing how childhood programming and conditioning prevent adults from making sound, sane, and independent choices?

CHAPTER THIRTEEN

"MIND" and PERSONALITY:
What Cultures Consider "Assets" Are Actually "Liabilities"

OFTEN, Type Sevens as children were trying to cope with a rigid or emotionally-unavailable or demanding parent (more often the mother). Sevens sense, rightly or wrongly, that the inflexible parent is never totally pleased with them or that the parent is never willing to fully accept their uniqueness. (That is generally a result of the fact that the mothers of many Sevens were either facing their own challenges at the time the Seven was a child; or had an attachment disorder; or were over-stressed because of circumstances but lacked the coping skills to deal effectively with those circumstances; or were preoccupied with their own agenda and interests.) Sevens as children become dedicated to trying to lighten the mood of the overly-serious parent. As a result, Seven's end up on a life-long quest to have fun and escape restrictions (such as those imposed by a rule-loving parent). Later, however, they also become hesitant to make commitments in their own adult relations, preferring to keep many options open instead.

Often, Type Eights as children were trying to cope with a mother in a battle for control. Typically, the Eights succeeded in getting their way as a child and they expect to always get their way throughout their adult years as well. They usually become domineering and controlling and often want both earthly and "heavenly" power in order to have all of the power necessary in order to try to control everything and everyone.

Often, Type Nines as children were dealing with excessively supportive or indulgent parents, so as adults they have a sense of entitlement that makes work unattractive and creates an expectation that others should take care of them.

Nines can become quite lazy and can use passive-aggressive methods to manipulate others to care for them.

(NOTE: It has been asked in the past, "If childhood and family conditions have such an influence on determining personality type, why do siblings so often have different personality types?" The answer is, "Because no two brothers or sisters are raised by the 'same' parents or in the 'same' family." Meaning? Meaning that parents are in a state of flux and families are in a state of flux. The dynamics are never the same for any two children, though they might be members of the 'same' family, since economic cycles rise and fall, since the parents' relationship ebbs and wanes, and since the addition of each child affects the character of the family unit.)

Thus, the most common personality defects (as revealed above) which mar the relative existence include the following: self-absorption; judgmentalism; giving, but only in order to receive even more in return; viciousness; being overly-competitive; being phony; being aloof; being unavailable; being morbid; being fear-based and insecure; being blindly loyal; being an escapist; being a control freak; being demanding; and being lazy. Those are the typical products of the basic personality types. Add the defects that appear when persons adopt another twenty or thirty ego-states ("spouse," "employee," "lover," "homeowner," etc.) and the fallout from personality becomes overwhelming, throwing the entire planet into chaos. Some have asked: "What about those who are 'healthy' and behave 'well'"? The answer is simple:

The very worst of each personality type in evidenced when persons are stressed, overly pious, or making money off their phony role-playing. How many on the planet are not either stressed, overly-pious, or receiving income for playing their roles? The negatives are prevalent—relatively speaking—and dominate the "human (persona) experience."

The more significant Advaita pointer is this: when strategies (a) originated in the mind of a child who was trying to cope with abnormal circumstances and when those strategies (b) produced a specific personality and when (c) those childhood strategies are still driving abnormal and subconscious behavior years later, then those are strategies that actually should play no part at all in the relative-existence lives of adults. For freedom to happen, the warped "mind" that generated personality during childhood must be dissolved and the personality (and its persona-driven behaviors) must be discarded.

Next, there are two or three specific personality disorders that are common to each of the basic personality types, so those will be discussed. In the meanwhile, are you seeing any of those examples of personality in your own conduct? Do you see any evidence of those remnants of a child within often controlling your thoughts and behaviors? Are you seeing why Advaitin sages recommend being free of body-mind-personality identification?

Are you seeing why Advaitins make the point that the problems of the relative existence are rooted in personality and that, in order to be free of chaos, all personal attributes and personal identifications must be discarded?

CHAPTER FOURTEEN

"MIND" and PERSONALITY:
What Cultures Consider "Assets" Are Actually "Liabilities"

THE "mind" has been shown to be the source of all assumed personality. Personality, in turn, has been shown to be the source of most of the relative existence problems on the planet, and each of the nine basic types generates a particular set of personality disorders. Before looking at the personality disorders that each of the basic types generates, a point should be offered that comes from the American Psychiatric Association's Diagnostic and Statistical Manual of Mental Disorders, 4th edition, 1994 (commonly referred to as "DSM-IV"):

A personality disorder is a pattern of deviant or abnormal behavior that the person doesn't change even though it causes emotional upsets and trouble with other people at work and in personal relationships. It is not limited to episodes of mental illness, and it is not caused by drug or alcohol use, head injury, or illness.

So, all of the (relative) negatives of personality, negatives which have motivated Advaitin sages for centuries to encourage the abandonment of personality, are becoming better understood. What additional motivation to Realize could possibly be required among those with any wisdom at all, once the facts about personality are understood: (1) to identify with the personality, formed as a childhood exercise, is a disorder; (2) the behavior that follows the assumption of personality is deviant and abnormal; (3) it is persons—not the Realized—who cling to false personas as identities; (4) emotional intoxication is rooted in personality; (5) relative existence problems, whether at work or at home or in between are rooted in personality; (6) personality has nothing to do with mental illnesses; and (7) personality problems are not caused by addiction, physical injury, or mental illness.

As a relevant example of the DSM-IV definition, apply it to the billions who are suffering from the Addictive Personality Disorder (APD). Take drug or alcohol abuse as an example. Per definition, the disorder is "not caused by drug or alcohol use." The drug or alcohol abuse is a symptom of a personality disorder. Neither the drug nor the alcohol is the core problem; therefore, if an alcoholic suffering from APD merely stops drinking, that will have no effect at all on removing the negative traits and behaviors of the personality disorder. The traits and behaviors will continue as a result of what the primary literature calls the "grave mental and emotional disorders" that APD's exhibit. (Also, note that the literature did not say that APD's have "grave mental and emotional illnesses," though some do. Most are suffering personality disorders, not mental illness. That applies to all APD's, no matter whether they are addicted to food, power, gambling, shopping, another person, alcohol, religion, drugs, sex, love, spirituality, chaos, money, etc.)

As noted earlier, the reason that persons with disorders typically do not change is because consequences are not imposed or because they are not imposed to a degree that inspires taking the necessary action to be free of the effects of one or more personality disorders. (That is another reason that few will ever seek Realization and why fewer still will ever Realize fully.)

Further, any rationalizations and justifications and denial and excuse-making in regards to those with personality disorders—such as "His/her behavior must be understood or tolerated as a result of mental illness" or "She/he is an alcoholic or drug addict and that must be considered" or "He/she has some injury or illness"—are (as shown by the definition above) totally unfounded, inapplicable, and irrelevant in regards to personality disorders. Tolerance of the warped thinking and warped behavior of persons with such disorders only prolongs their entrapment in personality and guarantees the continued manifestation of the effects of their disorders.

Now, pause to reconsider the information quoted above from the DSM-IV. Then, list all of the roles that you have assumed that are inspiring you to feel anxious or to fight. Are there certain self-images that are you trying to defend? Is there any evidence that you are forfeiting the fullness and freedom of AS IF living in order to maintain some assumed personality/persona? Are you having trouble in a relationship because "The Boss" persona is fighting for control? Are you angry with someone who is not supporting your false image?

CHAPTER FIFTEEN

"MIND" and PERSONALITY:
What Cultures Consider "Assets" Are Actually "Liabilities"

TO review the key pointers offered so far:

- For millions of years, human or human-like beings functioned in a manner guided by the brain (not unlike the deer today).

- The human brain began to expand in size and capability only recently (in evolutionary terms) and developed the capacity to store memories and to retrieve (natural) memories in order to recall information that could protect the body and perpetuate the survival of the species.

- Pre-language memories did their natural job: they created a "mind" that contained information which led to constructive behavior and helped avoid potentially-dangerous situations.

- After languages developed, persons with personal agendas began programming and conditioning the minds of persons in order to control them and influence opinion, beliefs, and conduct. Rather than storing natural information, the brain began storing unnatural teachings and magical teachings about supposedly "supernatural" beings and events. True freedom was lost because behavior came to be controlled by one's programmers and their teachings, even if they were not present. (If one is conditioned, then freedom is nothing more than a concept and certainly cannot be real if a person's actions and reactions are the unconscious result of programming and conditioning.)

- Once persons began storing ideas and beliefs and concepts in their minds (instead of recording fact-based observations that could assist in natural living), then memories became dualistic in their nature: "Our tribe is good, but their tribe is bad," and "We have the right to punish those whose memories contain information that differs from the concepts and beliefs in our memories." The "mind" became a distorted conglomeration of corruptions and lies.

- As human behavior became more deviant and abnormal as a result of dualistic beliefs and concepts, children began forming personalities in an effort to try to deal with abnormal family situations.

- As more dualistic beliefs and concepts were stored in memory because humans were being exposed to more and more programming and conditioning, a greater sense of separation from others and Self became more common as the "mind" became more corrupted and warped and as personas were attached to as an identities.

- As more adjusting was required among children who were trying to adapt to more and more abnormal circumstances, more personalities were formed. Then, children attached to their personalities (that is, to that childish set of "tools" being used to cope with the abnormal).

- As persons attached more and more to personality, which is rooted in childhood and in childishness, adults began to lose the ability to choose and instead fell under the influence and control of a childish personality. Childish ways were taken into adult-age situations. Adults, unconsciously driven by memories and programming and personality, began to behave more and more in childish and no sensible ways.

- Human behavior which is typically inspired by aberrations of personality now generates the majority of the "problems of the planet" as personality disorders determine (unconsciously) how persons emote, how they think, and, therefore, what they do. Each of the basic personality types eventually began to generate a particular set of personality disorders which then generated suffering for each of those types and for all of those who must try to deal with them.

- The result is this: billions of persons are walking about the planet, believing that they are choosing to do what they do when, in fact, they are sleepwalking...doing what their programmers would have them do; thus, all that they think and feel and do is determined by the emotional intoxication that they suffer as a result of unconsciously allowing a set of childish, childhood tools to guide them through adulthood. And all of that is based in illusion. Why? The past is an illusion. How can one possibly be free if everything being done, thought or felt in "the present" is a reaction to false perceptions formed in "the past"?

- The solution to "the problem of the planet" is Realization, including the discarding of all body-mind-personality identifications.

The discussion will now focus on the specific personality disorders that are common to each of the nine basic types, beginning with Personality Type Ones who can exhibit a God Complex Disorder, the OCD Personality Disorder and the Depressive Personality Disorder. Again, those happen most often when Type One persons are stressed, when they are overly-pious or seeing themselves as being highly-spiritual, or when they receive money as a result of their role-playing.

Type Ones (and Type Sevens who disintegrate into Type Ones) can be prone to perfectionism, including the belief that they are perfect and that all others should be perfect, according to the Ones' definition of "perfect." The God Complex Disorder inspires persons to act arrogantly, as if they have been appointed by a god or sent on a mission by a god. In the extreme, they act as if they are god, deciding who should live, who should die, judging who is right and moral, or determining who is wrong and immoral (using criteria based in childhood programming). Their sense of being perfect supports duality as they feel separate from—and superior to—"others." Note how duality is fostered by the assumption of personality.

The Obsessive-Compulsive Personality Disorder drives persons to accept mortgages on homes that are larger than they can afford, drives addictive behavior, and inspires persons to rush into or out of relationships. Professional researchers claim that OCD is one of the top causes of lost income and relative existence problems. The Depressive Personality Disorder is another common result of this personality identification, and while 95% of the earth's population suffer the defect to one degree or another, most are in denial and claim that they are "really happy" and "have a great life."

In fact, the Depressive Personality Disorder is marked by duality, so there are constant shifts between states of happiness and unhappiness, high esteem and low esteem, optimism and pessimism, acceptance and rejection, and all of the chaotic movements that mark the instability in the lives of persons trapped in personality and in each personality type's companion disorders. Is it becoming clear that almost all of humankind's relative existence problems are related to body-mind-personality identification and the nonsense that such identification generates?

CHAPTER SIXTEEN

"MIND" and PERSONALITY:
What Cultures Consider "Assets" Are Actually "Liabilities"

THE focus now is on the particular personality disorders that develop among each of the nine basic personality types. Personality Type Twos can eventually exhibit the OCD Personality Disorder, a God Complex Disorder, and the Histrionic Personality Disorder and, as always with personality assumption, deeper attachment to false identities happens when persons are stressed, are absorbed in the ego of religiosity or the spiritualized ego, or receive payments for their role-playing.

Personality Type Two's especially display the Histrionic Personality Disorder (a.k.a., Dramatic Personality Disorder) as they fall more and more under the influence of their personality. Again, the relative effects of personality are proven when you observe this disorder in action and see Two's who suffer instability and emotional intoxication and a distorted self-image. You can see persons suffering this personality defect as their desire to be noticed inspires then to act (and over-react) in ways that are overly-dramatic, highly-theatrical, and generally inappropriate. They become self-ish givers since they intend to get back more than they give, desiring more attention, more "love," more "respect," more self-worth, etc. All of that supports duality, desires, and fears.

Personality Type Threes can eventually exhibit the OCD Personality Disorder and the Narcissistic Personality Disorder, along with a God Complex Disorder and, as always with personality assumption, deeper attachment to false identities happens when persons are stressed, are overly-pious or highly-spiritual, or receiving monetary gain for their role-playing.

OCD and the God Complex have been covered. Now the discussion turns to the Narcissistic Personality Disorder, which many professional therapists agree is the personality disorder that they have had the least success in treating. Threes more than any other groups account for the majority of those on the planet who exhibit the traits of narcissism. According to the DSM-IV, they have an exaggerated sense of self-importance; expect to be recognized as superior; are grandiose; seek unlimited success, power, and beauty; and believe they are special. All of that, of course, generates belief in duality.

They seek out high-status persons or institutions for company; require excessive admiration; have a sense of entitlement; are users, not givers; lack empathy; and are envious, arrogant, haughty, patronizing, and contemptuous. In short, they are the epitome of the egotism that is generated when phony images are cultivated and maintained. These attitudes also support duality to the highest degree with their "better than you" and "different from all others" mentality.

Personality Type Fours can eventually exhibit the Depressive Personality Disorder, the Avoidant Personality Disorder, the Narcissistic Personality Disorder and the God Complex Personality Disorder, especially when stressed, absorbed in the ego of religiosity or the spiritualized ego, or receive payments for their role-playing.

Visitors can read earlier information shared on all of the disorders common to most Fours except for the Avoidant Personality Disorder (APD). Those suffering from APD are inhibited socially and have feelings of inadequacy. They are hypersensitive to criticism and/or rejection which might drive their tendency to isolate or to avoid social contact rather than risk a chance of being abandoned. They are slow to commit as a result of that fear of abandonment. They can develop a sense of inferiority and, therefore, a dualistic sense of separation.

Personality Type Fives can eventually exhibit the God Complex Disorder or the Schizoid Personality Disorder (SPD), especially when stressed, overly-pious, highly-spiritual, or being paid to play their roles. See earlier entries for information on the God Complex. SPD sufferers have trouble establishing relationships and experiencing feelings. They avoid close relations, pleasurable experiences, and family connections...preferring to isolate instead. They seem numb, not caring at all about either praise or criticism.

Personality Type Sixes can eventually exhibit the Paranoid Personality Disorder (PPD), the Passive-Aggressive Personality Disorder (PAPD) and the God Complex Disorder when persons are stressed, are absorbed in the ego of religiosity or the spiritualized ego, or receive payments for their role-playing.

See earlier entries for information on the God Complex. Those suffering from PPD are distrustful and suspicious of "others," reinforcing their belief in duality. They feel they are constantly being deceived or harmed or exploited by "others" and regularly question the loyalty of friends and family. They take offense over comments not intended to offend, they bear grudges, and they seldom forgive. They react angrily to the slightest of slights. All of that reinforces their dualistic beliefs. PAPD's are resistance to instruction and responsibilities. They become resentful, stubborn, negative, and sullen. They use procrastination as a way to avoid meetings, deadlines, events, or responsibilities.

Personality Type Sevens can eventually exhibit the God Complex Disorder, the Bi-Polar Personality Disorder (BPPD) known in the past as the Manic-Depressive Personality Disorder and the Histrionic Personality Disorder when they become stressed, overly-pious, or highly-spiritual, or when paid to play a role.

Earlier discussions covered all except the BPPD, often marked by extreme states of mood. High vs. low moods can change throughout a day or over the course of months. They tend to develop highly dualistic perspectives and see everything as all black or all white, meaning everything is totally positive or totally negative. The disorder can appear with levels of seriousness but, by definition, supports duality to the extreme.

CHAPTER SEVENTEEN

"MIND" and PERSONALITY:
What Cultures Consider "Assets" Are Actually "Liabilities"

PERSONALITY Type Eights can eventually exhibit the Anti-Social Personality Disorder (ASPD) when they become stressed, overly-pious, highly-spiritual, or role-players, along with a God Complex Disorder.

See earlier entries for information on all except the ASPD. Those with the ASPD have little or no regard for the rights of others, the feelings of others, or for any of society's norms and rules and laws. That "me vs. them" mentality fosters duality. ASPD's are typically quite impulsive, have limited feelings and little empathy, and have little regard for the consequences of their actions. They are especially deceitful and thus quite effective at conning people. They are irritable and aggressive and irresponsible while being able to rationalize and justify all of their conduct.

Personality Type Nines can eventually exhibit the DID Personality Disorder and the Dependent Personality Disorder and the Schizoid Personality Disorder along with a God Complex Personality Disorder when they become stressed, overly-pious, or identified with a spiritualized ego or any other role.

So, the Advaitin understands that personality identification comes from a twisted and warped "mind" and that almost all relative existence suffering and misery stem from personality. As reported by the APA, the defects that result from personality have nothing to do with mental illness. Trained professionals are required to assist the 1%-5% with clinical mental illnesses. A Realized teacher could guide the remaining 95%-99% to freedom from personality disorders if that 95%-99% recognized that they were suffering from such disorders and truly wanted to be totally free of the effects. Yet few will ever understand their disorders, and fewer still will be willing to discard all that must be discarded in order to be truly free and joyous.

The modern understanding of personality disorders discussed above support the ancient pointers that have been offered by Advaitin teachers for centuries as they have recommended detaching from personality identification and then Realizing fully. Review the following summary of the relative existence results of personality identification and the subsequent personality disorders:

Obsessing; playing god; perfectionism; judging; criticizing; financial problems; relationship problems; arrogance; depression; instability; emotional intoxication; distorted self-images; hysteria; an exaggerated sense of self-importance; a sense of superiority; grandiosity; a sense of entitlement; using others; lacking empathy; envy; blind faith; childish behavior among adults; and egotism.

Next, an understanding of the personality types—and the obstacles to Realization that are generated by each personality—can reveal why so few will ever Realize. 50% of the earth's populations are Type Sixes. When Sixes are programmed with dogma, as nearly 99% on the planet are, they will remain loyal to those beliefs, unquestioningly, and will accept what they have been told. Why? Being fear-based, they become trapped by their programmers' threat: "If you do not have faith in what we say or if you doubt any part of it at all, you will be punished and you will suffer now and forevermore." Therefore, the tally of those who will never be enlightened starts with that 50% who most likely will never give up their beliefs in dogma and nonsense. In an essay on his website, Mark McCloskey had this to say about "faith":

Faith is a crutch that humans have used for millennia as a way to explain the unexplainable...." (During a session in 2006, a similar reference was made to religious leaders who have historically dreamed up "concepts and ideas and teachings and beliefs that were used to convey false and supernatural explanations for events that were totally natural happenings." Such is the essence of childish, magical thinking. Only if you mistakenly believe that an imagined "world" is real will you also be required to mistakenly believe that an imagined god—who was actually "created" by man in man's image—is real.)

McCloskey continues, "If you stay with a crutch when you do not need it, you can become lame by reason of the crutch itself. The crutch must be abandoned, thrown away and then you can walk freely again...." He says, "Faith or any belief system as a whole is the final hurdle to overcome in the human path towards freedom and joy. Let me say it on a very personal level. Until you, as a human being, are able to completely abandon what you believe, have been told or taught what to believe or believe in, you will never experience this moment of reality as it is. You will never be fully free. You will be conditioned to experience present reality through a veil of the past…. This is not a joke, not any agnostic or atheistic principle. I am trying to point you to your own total human freedom to be able to live in this world joyfully….”

Sixes are especially prone to use the crutch that Mark speaks of, though all nine types can be programmed very easily. They will blindly and unquestioningly accept whatever they are told by anyone whom they take to be a “religious, spiritual, or political leader.” Relatedly, most Type Threes will live as a Six at times, exhibiting the Six’s blind loyalty to belief systems while being dedicated to image-building. By sheer numbers, most on the planet are living under the influence of a Three-Six personality. Threes are more interested in creating false images and maintaining those false images, actually believing that their images are real. With the preponderance of the Three-Six in the earth’s population, the majority on the planet will live like conditioned children, remaining loyal to whatever they were taught (Type Six) and always fighting to maintain image and always rejecting any invitation to get in touch with reality (Type Three).

Other types also face obstacles to enlightenment: Type Eights are prone to attach to supernatural beliefs since they think that such beliefs are another means to accumulating power (and thus control); therefore, they are not likely to abandon magical thinking and then Realize. Nines attach to the images that they use to manipulate others to take care of them. Two’s create a loving image in order to obtain what they think they lack and will attach to that image. Like Three’s, they are always “on stage.” Sevens have little desire to face reality and prefer to escape instead. Is it becoming clear why personality is a major hindrance to Realization?

Of all of the nine basic personality types, only Fours are geared toward the search for authenticity, toward attainment of a sense of unity, and toward the quest to discover the True Self, but Fours only account for about 1% of the earth’s population. As for Realizing fully, their dilemma lies in the fact that they are less prone to logic and more prone to seeing the dualities in the relative existence and seeking the “beautiful,” the “moral,” the “romantic,” or the “harmonious.”

So, the conundrum should now be obvious: the “mind” and personality must be abandoned to Realize, but persons value the “mind” and identify with personality; thus, both continue to be the great obstacles to Realization.

CHAPTER EIGHTEEN

"MIND" and PERSONALITY:
What Cultures Consider "Assets" Are Actually "Liabilities"

IT has been shown that the "mind" supports the assumption of personality and that personality is at the root of most relative existence problems. It has been asked, "Doesn't all this talk about the mind and personality and personality disorders deal with the relative, and isn't the relative an illusion?" The answer: Of course; however, if one believes in mirages and continues to suffer from automobile accidents that result when the driver takes evasive action to dodge mirages that seem to appear in the road, then mirages have to be discussed. They also have to be understood by the person driving and swerving and suffering if that destructive behavior is to end. Thus, this discussion.

FINAL SUMMARY

- For millions of years, humans survived and functioned well enough with a small, primitive brain and with no mind.
- Over the last four million years, human brain volume has increased from about 400 ml to about 1400 ml. Only recently during the evolutionary period did the brain develop the capacity to store memories and to retrieve memories, allowing for the formation of a "mind" which could store and retrieve information which could help avoid potentially-dangerous situations.
- After languages developed, persons with personal agendas began programming and conditioning the minds of persons, and the corrupted "mind" began overriding the brain, motivating foolishness and/or

dangerous conduct (such as the brain saying, "Alcohol poisoning is killing the body and making it feel ill" but the "mind" overruling the brain and saying, "It will be used anyway since it will make me feel better"; or the brain saying, "This dogma is self-contradictory nonsense" but the programmed "mind" saying, "I have to believe all of my religious and spiritual teachings or my body will be tortured with fire forever").

- When one has been programmed and conditioned, freedom does not exist since the power to choose does not exist.

- Once persons began storing in their "minds" the memory of ideas and beliefs and concepts that are taught by persons with agendas, then memories became dualistic in their nature.

- As human "minds"—and therefore human behavior—became more abnormal as a result of dualistic beliefs and concepts, children began forming personalities in an effort to adapt to abnormal family situations.

- With its belief in personas, the "mind" became more corrupted and warped and personas were attached to as identities. Personality then began to generate a variety of personality disorders, and personality disorders now generate most of the insane-like thinking and behavior of humans.

- Some claim, "A mind is a terrible thing to waste?" Nowadays, it would be far more accurate to say, "A mind is a terrible waste." As Dennis Waite puts it, "The purpose of j-nAna yoga is to remove the obstacles to Truth." The content of the "mind" has become the obstacle to seeing the Truth. Maharaj advised: "Go to zero concepts."

- Adults, unconsciously driven by memories and programming and personality, behave more and more in childish and nonsensible ways.

- Personality now generates the majority of the "problems of the planet" as personality disorders determine how persons emote and think and, therefore, determine how they behave.

- Billions of persons are blindly and unquestioningly doing what their programmers would have them do.

- The solution to "the problem of the planet" is Realization, including the discarding of all body-mind-personality identifications.

- Anything offered by Advaitins can only have "applicability" during the relative manifestation.

- Post-Realization, AS IF living can happen. When the ego dissolves via Realization, then happiness begins because fear and desires end.

- Full Realization will result in complete freedom…even freedom from believing in power or free will or choice. Seeing clearly, it becomes understood that the "problems of the planet" are illusory and that there is no "you" that has any problems.

- Only post-Realization can persons be free of the insane-like condition of not even knowing Who/What They Truly Are…and what they are not.

- It is "the direct path approach to Realization" that is offered here. Following the direct path requires no worship, no practices, no sacrifices, no giving or taking, no adherence to rules or dogma, no daily or weekly meetings, no fund-raising, no special buildings or special clothes, no robes, no special haircuts, no physical posturing, no holy texts, and no accoutrements. (It is because of the "no holy texts" part of this path that some suggest "vedanta" is not even applicable.) Pointing to the Original Understanding, which is the same understanding attained via Realization, makes the approach vary from other methods. That said, there is no suggestion that any path is "superior" to any other.

- The direct "path" that is being illuminated here allows a seeker to remove misperceptions via an objective investigation of all personally-held concepts; allows the continuation of the "journey" once it is understand that the highly-valued "mind" is to be devalued and discarded; and allows the seeker to advance along the way by removing the obstacles on the "path" (specifically, the psychological abnormalities) which support the erroneous belief in personas and which enable a childhood set of tools called "personality" to control the entire relative existence of adult-age persons across the face of the planet.

- Moreover, the direct path as expounded here is the path to natural—rather than unnatural or supernatural—living. Rather than "setting a goal" to worship god(s) or to know the Self, the direct path allows an awareness of the no-self, the no Self, the no-Being, the non-beingness, and the no-concept, non-dual Reality.

- If the content of the "mind" (which is a conglomeration of distortions and misinformation) is discarded, then the effects of personality can be discarded. If both the "mind" and the "personality" are discarded, then the remaining steps of the Seven-Step Journey to Reality can be completed and abidance as the Absolute can happen. Only then can freedom during the manifestation also happen. But it all begins with questioning and then discarding attachment to the illusions of the body-mind-personality triad.

WHY THERE'S NO SUCH THING AS "PEACE OF MIND": The Conclusion

First, consciousness is energy, and energy is always in motion. To try to "still" the consciousness is an exercise in futility.

Next, the "mind" was never intended by nature to be "at peace." The "mind" was intended by nature to be on guard. The peace that so many seek happen among humankind in the pre-mind days. A brain of small volume allowed humans to function, but it did not prepare them for the obstacles they would face. In order for the species to survive, nature began to adapt the brain.

As nature saw a need for memories to be stored and retrieved in order to protect the body and assure continuance of the species, the brain expanded in volume. The "mind" came into being, and its purpose was not to be "at peace." Its task was to be prepared, to be on guard, to be vigilant. Eventually, it would become hypervigilante as more and more memories triggered more and more opportunities to experience "fears."

With the advent of languages, persons began using conditioning and programming in order to plant into the "mind" certain concepts that would allow programmers to control behavior. Humans functioned for millions of years without a mind and then for years with a mind. Prior to language and program-ming, the functioning was all-natural. After the development of language, the functioning began to be unnatural (see the earlier discussion of personality disor-ders) and supernatural as more and more concepts were dreamed up to explain that which the ignorant masses could not otherwise explain. Thus, gods were invented and tales of those gods would be passed down for at least 5000 years. Modern versions of those ancient pagans gods have evolved, and "minds" are filled with nonsense rooted in ancient myths and superstitions and misunderstanding.

Now, the typical "mind" is so filled with dualistic nonsense and learned ignorance that it is never "art rest." It is no longer being used to generate self-constructive behavior but is being used to label and judge: "right vs. wrong"; "good vs. bad"; "ally vs. enemy"; and "deserving to live vs. deserving to die."

Whereas fighting in ancient days might have dealt with the life-death issue of water rights as new settlers tried to take over living space settled by an earlier tribe, fighting today is based in ideas, concepts, and supernatural beliefs. As more and more dogma and concepts were taught, a study of the history of humans reveals that, other than natural causes, fighting over religious or spiritual ideas implanted in the "minds" of persons has become the number one killer of people.

Now, the 'problems of the planet" are rooted in personality and the personality disorders that they generate. Persons are stressed, playing religious roles, assuming their spiritualized ego to be who they are, all of which is nonsense rooted in personality.

Personality, in turn, is rooted in the modern "mind," and the modern mind is an aberration of what nature intended to be an assets. That which evolved from nature an which was intended to be an asset has not become a major liability.

Now, people are being killed as a result of disagreements rooted in the content of their "minds"—content that relates to which of the dreamed up gods is the right one to worship. Among the masses, there is no "peace of mind" as concerns about "reward vs. punishment" and "right vs. wrong" result in a planet-wide sense of separation from 'others" and from Self. "minds" are restless as persons try to behave in unnatural ways in order to assure eternal continuity for a body that is only a temporary manifestation.

The unnatural and the supernatural work together to insure that no "peace of mind" will happen, so children are taught that they are not to engage in anything as natural as masturbation unless they are willing to suffer the penalty of eternal damnation into the fires of hell. And when that natural act happens, the unnatural state of a mind with no peace and no rest follows.

Thus, this consideration been offered to protégés:

The "mind" is the instrument that supports your personality with thoughts, and those thoughts are the instruments that will forever prevent "peace of mind"; in fact, there is no such thing as "peace of mind." There is only peace if freed of the "mind.

May you find the wherewithal and the courage to begin to question the nonsense that is being used by persons in your culture to create a "mind" that can never be "at peace" but that will always insure that no peace of mind ever happens. And then may this be realized:

Among religions and philosophies, there is no other means that can produce the necessary brain-flush save completion of the entire Advaita "journey" which invites the dissolution of all of the contamination that is "the mind."

QUOTATIONS BY FLOYD HENDERSON REGARDING THE "MIND"

Efforts to quiet the mind or to ignore thoughts cannot succeed with any consistency. Only when Full Realization strikes, only when the "Oh my gosh!" moment happens—only then does the mind dissolve. What to consider meanwhile? It is true that, if you are instructed to "avoid thinking about an elephant," the only thing that you can think of is an elephant. So, what is the answer? The answer is not to try to be rid of a disturbing thought. The answer is to ask when a thought is interrupting the peace, "WHO is thinking that thought?" Only by relinquishing belief in the false identities that inspire thoughts can the thoughts come to an end. Only by abandoning the "this" and "that" in such beliefs as "I am this" (role) or "I am that" (role) will the peace and quiet of only the "I Am" ever happen.

The "mind" is the instrument that supports your personality with thoughts, and those thoughts are the instruments that will forever prevent "peace of mind"; in fact, there is no such thing as "peace of mind." There is only peace if freed of the "mind."

Consciousness is rooted in the Absolute. The brain is rooted in the elements. The 'mind' is rooted in wrong programming and faulty conditioning and lies and concepts and ideas and superstitions and falsehoods.

You are in a play, playing a role, and believing that the role and the play are both real. Why would you believe such nonsense? Because "your mind" is the playwright, the author of every scene.

When Maharaj said, "You are not in the world...the world is in you," what did he mean? He meant, "You are not in the world," that is, there is no "you" that is real or in any world. "The world is in you" means that the world is in your "mind" and is nothing more than a figment of your programming-and-conditioning-induced imaginings.

Everything that is said here is to be used to get rid of another false belief until all ideas and emotional intoxication and beliefs are gone and nothing remains but the unstated understanding. Only then can the constant churning and re-churning of the false beliefs of the corrupted "mind" finally cease.

BOOK THREE OF SIX IN
"THE BLISSFUL ABIDANCE SERIES"

LIBERATION
(ATTAINING FREEDOM
FROM PERSONALITY
VIA REALIZATION)

FOREWORD

VARIOUS teachers use various approaches (or various yogas) for guiding protégés to Realization and Liberation. Why? Because there are three types of learners: auditory, visual, and kinetic. Also, the three body types among humans call for different approaches for different persons. The first body type is contemplative while a second type is more active. The third type includes students or protégés who are driven to be vigorously active. A variety of approaches are justified as attempts are made to provide methods that take into account the variety among protégés and their varied learning methods.

FROM THE I TO THE ABSOLUTE (A Seven-Step Journey to Reality) is an approach that can work well with contemplative and analytical seekers.

For those who are prone to action and who learn best by an action-based approach, the book LIBERATION (Attaining Freedom from Personality via Realization) offers specific actions that can taken by those seeking to be free.

CHAPTER ONE

BEING TRAPPED IN PERSONALITY
VS. BEING REALIZED AND FREE

PERSONALITY is (1) that which generates personas and (2) that which allows things to be taken personally.

A persona is an assumed social role or a character played by an actor, the term having been derived from the Latin word for "mask" or "character." Personas are all of the false identities that persons think define "who they are." In fact, they define everything that one is not.

"Taking anything personally" can only happen when a persona assumes a false identity and then assumes offense at the words or actions of another. When do personas take offense? When an assumed identity assumes that it is being hurt, interfered with, or threatened. What conclusion can be drawn from knowing that? All instances of feeling hurt, interfered with, threatened, fearful, desirous, miserable or in pain originate from assuming false identities and then wanting to defend or protect false identities. Therefore, to be free of feeling hurt, interfered with, threatened, fearful, desirous, miserable, in pain or defensive requires being free of personas...being free of the entrapment in personality.

Thousands of personas are assumed by persons: husband, lover, homeowner, employee, employer, wife, son, ad infinitum; however, as a result of genetics and environment and other factors, all persons develop one dominate persona while assuming scores of others. Often, that dominant persona is overlaid onto (or combined with) all other assumed roles.

Only nine primary personality types exist, and since persons become most driven by that type and most separated from Self by that type and most absorbed in "self" via that type, then the "journey" to liberation can begin with an effort to be rid of the influence of the dominate personality type. Then the secondary types and personas might be abandoned more easily.

Why Understand Personality Types?

Psychotherapist Marie Lachney explains it this way: "You may as well learn all that you can about your primary personality type as well as the related types that influence you. For most people, it will determine everything they do and everything they feel during their entire lives. Only a small percentage will ever be liberated from the dominance of personality."

Dictating Behavior

Of course each individual is "unique," but unless people understand the way that personality type dictates behavior, then they will never fully understand why they do the things they do and why they feel the way they feel. Nor can they understand why others do the things they do and why they feel the way they feel—which can be quite different from person to person—depending on personality type. Nor can they ever break free of unconscious influences.

Personality Formation

Early in life, we learned to feel safe (and to cope with unhealthy family situations and circumstances) by developing a strategy based on natural talents, genetics, and abilities.

Personality's Power over Behavior and Feelings

People of the same type have the same basic motivations, the same basic liabilities and assets, and the same basic view of the world in some fundamentally similar ways. It's almost "textbook" the way people demonstrate the exact traits of their type. It is amazing to see how infrequently people choose to do the things they do and how often they are predisposed to certain behavioral patterns. (When you add programming, conditioning, enculturation, and the effects of trauma to the mix, "free will" and "choice" become reduced to the level of theory.)

The Benefits of Knowing and Understanding Your Type

This understanding can provide release, if not comfort, in knowing that millions of people who share your personality type have the same coping strategy as you and have done exactly what you did when faced with the same circumstances. But by understanding personality, millions have also been able to say, "Oh my gosh! So that's why I do what I do!" and then they have become free of the overwhelming influence of personality which has unconsciously driven them. At some level, "That's totally insane" can give way to "That's perfectly understandable, all things considered." Blame and guilt and anger directed at self can end and a shift toward sanity can begin.

CHAPTER TWO

What is the Enneagram and What Are the Nine Personality Types?

IN geometry, the enneagram is a star polygon with nine sides. In psychology or philosophy or sociology, it is a means for studying the nine basic personality types that have been recognized for hundreds, if not thousands, of years.

Some believe that the Sufis first used the tool in the Middle East hundreds of years ago. Others believe that the roots can be traced to the Far East and were transmitted orally even thousands of years ago.

It is known that the modern use of the enneagram can be traced to the Russian teacher Georges Ivanovich Gurdjieff in the 1920's. The tool has been used in the U.S. since the 1960's.

More significantly as far as the pointers in this book are concerned, it is just that…simply a tool. The tool can be used to understand the forces that drive persons to do the things they do and to feel the way they feel. It can also be used to promote understanding of others and their behavior and also to catalogue the disintegration of persons who move downward from the stages where they can function in society through the declining stages and into the dysfunctional stages. It can also provide a series of actions that can be taken to "undo" that process and return to a stage where one can be functional or even totally liberated via Realization.

The nine types (and their interactions with each other) are typically illustrated by use of a star polygon. For the purposes of this study, little explanation will be offered to explain the ways that the types adjacent to your own influence behavior or the way that other types connected by lines to your own affect your conduct. Much information is available on the web if you are interested in those other aspects.

CHAPTER THREE

Traits, "Assets," and "Liabilities" among the Nine Personality Types

[TYPES 2, 3 AND 4 ARE CENTERED IN THE HEART, IN FEELINGS, IN IMAGE]

2
THE HELPER
WHEN HEALTHY: Demonstrative, Sensitive, and Generous.
WHEN NOT: People-Pleasing, Martyr-like, Manipulative, Hysterical, and Possessive.

3
THE ACHIEVER / THE PERFORMER
WHEN HEALTHY: Adaptive, Energetic, Optimistic, Assured, Excelling, Goal-Oriented, Driven.
WHEN NOT: Image-Conscious, Vile-Tongued, Narcissistic, Pretentious, Vain, Superficial, Vindictive and Overly-Competitive.

4
THE INDIVIDUALIST / THE ROMANTICIST
WHEN HEALTHY: Expressive, Strong Feelings, Warm, Dramatic, and Perceptive.
WHEN NOT: Self-Absorbed, Depressed, Guilt-Ridden, Moralistic, Isolationistic, Stubborn, Moody, and Temperamental

[TYPES 5, 6 AND 7 ARE CENTERED IN THE HEAD, IN THINKING, IN FEARS]

5

THE INVESTIGATOR / THE KNOWLEDGE SEEKER / THE OBSERVER
WHEN HEALTHY: Analytical, Persevering, Wise, Objective, Perceptive, and Innovative.
WHEN NOT: Secretive, Intellectually-Arrogant, Stingy, Distant, Critical, Unassertive, and Negative.

6

THE LOYALIST / THE QUESTIONER
WHEN HEALTHY: Engaging, Responsible, Loyal, Caring, Compassionate, and Practical.
WHEN NOT: Anxious, Suspicious, Controlling, Unpredictable, Paranoid, Defensive, Rigid, and Self-Defeating.

7

THE ENTHUSIAST / THE ADVENTURER
WHEN HEALTHY: Spontaneous, Energetic, Optimistic, Versatile, and Lively. WHEN NOT: Distracted, Scattered, Impulsive, Histrionic, Undisciplined, Self-Destructive, and Restless.

[TYPES 8, 9 AND 1 ARE CENTERED IN THE GUT, IN INSTINCTS, IN ANGER

8

THE CHALLENGER / THE ASSERTER / THE BOSS
WHEN HEALTHY: Self-Confident, Direct, Self-Reliant, and Decisive.
WHEN NOT: Willful, Confrontational, Controlling, Domineering, Aggressive, and Self-Centered.

9 THE PEACEMAKER / THE PASSIVE-AGGRESSIVE AVOIDER
WHEN HEALTHY: Receptive, Good-Natured, Reassuring, and
Agreeable. WHEN NOT: Passive-Aggressive, Complacent, Lazy,
Spaced Out, Obsessive, Judgmental, and Users w/ a Sense of
Entitlement.

1
THE REFORMER / THE PERFECTIONIST
WHEN HEALTHY: Principled, Purposeful, Self-Controlled, Realistic,
Conscientious, Productive, Honest, Orderly, and Self-Disciplined.
WHEN NOT: Extremely Perfectionistic, Judgmental, Inflexible,
Dogmatic, Obsessive-Compulsive, Critical, Overly-Serious, Anxious,
and Jealous.

If you notice that all nine types are centered in some areas that are not especially conducive to being at peace and at ease (IMAGE, FEAR, OR ANGER)
then one can understand the rationale behind the statement that:

THE LESS WE ARE INFLUENCED OR DRIVEN BY PERSONALITY,
PERSONAS, EGO, or EGO-STATES, THEN THE GREATER CHANCE
WE HAVE OF BECOMING TRULY FREE AND TRULY HAPPY;
ADDITIONALLY, IT CAN ALSO BE SAID THAT THOSE WHO
ARE HEALTHY AND INTEGRATING CAN EXHIBIT "THE BEST"
OF ALL NINE TYPES AND THOSE WHO ARE UNHEALTHY AND
DISINTEGRATING CAN EXHIBIT "THE WORST" OF ALL NINE
TYPES.

CHAPTER FOUR

THE RELATIVE EFFECTS OF PERSONALITY:
FEARS, DESIRES AND INTERRUPTED HAPPINESS

MANY questions raised by protégés over the years originated from that which is as far removed from Full Realization as possible: body, mind, and/or personality identification. Questions or comments about "fear of death," about "the well-being of the body," about "religious and spiritual concepts and beliefs," and about their desires for "the eternal continuity of the body and mind" have revealed just how absorbed persons are in their false identities. The "self" is always about body-mind-personality, and the body-mind-personality is always about self...self-absorption, self-centeredness, and self-concern.

One therapist who uses the Enneagram method to teach her clients their personality types has been asked by some why they need that awareness. She explains, "Because if you do not abandon the belief that your personality has anything to do with Who You Truly Are—and 95% never will—then it will be the force that will blindly drive you through life, that will determine what you do and how you feel, and that will cause that misery which brought you to this office to continue."

In fact, it is the phenomenon of personality that sustains the belief in duality and prevents the Realization of the truth of non-duality. All "personal assets and liabilities," and all notions about the "good qualities and bad qualities of people," are actually dealing with nothing more than personality traits which are always dualistic by definition. Thus, the Advaita teachings always include certain pointers about personality (along with an invitation to abandon all belief in personality—and personas—while abandoning body and mind identification as well).

While on a trip through Europe, much discussion was overheard as people talked about the content of a report released at that time from the United Kingdom that studied "the reasons that women over 40 have sleepless nights." In the order of importance, the results showed their lack of sleep resulted from the following fears:

1. Children's future - 55 %
2. Health risks - 45%
3. Financial difficulties - 43 %
4. Breast cancer - 36 %
5. Rising crime - 27 %
6. Immigration - 19 %
7. Threat of terrorism - 12 %
8. Menopause - 12 %
9. Losing their partner - 11%

So what does each of those really deal with?

1. Fears about "Children's future" deal with BODY AND MIND AND PERSONALITY IDENTIFICATION: (Reproduction is a BODY function. "The Mother," which automatically becomes "The Super Mother" once the role is assumed as an identity, cannot exist without children, so MIND and PERSONAS are also involved.)
2. Fears about "Health risks" deal with BODY IDENTIFICATION
3. Fears about "Financial difficulties" deal with PERSONALITY IDENTIFICATION AND MIND IDENTIFICATION
4. Fears about "Breast cancer" deal with BODY IDENTIFICATION
5. Fears about "Rising crime" deal with BODY IDENTIFICATION
6. Fears about "Immigration" deal with BODY AND MIND IDENTIFICATION
7. Fears about the "Threat of terrorism" deal with BODY IDENTIFICATION
8. Concerns about "Menopause" deal with BODY AND MIND IDENTIFICATION
9. Fears about "Losing their partner" deal with PERSONALITY AND MIND IDENTIFICATION

So much for "True Love," partners. The women surveyed admitted that they are five times more concerned about losing their children than about losing their partners, four times more concerned about losing money than about losing their partners, and three times more concerned about problems with their breasts than about losing their partners. And if men answered honestly the same types of questions in an anonymous survey, the priorities of men would be just as focused on body-mind-personality "issues" and therefore just as "self"-centered as the women interviewed in the study cited above.

Belief in one's personality/personas results in not knowing Who/What You Truly Are. That, in turn, results in the dualities revealed above…and all duality then results in delusional fears and unmet desires. And of course all fears and desires result in dis-ease. While Realization cannot guarantee that the Realized (living out an AS IF existence) will never witness any relative existence happenings that will provide opportunities to observe feelings as they rise and fall, the absence of Realization will guarantee that persons will be absorbed in the types of emotionally-intoxicating issues that are causing the women surveyed to lose sleep and to have their relative existence dominated by preoccupation with fears and desires. The same applies to men. Worry and fear and desire are merely the toll to be paid when body-mind-personality identification exists.

Yes, personality typing amounts to nothing more than another set of concepts, but since Advaitins employ thorns to remove thorns—concepts used to eventually remove all concepts—use of the Enneagram methodology can stimulate the Realization process among protégés. Too, it was observed during certain satsanga sessions in the past that the pointers offered to one personality type about her/his basic desires and basic fears were ignored as irrelevant by those present whose personalities were among the other eight types and who had different fears and desires that were driving them. Thus, the basic fears and the basic desires of each of the nine personality types will be discussed.

By the end, each should have discovered the single most basic fear and the single most basic desire that is driving him or her, that is interfering with realization and happiness, and that is supporting the attachment to personality identification. To identify the source of the dis-ease is the first step to eliminating that source and the dis-ease.

By comparison, the colon cancer that had manifested in this space was not addressed and removed until its presence and nature were diagnosed and understood. Freedom from cancer followed understanding the exact nature of the problem…it did not precede that understanding. So it is with personality and the fears and desires that personality identification generate: freedom from the relative effects of fears and desires cannot happen until persons are aware of the illusions surrounding their personality type, are aware of the effects, and are freed of the false beliefs about personality that will otherwise drive all of their relative existence behaviors and "feelings."

CHAPTER FIVE

The Relative Effects of Personality: Fears, Desires and Interrupted Happiness

WHY do the Advaita teachings invite persons to discard their identification with personality? (A) The influence of personality results in specific but illusory fears and in specific but unattainable desires. How could happiness possibly happen in a relative existence littered with the anxiety of illusory fears and the frustration of unmet desires? (B) Trapped within the sphere of personality identification, duality manifests. Why? To believe that any of the various personas that evolve from belief in the personality types can define who you are (for example, "The Perfect One" or "The Helper" or "The Boss," etc.) will prevent your knowing Who/What You Truly Are. Too, since the cataloguing of personality traits always lists "assets" vs. "liabilities," then belief in duality is fostered. (C) The lie of multiplicity is reinforced by assuming identification with personality. How? When trapped in the sphere of personality, a person does not exhibit traits of only her/his dominant persona type. When "mentally healthy," one unconsciously integrates the traits of another type. If stressed or pious, one disintegrates into the mode of a third type. Further, personas adopt the traits of their two adjacent types, so a Type Three will exhibit Type Two traits as well as Type Four traits. All personality identification, therefore, will ultimately foster the chaos and disorder of living with "multiple personalities."

The Advaita teachings can (1) provide release from illusory fears and unmet desires via elimination of the belief in the personality and can (2) free persons of the misery generated by personality identification via Full Realization. The process invites protégés to answer certain key questions: WHO has a fear? WHO has a desire? WHO wants to be perfect? WHO is taking himself/herself to be a persona with a personality? To be free of believing that a mirage is real, one must first understand what a mirage is, so today, the basic fear and the basic desire of Personality Type One—"The Perfectionist"—will be discussed. Russ Hudson pointed out the following about Personality Type Ones:

BASIC FEAR AND BASIC DESIRE
The Type One's BASIC FEAR is being corrupt or evil or defective
The Type One's BASIC DESIRE is to be good

THE IMPACT OF THAT PERSONALITY TYPE ON THE RELATIVE EXISTENCE

Consider the effects of trying to live out a relative existence while being trapped in the belief of dualities that tell you that sometimes you are "good" but that more often you are "bad." Consider the misery of being programmed and conditioned to think that you are really "corrupt" (as opposed to "honest"), "evil" (as opposed to "moral"), or "defective" (as opposed to "perfect"). What a nightmarish existence has to result if one does not Realize and thereby free the "self" of the effects of the messages that "you are not good enough," "you are corrupt and immoral" or "you are nothing more than a living and breathing defect, personified." (Also, understand that those messages might be delivered with words but that they can as easily be implanted with a particularly harsh facial expression, by other "body language," or by other forms of abuse.)

Imagine all of the relative existence pleasures that such a mindset precludes as one spends a lifetime trying to attain the "positive" images in those sets of dualistic evaluations that result when enculturation and programming and conditioning instill the desire to be perfect in order to prove to early critics (as well as current critics) that they are wrong in applying such "negative" labels to you. Imagine how often natural conduct is blocked and how often supernatural conduct is inspired by what becomes a life-long, unconscious effort to prove that one is good and honest and moral and perfect.

WHY HAPPINESS IS INTERRUPTED FOR PERSONALITY TYPE ONES

Note how acceptance of the influence of this personality type will automatically force persons to be stressed and apprehensive and overly-serious; note how the influence of this personality type will drive personas to always be dissatisfied with themselves; see how they will be driven to believe that they can never do anything well enough; see how the influence of their personality will drive these persons to feel burdened and unacknowledged and compulsive. Then, you'll understand why persons living under the influence of a Type One Personality might claim all day long that they are happy, but with the above factors at work, that belief is just another lie that they take to be truth. Sure, some fleeting moments of happiness or pleasure might manifest, but as long as the personality is allowed to have its influence, then personality will interrupt happiness and deny the enjoyment of the pleasures of natural, AS IF living.

FREEDOM FROM PERSONALITY TYPE ONE EFFECTS VIA REALIZATION

To be free of the frustration of living out a relative existence while being trapped in the dualities of "good" vs. "bad," "corrupt" vs. "honest", "evil" vs. "moral", or "defective" vs. "perfect," then attainment of the non-duality understanding is required. "Good" and "bad" are relative. Being relative, they are lies and cannot be defined with any continuity. What is "good" to one person is "bad" to another. So-called "universal truths" or "moral standards" are just as relativistic. The same person who claims that "lying is bad" would likely have advised those hiding Jews in WWII to lie if a Nazi asked them if they knew where any Jews were hiding. If a Type One finds the answer to "Who Am I, really?" then no WHO will remain that can suffer the duality of sometimes feeling "good" and sometimes feeling "bad." If Realized, that person will no longer suffer from the duality of sometimes feeling "evil" while sometimes feeling "moral" or the duality of sometimes feeling "defective" while at other times feeling "perfect." The former Type One can then be freed from being driven to try to reach the unattainable state of being "perfect" or from being driven to try to meet the unreasonable, dualistic expectations that were set forth by other delusional personas.

CHAPTER SIX

THE RELATIVE EFFECTS OF PERSONALITY: FEARS, DESIRES AND INTERRUPTED HAPPINESS

THIS discussion focuses on the personality type that desires love but that lives in the fear of not getting it and with the unhappiness of never having enough of it. A pointer offered in the past said: "Desires and wants and fears and imagined needs are generated by illusory ego-states. Who could be satisfied if constantly experiencing the sensations of desire, want, fear or need?" Ego-states, in turn, are the result of the personality influences being discussed in this series (which also generate all dualistic beliefs, including: "good vs. bad," "loved vs. not loved," and belief in "a god of evil in opposition to a god of morality.")

Sri Nisargadatta Maharaj offered this pointer: "Only at word level does one think something good or bad will happen; when one identifies with the space, it is the end of good and bad. First of all you identify something as being good or bad for yourself. Then, in an effort to acquire good or to get rid of bad, you have invented a god. Then, you worship such a god...and you pray to that god for something good to happen to you."

Those pointers having been offered, the focus today will be on the basic fear and the basic desire of Personality Type Two—"The Helper." The consideration for Type Two's is this: WHO thinks she/he needs love? WHO thinks that he/she is in any position to "help" "others"? WHO is so arrogant as to believe that "others" are obviously far less intelligent, far less capable, and far less gifted than the persona who thinks she/he is most qualified to provide "help" to "others"? WHO is so egotistical that he/she believes that they know so much that they have the answers for everyone else's relative world problems? WHO believes that she/he knows what "others" need? And WHO believes that he/she is the most competent to provide "help"? Russ Hudson pointed out the following about Personality Type Twos:

> BASIC FEAR AND BASIC DESIRE
> The Type Two's BASIC FEAR is the fear of not being loved
> The Type Two's BASIC DESIRE is to be loved

THE IMPACT OF THAT PERSONALITY TYPE ON THE RELATIVE EXISTENCE

A Type Two will try to get the love she/he desires by manipulating others into believing that they need the Type Two, that they need what only that one person can offer, that they need the insight that only that one Type Two has, and that they cannot survive without that Type Two person. That mindset will attract what type persons for Type Twos to deal with on a daily basis? Needy, dependent, easily-influenced persons. The resulting co-dependency and chaos from dealing with the needy people that Twos attract will mar the relative existence of the Type Two. Why? Because Twos eventually resent all the demands being made upon them by the needy, exploitative persons that their dependency-fostering persona creates, even though the Twos were aggressively seeking out needy people with an excess of relative existence problems and who need the "help" that Type Twos believe (in their huge conceit) that only they can provide.

The resulting dependency preempts independence for the Two and for those persons who accept the Two's "help," and persons who are not free cannot possibly be happy—their baseless protestations to the contrary notwithstanding. The relative existence of those trapped in the Type Two sphere becomes marked by a lack of energy as Type Twos try to do so much for "others"; becomes marked by selfishness as Twos are really giving with the ulterior motive of trying to get back even more; becomes marked by working to "help" "others" while Twos ignore their own basic, relative requirements; becomes marked by the building up of resentments since Twos never feel that "others" appreciate adequately their sacrifices; and becomes marked by the passive-aggressive behavior that always follows when the Type Two believes that he/she is not getting the degree of love and gratitude that is deserved after all the "help" they have offered.

WHY PERSONALITY TYPE TWO INTERRUPTS HAPPINESS

Imagine the frustration of needing love, of constantly wanting love, of constantly trying to find love, and of trying—always in vain—to hold onto love in a culture where 62% of those persons who pledge "to love 'til death do us part" . . . don't. Yet the transient nature of "love" is not confined to the U.S. Across the globe, the typical pattern of relationships is to move through the following phases: "stranger" to "acquaintance" to "friend" to "lover" to "spouse or partner" to "enemy" to "mortal enemy." The same intransigence marks not only "love relationships" but friendships and partnerships as well. How, therefore, could a Type Two ever be consistently happy when the desire is "to be loved deeply by everyone" while "self"-absorbed persons have no ability to love unconditionally at all and while persons mistake all sorts of personal agendas for "love"?

Much has been written about the illusion of "need." Much has also been written about the illusion of "love." As long as a person has a desire to be needed, happiness cannot happen with any degree of continuity. As long as Type Twos are overly-accommodating, are acting like martyrs, or are being possessive and manipulative, then happiness cannot happen with any degree of continuity. As long as Twos are behaving as overly-sensitive pleasers and controlling manipulators, happiness cannot happen with any degree of continuity. The misery that accompanies such entrapment in this personality type—or in any of the other eight types—should make clear why those who offer Advaitin pointers consistently invite protégés to abandon identification with body, with mind, and with personality.

FREEDOM FROM PERSONALITY TYPE TWO EFFECTS VIA REALIZATION

With Realization comes (A) the understanding that there is no "one" that has any need. With Realization comes (B) the understanding that no "one" can help any "one." With Realization comes (C) clarity about what love is not and then (D) an end to wasting energy in the search for anything that is illusory. Lies are stored in the mind; truth can be accessed via the inner resource, contact with which is typically blocked by assumption of personality. When that inner awareness springs forth into the consciousness, then all beliefs about being a person in need, about being a person who needs help, and about being a person who has great ability to help others…all that will end and a lightness of being can happen for the remainder of the manifestation. But whether Realization (and an accompanying lightness of being) happens or not, neither case changes the fact that no "one" exists that can "help," that no "others" exist that are "separate from" and needing "help," and that no "one" exists that needs "help"…or anything else.

Next, any lightness of being that does happen during the relative existence only comes about after Realization, which is then followed by an acceptance of these facts: first, if something happens, such as "being loved," it happens, and, secondly, if it does not happen, so it is. Furthermore, the Type Twos' belief in the dualistic concept that they have a "need to connect" reveals that the Oneness is not understood at all by Type Twos. That failure to understand the unicity fosters a belief in duality and a desire to create dependencies and connections. To commit to finding the lies and thereby to finding the truth via Realization is the course that can free Type Twos of (1) their constant sense of feeling rejected, of (2) their typically feeling hurt, of (3) their feeling that they need to win over everyone and be loved by all, of (4) their egotism, revealed by their belief that they are so much better than "others" that they are in a position to "help" "others" and of (5) their frustration that results from that constant, nagging sense that they lack the love, the esteem, and the sense of worth that their personality convinces them that they need.

With the coming of Realization and the subsequent freedom from being driven by personality, all such nonsense goes.

CHAPTER SEVEN

The Relative Effects of Personality: Fears, Desires and Interrupted Happiness

THE following was offered in response to a question about coming to really know or understand another person: "…You'll never 'know' or 'understand' any person [because] you'll never know 'which person' (which persona or which personality type) you're dealing with on any given day. Have you ever met someone and thought you 'really knew' him/her…only to scream later, 'I don't even know who you are!' Millions in 'relationships' eventually feel like fools, like they were 'fooled' by someone who put up a false front, a false image, only to discover that their mate, friend, lover, spouse, etc. is a fraud. Of course that will happen, because all personas are fraudulent." Thus, to be free of fear, desire, foolishness, and unhappiness, personality must be transcended. But before such transcendence can happen, personality and its fraudulent nature must be understood. Of all the personality types, none put up that false front or false image more than the type discussed today. The basic fear and the basic desire of Personality Type Three—"The Performer/Achiever"—will now be discussed. Russ Hudson pointed out the following about Personality Type Threes:

BASIC FEAR AND BASIC DESIRE
The Type Three's BASIC FEAR is the fear of being worthless
The Type Three's BASIC DESIRE is to feel valuable

THE IMPACT OF THAT PERSONALITY TYPE ON THE RELATIVE EXISTENCE

Because they fear that "the way they really are" makes them worthless, Threes above all else engage in (1) "image-building" and in (2) seeking an audience to display that image and thereby receive praise or positive feedback. When Type Three Performers/Achievers act or sing or perform or accomplish, they are seeking the applause or praise that their personality desires. Then, in an act of self-delusion, they take the applause or praise as a sign that they are truly loved and therefore valued and worth something. A Three will, therefore, do all within her/his ability to create and maintain what they take to be a "positive" image. "Style over substance" is the hallmark of these persons trapped in their love of their relative world existence, identified as they are with their physical bodies and their "good looks" and thus having little chance of ever understanding the Absolute.

These personas lose contact with the True Self, with reality, far more than most other types. They suffer from distortion, from faulty perception, and from their inability to differentiate between what is true and what is false…between what is real and what is unreal. They will literally live out their lie throughout their relative existence if they do not Realize, believing all along that their false image really defines who they are and never having the slightest clue about Who They Truly Are. They become susceptible, if exposed to religious or spiritual teachings, to adopting with a vengeance the false personas that are generated by religious or spiritual beliefs and concepts and dogma. Ironically, even as they proclaim to love, they are the most capable of hating when they think they are not getting enough honor or respect or praise. Their need for praise is limitless, but since they cannot get limitless praise, they develop deep resentments and anger. To maintain their image of being wonderful and charming, however, they suppress that anger and rage builds within. The result is a continual series of explosive, raging episodes through their lives. Eventually, if they adopt a "Religious Giant" or "Spiritual Giant" persona, they come to believe that they are perfect; therefore, they fail to see any need to look within; thus, they will typically never see the defects that characterize their personality type. They are so capable of hating that they can become quite capable of destroying anything that they think is interfering with their two, primary preoccupations: image-building and image-maintenance. Few are as invested as Threes are in creating false selves, in adopting false identities as definitions of "self," and with ruthlessly destroying anyone or anything that interferes with their desire to be the epitome of what their culture considers "attractive," "good," and "valuable." (Note: If you study the enneagram, you see that Threes are part of the "Type 3-6-9 triangle," so those other two types can display the same type behavior as a Three. Some estimates are that 80% or more of the population of Aryan nations such as Germany, Austria, Great Britain and the U.S. are either Threes or persons inside the 3-6-9 triangle who behave as Threes behave.)

WHY PERSONALITY TYPE THREE INTERRUPTS HAPPINESS

That desire to be the epitome of what their culture considers "attractive," "good," and "valuable" results in a never-ending drive to be more, to be better, to be better than, and to be perceived as "the best." Such egotistical pursuits place them in a competitive mode and drive Threes to feel they are being challenged or threatened in most situations. They demand the spotlight and resent people and situations that force them to share the spotlight. In their effort to look perfect and to say the perfect thing in each case and to appear to be the best, the result is an inordinate fear of failure and a consequent need to exploit and control or manipulate in their effort to maintain their image and their sense of superiority. They become charming actors, performers who are always "on stage" or who are in need of finding an audience if an audience is missing. In their effort to stay in the spotlight, they become jealous, vindictive, deceptive, narcissistic, vain, and self-righteous. They become obsessed with being the center of attention and receiving crowd approval in order to believe that they really are "OK." They project their personality defects onto others and then do all that is possible to destroy other persons who evidence the Three's own personality traits and phony personas. On some level, they really hate their false self, even as they work so diligently to create it and to maintain it. (That is the typical discontinuity that exists for all persons identified with the body-mind-personality triad, and that is the reason to see these influences that personality has on the relative existence and then discard identification with personas.) Threes will appear to be the most charming among the nine types, and though they are the opposite at their core, their use of denial results in their believing their own lies. Far from being truly charming, they can say the vilest, most hurtful things, can spin their failures into success stories in an instant, and can literally kill when angered over not receiving the degree of honor that they think they deserve or when someone questions them or exposes their faults. "Isn't all this relative existence stuff?" it has been asked. Of course. It's always the "relative existence stuff" that must first be seen in order to realize what must be discarded. Only then can the "absolute stuff" be understood.

FREEDOM FROM PERSONALITY TYPE THREE EFFECTS VIA REALIZATION

Along with realization comes authenticity as images are seen to be images and nothing more. With realization, honesty replaces the lie that the relative existence of most Type Threes eventually becomes. The distorted thinking and twisted perspectives that prevented the manifestation of happiness disappear. That said, with the degree of attachment that Threes have to image, few will ever see all of the lies that must be seen before the truth can explode into consciousness. Again, the justification for the teachings to invite protégés to recognize the influences of personality on relativistic behavior and to then be free of it should be clear.

CHAPTER EIGHT

THE RELATIVE EFFECTS OF PERSONALITY: FEARS, DESIRES AND INTERRUPTED HAPPINESS

THE following pointer was offered in response to a question regarding personality-driven fears and desires: "...Fear and desire are the sources of anger, and anger is the source of all hostility. Hostility becomes the source of all harm," relatively speaking, of course. To be free of the anxiety of fears as well as the frustration of unmet desires, one must be free of identification with personality. Today, the basic fear and the basic desire of Personality Type Four—"The Romantic/Individualist"—will be discussed. Russ Hudson pointed out the following about Personality Type Fours:

BASIC FEAR AND BASIC DESIRE

The Type Four's BASIC FEAR is the fear of having no identity

The Type Four's BASIC DESIRE is to find Themselves

THE IMPACT OF THAT PERSONALITY TYPE ON THE RELATIVE EXISTENCE

In their need to understand themselves, Fours developed a related desire to be understood by others. Since most "others" do not understand themselves, how could they ever understand the Fours? They won't, so the Four's frustrated desire to find "Self" and to be understood leaves him/her feeling depressed...yet stubborn about continuing to try to have those desires met. The result is that, eventually, Fours tend to withdraw and to isolate and to become depressed as they remain misunderstood and as they fail to find the answer to "Who Am I, Really?"

WHY PERSONALITY TYPE FOUR INTERRUPTS HAPPINESS

Because of their frustrations, Fours can eventually suffer dark moods, a variety of perceived hurts, the angst of unmet expectations, a constant fear of abandonment as a result of not being understood, and an uncomfortable sensation of longing as a result of knowing that "something is missing" but not having a clue what that is. In Advaita terms, the desire of the pre-Realization Type Four could be described as an inner yearning to find the True Self (or to find out what THAT is which is actually beyond any "self-ness" or Self-ness.") Yet all yearning, wanting, and desiring interrupt any opportunity for consistent happiness to happen in the relative existence.

Next, by focusing on their "quest," Fours generate relative-existence problems as a result of their self-absorption. They obsess on finding the answer to "Who am I?" which often prevents their asking, "Also, what about you?" Fours, since they disintegrate to the Type Two personality if stressed or pious, can behave as a Two and become jealous, self-righteous, and critical or can feel hurt as a result of feeling "rejected." Their pre-Realization state leaves them frustrated as they know that they cannot answer accurately the question "Who Am I, Really?" That leaves them searching but not finding, and that—in turn—leaves them dark, moody, empty, resentful, and longing. Depression and withdrawal and isolation often follow.

FREEDOM FROM PERSONALITY TYPE FOUR EFFECTS VIA REALIZATION

Some claim that Fours have an advantage in moving along the "path" to Realization because of their innate drive to search for identity and to uncover what "self" is not and what "Self" is. If they succeed in their quest and attain Full Realization, they can live out an AS IF existence with greater ease than most...the silence, the solitude, and the lack of need being quite comfortable for Fours, relatively speaking. Post-Realization, the earlier drive to find themselves ends, so the basic, unmet desire ends and the basic, illusory fear disappears as they understand their "true identity," namely, THAT. For the remainder of the manifestation, then, the AS IF existence of Realized Fours is no longer driven by personality but functions naturally under the auspices of the intuitive sense. The inner resource and the natural drives move Realized Fours through the remainder of their manifestation, as happens with all types...post-Realization. Learned ignorance and supernatural thinking disappear and natural living begins.

Always having been interested in their feelings—but too often driven by their emotions when not Realized—the Realized Fours can witness their feelings as they rise and fall but can be free of the emotional intoxication that identification with body and mind and personality had generated in their pre-Realization days. As opposed to the isolation that was previously experienced—along with its misery and self-absorption—both the sense of feeling separated and the sensation of experiencing the aloneness end as the all-oneness is understood after Realization. Though seclusion no longer happens unconsciously, solitude does happen, consciously. Then, the silence of private periods of tranquility can be enjoyed with peace as opposed to earlier times of withdrawal that were marked with anxiety or depression. The same outcome awaits all who would be free of the influence of personality and who discard their personas, their false identities, their roles.

CHAPTER NINE

The Relative Effects of Personality: Fears, Desires and Interrupted Happiness

IN one discussion, the following was offered: Who could have cares if free of the fear of death and punishment, if free of the uncertainty of what happens when your body "ends," if free of the desire and hope for eternal reward, and if free of the constant struggle to meet man-made definitions of "good vs. bad," "right vs. wrong," and "moral vs. immoral" in order to get rewards both now and later? All of the struggling ends [when Realization happens].

Relatedly, the subject of today's Personality Type comes to a very early and profound awareness of "death," of the transitory nature of the elemental body, and of wondering about "post-life" events. Today's discussion will focus on the basic fear and the basic desire of Personality Type Five—"The Investigator." Russ Hudson pointed out the following about Personality Type Fives:

BASIC FEAR AND BASIC DESIRE

The Type Five's BASIC FEAR is the fear of being overwhelmed by reality

The Type Five's BASIC DESIRE is to be competent and knowledgeable

THE IMPACT OF THAT PERSONALITY TYPE ON THE RELATIVE EXISTENCE

As a result of their early awareness of death and the transitory nature of the physical body, Type Fives focus on the relative world and its finite aspect and become overwhelmed by (a) knowing all of "this" is relative but without (b) understanding at all that which is "after this." They can, therefore, become cynical and schizoid at an early age. They can feel as if they don't belong…not to their family, not to their culture, and not even on the planet. They become acquainted with the duality of a sense of separation even as children. More sense of duality results and can leave Fives feeling intellectually arrogant, distant, critical, and negative. The isolation of the unhealthy Four can be practiced to the extreme by the non-Realized Five. The duality of feeling "separate" sets them up for belief in more and more dualities of the types described in the 2005 quote above. Rather than being free of the "thinking mind," "thinking" becomes their very raison d'etre. That further separates them from being in touch with the natural, intuitive, sixth sense. As a result of not being able to shut down the illusion-filled "mind" and its endless gyrating, sleep disorders and dreadful nightmares result and levels of madness eventually seem to manifest.

WHY PERSONALITY TYPE FIVE INTERRUPTS HAPPINESS

In their quest to be seen as competent and knowledgeable, Fives develop a love of titles that reinforce the image of their being "experts" in one or more fields. That seeking of labels reinforces duality and blocks any effort to seek the "True Self." They become "self"-contained instead of finding the Real "Self." Focusing on a fictional, frightful "future" and on the finite nature of a body that has no continuity, how could any sustained happiness possibly happen?

FREEDOM FROM PERSONALITY TYPE FIVE EFFECTS VIA REALIZATION

Their independent and challenging nature can allow Fives to question not only what they observe but to question authority as well. That challenging of authority provides an opportunity to Fives—a chance to become free of the programming and conditioning that authorities impose on members of all cultures and that reinforce belief in concepts and ideas and dogma and all else contained in that unlimited pool of nonsense that has been dreamed up by men who would control. Fives' ability to observe with detachment can initiate their movement along a "path" to Realization that results in their living out the remainder of the manifestation in an AS IF fashion. Via Realization, Fives (as is the case with all personality types that finally Realize) can be freed of the incessant whirling and twisting and movement of the "mind." They can get in touch with their instincts, can be freed of the effects of their programming and conditioning, and can begin living in a reasonable, sane, AS IF fashion. Realization allows Fives to transcend their focus on a fictional, scary "future" and to live more in the present…in the moment. As with all types, Realization can allow Fives to be less "self"-conscious and less "self"-absorbed.

Then, rather than having a fear of being overwhelmed by reality, Realized Fives will understand Reality (and will enjoy the AS IF living that accompanies being in touch with Reality). They will no longer be driven to create and sustain an appearance of extreme competence or be driven to display all of their vast "knowledge." Learned ignorance will be set aside and natural living will happen. No matter what your personality type, would that not be preferable (relatively speaking) to the chaotic existence that results when persons believe in dualities?

CHAPTER TEN

THE RELATIVE EFFECTS OF PERSONALITY: FEARS, DESIRES AND INTERRUPTED HAPPINESS

MANY persons read Enneagram descriptors of personality types and find that they're unable to "pin down" the one exact category that is their dominant personality. That is understandable. It was pointed out earlier that all personas are driven not only by their own dominant type but also by the two adjacent types/wings and by two other types that they attach to either via integration or via the disintegration that happens when persons become stressed or pious. (Research shows that stress or piety lead to the same result: either will trigger disintegration into the worst traits of another type.)It should be seen, therefore, that these discussions of personality types are not the pointers, whether the listings are found in the enneagram or on some astrological chart. The pointer is that any person (that is, any persona, any "one" trapped in personality identification) will be impacted by personality, will suffer throughout their relative existence from behaviors and a thought-life that are driven by personality, and will never know the true happiness of AS IF living. The pointer is not that you will receive any benefit from understanding which type you are or which types influence you. The pointer is to see that identification with personality is insane, that the "you" which can be influenced by personality is not real, that allowing something as nebulous as "personality" to control every facet of an existence will prevent personas from ever being in touch with reality, and that identification with personality will preclude any opportunity for living out the manifestation in a sane manner that is characterized by reason and logic. As with all Advaita teachings, therefore, the point is to see the concepts being discussed as concepts, to use the discussions to free persons of the influence of forces that are unconsciously driving them, to discard all of those influences, and then to be truly free. That point having been offered, today's discussion will focus on the basic fear and the basic desire of Personality Type Six—"The Loyalist." Russ Hudson pointed out the following about Personality Type Sixes:

BASIC FEAR AND BASIC DESIRE

The Type Six has a BASIC FEAR of having no support or guidance

The Type Six has a BASIC DESIRE to have support and guidance

THE IMPACT OF THAT PERSONALITY TYPE ON THE RELATIVE EXISTENCE

Because Type Sixes can disintegrate into a Type Three—especially when stressed or pious—they often exhibit many of the traits of an unhealthy Three. [See entry on 23 October 2006 for details on Type Threes.] Because the Type Six personality generates high-stress situations—and because their type automatically listens to anyone who seems to know what he/she is talking about—they often allow persons to control them. They are frequently stressed and frequently pious, so they frequently exhibit the worst traits of Type Threes who have adopted religious or spiritual personas as their identity. Non-Realized Sixes have no ability to discriminate, so they listen to anyone in a position of authority. That leaves them especially vulnerable to the effects of programming, conditioning, and enculturation; thus, they are very susceptible to influence from those who would control them. That susceptibility to accepting blindly the influence of persons (specifically, the influence of egotistical persons who assume positions of authority) also leaves Sixes especially prone to accepting as truth the false, non-duality teachings of the authority figures in their cultures. The persons that Sixes often listen to unquestioningly can include preachers, priests, politicians, military officers, police, speakers in spiritual movements, other so-called "religious leaders," etc. Their openness to influence and loyalty to "leaders" or "experts" also deprives them of that skill that is required for even beginning the "journey" toward Realization, namely, the willingness to question authority or to suspect the validity of superstitions or beliefs or dogma or myths. The fact that some estimates suggest that 50% of the persons on the planet are Type Sixes makes clear why so few persons will ever Realize and why so many persons can be compared to sheep, walking willingly off to the slaughter and cheerfully behaving in the most nonsensical manner in order to please their "shepherds." These are the types who become cannon fodder for their political and military leaders, the ones who shout, "I will follow any order that is given to me," as was the case in Germany in the '30's and as is still the case in many nations today. These are the ones who proudly proclaim that they are "willing to die for god, for country, for their beliefs, for their concepts, for their leader" or for any one of a thousand other "causes" that are dreamed up as a result of the egomania of the controlling personas who influence Sixes.

WHY PERSONALITY TYPE SIX INTERRUPTS HAPPINESS

Their personality can leave Sixes in a constant state of hyper-vigilance. They can become bad-tempered, paranoid, controlling, rigid, defensive, disparaging, and volatile. Identified with body and personality, they can become obsessed with obtaining a sense of security (but trusting in leaders or leaving it to the authorities to protect them rather than being independent, rather than meeting their relative existence needs themselves, and instead of finding truth themselves as opposed to taking the word of leaders who would control them). Often, these types are self-contradictory. Typically the types who are most often loyal to religious leaders, to political leaders, and to a god, they ironically claim on one hand that they "are turning it all over to god" while occasionally admitting on the other hand that "god will not do for you what you can do for yourself." They will give blind loyalty to their politicians but can become stressed and bitter when (a) their politicians fail them but when (b) they still feel driven to continue to support them or their ruinous policies.

Because of their obsession with security, their basic, constant desire is to seek out support and guidance from others, mostly those they see as authorities. Being so dependent gives controlling persons the ability to manipulate Sixes quite easily. Losing all confidence in their own abilities, they can reach a point where they can do nothing without getting advice or approval from the figures they respect as "experts" or "authorities." They can become burdened by doubt and will question their own judgment while refusing to question the judgment of the authorities they remain loyal to and dependent upon. How blind can "Loyalists" actually be? Being drawn as they are to religion, they can see no contradiction in such teachings as "God loves you unconditionally but He will also subject you to eternal torture in the flames of hell." Thus they become studies in contradiction, sometimes following rules but at other times breaking rules and then trying to hide that conduct. They can be fearful at times and at other times can confront their fears, but only with assistance from their advisors. (Is it becoming clear why so many are prone to accept dualities as truth?) They seldom have an ability to "make up their minds about anything" and are constantly under the pressure of being pushed in one direction while being pulled in another. They often worry and are always on guard—watching out for danger and fearing that persons are out to take advantage of them. That leaves them susceptible to such lies as "I will take care of you for all your life" or "I can show you the way to save your soul and to have eternal life." Sixes are especially drawn to those who make the illogical claim that they know how to provide continuity for the body-mind-personality triad. Who could possibility be happy with those personality traits and the behavior they inspire?

FREEDOM FROM PERSONALITY TYPE SIX EFFECTS VIA REALIZATION

Realized, the Type Six will no longer be obsessed with a search for support and guidance. The desire for support will dissolve as independence manifests. The search for external guidance ends as contact with the inner resource manifests. Being in touch with reality restores sanity, and being restored to sanity frees Type Sixes—and all other personas as well—of their tendency to accept the nonsensical as sensible. Natural, innate awareness will replace dependency on outer authority figures and external "power sources" that have been dreamed up by men over the ages. Magical, supernatural thinking will end and then the (former) Sixes will live naturally instead. True independence, the prerequisite for true happiness to happen, will manifest.

CHAPTER ELEVEN

THE RELATIVE EFFECTS OF PERSONALITY: FEARS, DESIRES AND INTERRUPTED HAPPINESS

"BODY," "mind," and "personality" are concepts, rooted in ideas dreamed up—typically—by controlling men and passed on today via programming, conditioning, and enculturation. Among the masses on the planet, little progress has been made in eliminating belief in concepts and dogma and myths and magical, supernatural thinking since those early times when an eclipse was perceived to be the result of an action taken by an angry god (the same explanation many modern persons cited as the cause of Hurricane Katrina and the subsequent damage and deaths). Any discussions of any concepts—including these on personality—are offered, therefore, in the spirit of thorns being provided for use in removing thorns. To see that archetypes, programming, personality traits and conditioning can drive persons subconsciously and/or unconsciously to think and behave in certain ways is a prerequisite for being free of those subconscious and unconscious influences. Only by being free of those influences can one move into a state of enlightenment and awareness and then live out the remainder of the manifestation in the type of AS IF living that happens after the consciousness has been re-purified. This discussion will focus on the basic fear and the basic desire of Personality Type Seven—"The Adventurer/Enthusiast." Russ Hudson pointed out the following about Personality Type Sevens:

BASIC FEAR AND BASIC DESIRE

The Type Seven has a BASIC FEAR of being trapped, deprived or in pain (be it mental, emotional, or physical)

The Type Seven has a BASIC DESIRE to be free, to have the "need" for exciting or enjoyable activities fulfilled, and to avoid all pain (be it mental, emotional, or physical)

THE IMPACT OF THAT PERSONALITY TYPE ON THE RELATIVE EXISTENCE

Type Sevens are busy, fun-loving types who enjoy the spontaneous but hate the routine. While they can be free-spirited at some point, they can eventually deteriorate into excessiveness and becomes escapists. In the extreme, they can disintegrate into manic compulsiveness, and their relative existence can become marked by panic attacks and fits of hysteria and histrionics. Sevens can become the "bliss seekers" of the relative existence or the "bliss seekers" among evangelical extremists or even the "bliss seekers" among those on the Advaitin path. Of course, all such seeking and desiring eventually lead only to more frustration as all perceived (but unreal) "needs" are never fully met.

WHY PERSONALITY TYPE SEVEN INTERRUPTS HAPPINESS

Sevens would rather be excited than happy. They would rather be ecstatic than at peace. They will use activity and "doing" to treat their anxiety and can become "go-ers and do-ers and zoomers" in the style of Type Threes and Sixes and Eights. Their tendency to "anticipate" leaves them discontented with the present, and even when an anticipated activity eventually happens, Sevens are frustrated. Why? When that which was anticipated eventually comes about, it is never as great as what was anticipated. They are constantly "living in the future" and are, therefore, deprived from living in the moment...similar in that way to many Type Fives. Living in the illusion of their "mental future," NOW becomes anathema and further separation from reality results. Sevens want to find "that magnificence that IS," but they are actually in fear that they'll never find it; therefore, they can become cynical and can turn to drugs or alcohol to deaden any pain or frustration that they might be feeling. They can become so determined to avoid all pain and all uncomfortable situations that they can engage in impulsive, insane relative existence conduct to avoid pain and all physical, mental, or emotional discomfort. That leaves them "emotionally unavailable" in their relative existence "relationships." They hate commitment and seriousness and confronting and analysis and suffering so much that they, ironically, induce more suffering in their efforts to avoid or to escape. Eventually, they can become more impulsive, restless, and self-destructive in economic, emotional, or social ways (but their hatred of slowing down and analyzing the things that are driving them and finding out Who/What They Truly Are prevents many Sevens from ever reaching a state of Full Realization). Who could possibility be happy with those personality traits and the behavior they inspire?

FREEDOM FROM PERSONALITY TYPE SEVEN EFFECTS VIA REALIZATION

If Sevens Realize, their basic fear of being trapped disappears. They are able to ask "WHO feels trapped?" and are able to understand that no "one" exists to feel trapped. The fear of being deprived ends as they are able to ask "WHO feels deprived?" and can then understood that no "one" exists to feel deprived. And the fear of mental or physical or—especially—emotional pain ends. Why? With Realization, feelings are witnessed as they rise and fall, but no ego-states exist that stimulate emotional intoxication. There is no longer any "one" to "experience" anything. The ego prefers the search, the going, the doing, the zooming. When the "magnificence" which they were searching for is finally found in the "magnificence" of knowing the True Self and then living in an AS IF style, then ego dissolves. The overwhelming pain of the frustrating search (which in the past had ended so often in futility) comes to an end

Only the re-purified consciousness can result in the bliss that the Sevens had sought for so long with such vigor. The desire to be free ends as freedom truly manifests. Exciting or enjoyable activities can happen, but even if they don't (and even if a state of bliss is never maintained) the Sevens can still be content. And then, for those who could never find enough of what they had been seeking, merely being content suddenly becomes…enough.

CHAPTER TWELVE

THE RELATIVE EFFECTS OF PERSONALITY: FEARS, DESIRES AND INTERRUPTED HAPPINESS

THIS pointer about remote tribes people and their language was offered: The personal "I" is avoided by the members of that tribe because they consider its use to be a sign of arrogance. Find a person who is arrogant and you'll have found a person self-absorbed and totally occupied with the "I," with the "ego" (Latin for "I"). A Jiukiukwe child would not say, "I want water" but would report instead, "There is thirst." The focus is on the thirst, not on the wants or desires or needs of a personal "I"—of a persona or a "personality."

This section will focus on the basic fear and the basic desire of Personality Type Eight—"The Boss/The Challenger/The Asserter," another of the types that is often driven by arrogance and by the false perception of the wants or desires or needs of a personal "I"—of a persona or a "personality." Russ Hudson pointed out the following about Personality Type Eights:

BASIC FEAR AND BASIC DESIRE

Type Eights have a BASIC FEAR of being harmed, violated or controlled by others

Type Eights have a BASIC DESIRE to protect themselves, to gain control of their lives, and to control all other persons

THE IMPACT OF THAT PERSONALITY TYPE ON THE RELATIVE EXISTENCE

The observation that "The Bully is really a very frightened individual" can apply to Type Eights. They often become "The Boss" or "The Assertive One" in order to be in control. In their fear of being harmed or violated or controlled, they work diligently to place themselves in positions of authority. Once there, they can become insensitive, aggressive, and self-centered. As a result, they (ironically) harm, violate, or try to control others. Peace is never a goal for these fighters. They will take any steps required to appear to be strong and thereby avoid feeling dependent or weak. They can become blunt, impatient, resentful, demanding, defensive, intolerant, and over-reactive.

WHY PERSONALITY TYPE EIGHT INTERRUPTS HAPPINESS

Ultimately, these warriors can reach a state of fatigue that is debilitating mentally, emotionally, and physically. To assume the ego-state—the persona—of "Chairman of the Board of the Universe" leads to behavior that becomes very tiring. At least in a boxing match the fighters brawl for three minutes but then sit down and rest for one minute. Type Eights never take a break from engagement and hostility if they feel they are not in total control of all of the people they must deal with, of all places wherever they are, and of all situations. To be embroiled in identification with the personas of "The Boss" and "The Challenger of All That Seems a Threat" and "The One Who is in Charge of Space and Time" will eventually take a heavy toll. Type Eights wear themselves out and wear out people around them as a result of being so forceful, so insensitive, so hyper-vigilant, and so self-absorbed. In the office, their bluntness and "bottom line" approach might generate profits for a time, but their overbearing nature will eventually produce an environment of fear and hatred and passive-aggressive conduct among workers that becomes counter-productive in the end. In traffic, they are overly-aggressive, going into a rage if anyone tries to enter into "their" space. In "personal relations," they are dictatorial. Their belief that they are in charge and don't have to "put up with anything" leaves them completely intolerant. At their worst, these megalomaniacs become so hard-hearted that they can become ruthless. Like non-Realized, unhealthy Type Threes, they can "wish people dead" or actually become murderous. Also like Threes, when totally absorbed in the worst traits of their personality, they become sociopaths. Who could possibly be happy with those personality traits and the behavior they inspire?

FREEDOM FROM PERSONALITY TYPE EIGHT EFFECTS VIA REALIZATION

While Realization comes as rarely to unhealthy Type Eights as it comes to unhealthy Type Threes and unhealthy Type Sixes, it can happen. If they live long enough and suffer the consequences of their personality enough, Eights may become tired enough to seek another way. Should they follow a "path" to Full Realization, they—just as happens with all personas who abandon personality—can accept the vulnerabilities and limitations of the physical body and stop feeling the constant fear of threat. No longer self-absorbed, they can know the unicity and can care about "the welfare of others" (relatively speaking). They can become aware and can live deliberately but spontaneously, yet their spontaneity is of a nature that is diametrically opposite that of their spontaneous raging from days past. As with all who Realize, their conduct during the remainder of the AS IF living can take on the flavor of what dualists call "moral behavior." Why? They had lived with the fear of being harmed, of being violated, or of being controlled by others. By overcoming their false perception that everything is a threat—and by relinquishing identification with the physical body—they can also abandon automatically their false perception that they must fight constantly in order to protect themselves. WHO is there to protect? Their desire to defend (by engaging, controlling, raging, fighting, dominating and overcoming) dissolves if Full Realization happens.

CHAPTER THIRTEEN

THE RELATIVE EFFECTS OF PERSONALITY: FEARS, DESIRES AND INTERRUPTED HAPPINESS

IN March of '05, the following was offered in response to a question: The problem [in the relative existence] is always the personality—those ego-states that generate personas and the use of ego-defense mechanisms that they always generate. The Advaita teaching offers an invitation to put an end to ego and arrogance in the relative existence by ending all false beliefs in ego-states.

Identification with personality (which has been seen to include identification not only with the dominant type but with several of the other nine types) always results in the assumption of labels, personas, and ego-states. The phoniness of role-playing eventually mars the entire relative existence and prevents most persons from ever Realizing fully What They Truly Are. To be inspired to become free of the effects of personality, the malfunctionings of personality must first be understood, so today's discussion will focus on the basic fears and the basic desires of Personality Type Nine—"The Indifferent One/The Mediator/The Peacemaker/The Sloth." Russ Hudson pointed out the following about Personality Type Nines:

BASIC FEAR AND BASIC DESIRE
Type Nines have a BASIC FEAR of loss and of separation (and of not being taken care of)
Type Nines have a BASIC DESIRE for continuity and for "peace of mind" (and for reaping the benefits of their perceived entitlement and being taken care of)

THE IMPACT OF THAT PERSONALITY TYPE ON THE RELATIVE EXISTENCE

Type Nines are evidence of the fallacy of the concept "Blessed are the peace-makers"—at least as far as personality is concerned. As far as the Absolute is concerned, there are no blessings to be had at some future point since there is no future (and no future "one" to be blessed.) As far as the relative is concerned, nothing is farther removed from the concept of "being blessed" than personas living under the whims and the influences of identification with personality... with their assumed personas. And most certainly that is the case with non-Real-ized persons who are identifying with their Type Nine personality. Non-Realized Nines have an unstated motto: "Never do today what can be put off until tomorrow or that—better yet—can be avoided forever." Because they have a desire to avoid confrontation, to avoid ever having to be in a challenging situation with other persons, and to avoid any occasion that ever has the slightest possibility of leading to any degree of conflict, they can eventually avoid all of the relative existence functions that are required for meeting the basic requirements of food, clothing and shelter. That means avoiding regular employment and, instead, seeking out Type Two Helpers who will care for the Nine or seeking out Type Sixes or Threes who have assumed religious or spiritual roles. Those three types can find themselves being "used" by apathetic and lazy Nines in order for the Twos, Threes, and Sixes to support their own fabricated, altruistic image.

Eights can also be dragged into a Nine's game because Eights love to "jump in" and take charge of situations that "need fixing." Ones can be snared by Nines since Ones have a personality-driven desire to "make all things right." Fours can be "moved" by the eloquence of Nines who are masters at detecting Type Four personas with romantic ideals and who want to "make the world a better place" by helping those who "need help." (Since non-Realized Fours disintegrate to Type Two and adopt Helper traits, they fall into the Nine trap as well.) A Seven might consider it an "adventure" to move in a needy Type Nine person, having no idea that it's far easier to get a Nine to move in than it is to get them to move out. Thus, it becomes clear why Nines are able to find so many other persons who are willing to care for them: so many among the varied personality types are driven in ways that make them susceptible to manipulation. And Nines can become "The Great Manipulators" because they can "read" the other types and know how to appeal to that within each personality type that will elicit the support that Nines desire (and believe they deserve).

Being adept at rationalization, they can make a comment like, "I've surrendered completely because God will take care of me." If asked about when they might start looking for a job, a typical response would be, "In God's time... not mine." They can eventually become quite stubborn with those who would encourage them to exercise, to move about, or to seek employment. Still avoiding confrontation, they become passive-aggressive but will use their skill of apologizing or "making amends" in order to defuse anger in others and to reestablish codependency. Their laziness or apathy is often mistaken for "a state of divine peacefulness" that comes as a result of "working their religious or spiritual disciplines." One person said of an unemployed Nine, "He's my ideal. He lost his job, but his level of spiritual development has left him with such peace that he can live in the back of his car and be okay with that." The truly awake and aware did not see that Nine as a "Spiritual Giant" but as one who is really dedicated to avoiding work at any price.

WHY PERSONALITY TYPE NINE INTERRUPTS HAPPINESS

The toll on Nines is cumulative. Eventually, they are criticized for their refusal to mobilize by those who do not understand the effects of their personality type. After years of such criticism, Nines become disparaging of themselves, exacerbating the destructive traits of their type, relatively speaking. Their predilection for procrastination leaves them perpetually in a dependent state...often appealing to a god or some external power to intervene and take care of them. To meet basic requirements, Nines can become adept at impressing others, at making others believe that the Nines are special, at earning respect and admiration, and at creating through those actions a network of idealizing supporters who will be willing to take on the task of meeting the basic needs of the Nines. The Nine, at that point, is never freed from playing the game. When stressed or pious, Nines disintegrate to Type Threes. Embroiled as Threes are in the tasks of image-fabrication and image-maintenance, disintegrated Nines can eventually become exhausted.

They deplete their energy with (a) appeals to relatives and friends and acquaintances to meet their basic requirements or (b) with constant efforts to manipulate. Once they exhaust all sources of support, they can become frustrated and angry and fatalistic. Dissociation further blocks any possibility of coming to know the True Self. Rather than seeking awareness, they try to block out all awareness. Eventually, they can become totally dysfunctional. If they worked as hard at a job as they work at (1) avoiding work and at (2) finding other persons to take care of them, then Nines could be completely independent, but that is seldom their goal. Having no independence and thus never being truly free, who could possibility be happy with those personality traits and the behavior they inspire.

FREEDOM FROM PERSONALITY TYPE NINE EFFECTS VIA REALIZATION

Realized, Type Nines—just as is the case with all other types that Realize— can stop their avoiding and can become productive enough to meet their own basic requirements for food, clothing, and shelter. Being realistic for a change, Nines can function in the natural way whereby each meets his/her own basic survival needs. The Nine can then abandon the dependency-producing, supernatural, magical thinking that makes him/her believe that either some supernatural power, or something or someone external, is supposed to take care of the Nine. Then, the Nine can Realize, can meet his/her own basic needs, and can then live naturally. Naturally? Yes. The deer, which lives naturally instead of supernaturally, does not expect another deer to do its grazing for it. Post-Realization, an element of practicality begins to mark the relative existence of Type Nines...an element that had never manifested before. Realized, the Nines automatically stop the past behaviors that led to such a sense of separation. Taking care of their own physical requirements, the fear of not being taken care of disappears (along with the sense of entitlement that led them to believe that they deserved to be taken care of by others). They leave that fantasy world that they had "lived in" where they preferred the escapism of oblivion and the avoidance of reality. Contrary to what many persons imagine Realization can lead to—such as "not feeling anything" or "being fatalistic" or "never having any pleasure"—the Realized Nine (as is the case with all that Realize) can become truly free and independent. And only if truly free and independent can the fullness and pleasures and joys of AS IF living happen.

CHAPTER FOURTEEN

THE RELATIVE EFFECTS OF PERSONALITY: "HOW PERSONALITY ALWAYS (A) GENERATES FEAR AND DESIRE AND (B) PREVENTS SUSTAINED HAPPINESS"

ALL persons (being mentally and emotionally unhealthy as a result of non-Realization) can exhibit traits of any or all of the nine personality types. The prior descriptions of the varied personality types, combined with an understanding that anyone not Realized can exhibit the traits of almost any of the nine types, makes clear why persons suffer from multiple personality disorder and why their relative existence is marked by instability, chaos, and an inability to sustain any degree of true happiness. It has been seen that identification with the body-mind-personality triad will result in persons/personas—always trapped in their dualistic beliefs as a result of personality, programming and conditioning—experiencing the fear of being "corrupt" or "evil" or "defective"; the fear of not being loved; the fear of being worthless; the fear of having no identity; the fear of being overwhelmed by "reality"; the fear associated with the dependence of seeking external support and guidance from others; the fear of being trapped; the fear of being deprived or in pain; the fear of being harmed or violated or controlled by others; the fear of loss and a constant sense of separation; and the fear that their perceived needs will not being met. All of those will be experienced by the non-Realized who are trapped in their identification with personality.

Too, all persons trapped in personality identification will be frustrated by their unfulfilled desires...desires rooted in their wanting to be free of their fears. Trapped as they are in their false identity and duality—and driven by their fears,

as all personas are—all persons at one time or another can have the desire to be
seen as being "good"; can have a desire to be "loved"; can have a desire to prove
how valuable they are; can desire to understand Who/What They Truly Are; can
desire to prove that they are competent and knowledgeable; can desire external
support and can thereby become dependent on others for guidance and sustenance; can desire a level of freedom that they will never find without Realization;
can desire to gain control of others; and will desire freedom from the sense of
emptiness and misery that results from (1) desiring continuity of the physical
body, (2) desiring "peace of mind" when the "mind" is actually the source of
their lack of peace, and (3) desiring that their personality and assumed roles can
last eternally.

The reasoning behind the Advaita suggestion that personality identification should be abandoned should now be obvious. The Original Understanding
preempted the assumption of personas, roles, labels, concepts, dogma, and—
yes—even any rationale for offering teachings. The influence of personality
in regards to the manifesting of perceived fears, unmet desires, and forestalled
happiness should be clear.

CHAPTER FIFTEEN

HOW EGO/PERSONALITY CAN LEAD TO DISINTEGRATION AND DESTRUCTION IN THE RELATIVE EXISTENCE

THERE are nine stages of disintegration that each personality type can undergo. The farther removed a persona is from Reality, the more insane they behave in the relative existence. Please note the role that ego plays at each stage in the disintegration of the personality, recalling that "ego" is Latin for "I" or "I myself"; thus, "I" or "ego" = "my [false] self."

See, in fact, that personality identification prevents Realization and that Realization eliminates personality. As far as the relative existence is concerned, see that the more persons become trapped in personality and the more trapped they become in their ego-states, the more their relative existence lives degenerate through stages of delusion, chaos, and destruction. See that professionals know what the Realized know: "healthy" AS living happens only after Full Realization happens.

FUNCTIONING STAGES: 1-3

STAGE 1: LIBERATED
(At this stage, ego is transcended; therefore, truth, balance, freedom and awake-ness manifest; there is an ability to differentiate true from false; the True Self is known; Awareness, complete freedom, sanity, and independence manifest; AS IF living happens)
STAGE 2: IDENTIFIED w/ MIND-BODY-PERSONALITY

(At this stage, ego begins identifying with states-of-being as a result of programming, conditioning, and enculturation; co-dependency results)

STAGE 3: FUNCTIONING IN A "SOCIALLY-ACCEPTABLE" MANNER

(At this stage, ego operates, but in a manner considered "acceptable" within societies)

DECLINING STAGES: 4-6

STAGE 4: DISTURBED / "ASLEEP"

(At this stage, ego blocks any sense of Presence or Awareness; persons exhibit evidence of being irritable, restless, discontent or being disturbed by "others"; beginning of being "asleep")

STAGE 5: SCHEMING

(At this stage, ego works to control and manipulate other persons; ego expends more energy to defend roles/images/ego-states)

STAGE 6: AGGRESSIVE / DEFENSIVE

(At this stage, ego inflates; personas behave aggressively to defend false identities)

DISFUNCTIONAL STAGES: 7-9

STAGE 7: ABUSIVE

(At this stage, ego is so dedicated to "self"-preservation that persons become willing to violate self and others; persons become abusive if need be to fight for the preservation of identities and to exert power over "others")

STAGE 8: FANATICAL / IMPULSIVE

(At this stage, ego/self is out of control and out of touch with Reality; perceptions are 180-degrees in opposition to actuality; major mental disorders manifest)

STAGE 9: DESTRUCTIVE

(At this stage, persons become destructive toward self or others; acute mental disorders emerge; persons degenerate into sociopaths; persons can become willing to kill themselves or others)

CHAPTER SIXTEEN

NINE RELATIVE EXISTENCE ACTIONS THAT CAN HELP SHIFT PERSONAS FROM UNHEALTHY STAGES OF DISINTEGRATION TO LIBERATION

SINCE ego takes the composite of all of its false identities to define "who it is," there is a major emotional investment among persons in terms of the value given to their false roles and to the amount of energy that ego is willing to expend in trying to preserve and sustain ego's false images. The resulting emotional intoxication prevents the re-purification of the consciousness and prevents any shift from (a) the unhealthy stages of personality disintegration to (b) the highest level of liberation. (Liberation here refers to freedom from the influence of ego, freedom from the misery and suffering that are always generated by the corrupted consciousness, and then true freedom, period.)

Only a quality of consciousness—only the completely re-purified consciousness—can provide any quality of happiness. Ego dulls the quality of the consciousness; then, the ego-driven disintegration of the personality can lead not only to misery and suffering but also to physical destruction as well. For one to be happy, the lies of the ego must be abandoned (which will happen if the consciousness is re-purified).Even If you find that you're unable to reject immediately the influences of whichever of the Nine Personality Types are driving you, you can at least begin to wear those types with a lightness rather than as a weighty armor that the ego is using to shield its false identifications and personas. So what actions can free you from the unhealthy stages and shift you into a state of total liberation? The nine actions begin by providing a method to address the needs of those at level nine and then provide a step-by-step process to shift persons from there to the highest level: total liberation.

CHAPTER SEVENTEEN

THE NINE ACTIONS

(THE early actions on the list are about survival in the relative existence. The Later actions are methods for reaching a state of Full Realization and Full Liberation)

Action One
Action one is recommended for those who have disintegrated to the ninth level: intervene by relocating to an environment that can provide safety; move away from triggers

Action Two
Start to understand the personality and what causes it to disintegrate; begin to study the ego and its role in that process; seek out those who are in touch with reality

Action Three
Along with removing yourself from triggering people, triggering places and triggering things, begin to consider the possibility that a false "self" (or selves) might have been driving you throughout the entirety of your life and preventing You from gaining conscious contact with Your True, Real, Authentic, Actualized Self

Action Four
Engage in activities and exercises that can begin to deflate the ego; begin uncovering the personas (the states-of-being) that inspire aggressive behaviors in defense of ego-generated identities

Action Five
Continue to uncover the roles that you have been playing, the images
that you have cultivated (or accepted when assigned to you), and the
ego-states or states-of-being that have taken away from you an ability to
control your own behavior and life

Action Six
Engage in exercises and disciplines that lead to an awakening, to an
awareness of all that you have not previously been aware of; submit to
a process of inventory that allows the understanding of "psychological
projection" in order to inventory yourself (your "self"), to be free of "self

Action Seven
You are re-integrating by this point, but not totally free of ego-iden-
tifications; as you continue seeking to be totally free of ego and false
personas, consider ways in which your individual strengths and newly-
gained awareness might be employed in order to provide for your own
basic needs as well as to set the stage for your assets to be used to the
benefit of other

Action Eight
Commit to spending whatever time and effort is required to become
free of the illusions of false identities, of ego-states, of states-of-being, of
roles, and of anything that is artificial and that blocks Your awareness of
Your True Self

Action Nine
Read the following description of a vision:
Envision yourself standing at one end of an open field in a very remote area.
At the far end of the field is the edge of a forest. See yourself moving across the
field and toward the woods. As you walk closer to the edge of the forest, see a gap
in the trees that allows clear access to a trail. Follow that path through the woods,
noticing the sounds along the way. Walk until you reach the side of a small creek
bed. Turn to the right and see yourself walking along the bank of a "branch," one
of those small, usually V-shaped mini-gorges, cut into the ground ten to twelve

feet at its deepest, not as much by rainwater as by constantly flowing springs that surface from below.

Observe an emerald-green moss that covers the walls and the bed; it seems to shine with a luminescence in spite of the fact that the thickness of the overhead foliage prevents much sunlight from striking the creek bed or the sides of the chasm. The earthen walls look rough-edged, for stones jut out all along the way, their tips exposed by years of erosion. Colors typical of the region come into view along the way: earth-tones, rust-colors, and sometimes blackness, but always brightened by the ever-present grayish and fluorescent-green moss.

As you parallel the edge of the creek on the beginning of this journey, see yourself reaching a place where the land slopes sharply, and the watery swath cut into the earth follows the oblique contour of the land.

Next to the slanting branch rests a series of natural, sandstone steps descending to a granite arch twice the height of a human. From the arch shines a pure white light. An illumination this bright should easily blind you, but instead it soothes you. It seems to spotlight the steps, and as you move down the stones, first your feet and then your legs and then your torso become bathed in the glow. Eventually, by the time you reach the dead-flat area at the bottom of the natural walkway, you stand before the arch, and the luxuriance of the light baths you fully in its warmth. The clear spring waters from the branch flow through the archway, and you follow. Stepping inside, you look over your shoulder to see that your physical body has remained outside the arch.

You sense some degree of separation from the material. When you turn to see where the arch has led, you notice that the spring waters have suddenly multiplied into a slow-moving stream. The stream runs the length of a plateau and then cascades over the edge at the far end. You will soon see that the waters drop from the highland and then flow, in waterfall fashion, down the cliff side and into a pool some twenty feet below.

Trees line either side of the stream, and you begin walking through them toward the sounds of the water crashing below. Astonished, you noticed that you are literally walking through the trees. As you progress, fauna of several species join you: a black bear rubs against your leg in the manner of a docile housecat; a cougar does the same on the opposite side, and each playfully swats at the other as if to proclaim dominion over both of your legs; a lamb skips along ahead as a heron brings up the rear. He walks as if on stilts, taking more time than needed, looking rather judgmentally, it seems, at the wasting of energy by his peers. As you near the edge of the cliff, you walk across the top of the water, not becoming wet at all; your new companions either lead or follow.

As you approach the left side of the plateau, the animals nudge you toward a winding walkway of sorts, cut from the stone side of the cliff naturally, definitely not made by man. After swinging down and around and back to your right, you find yourself on a level piece of ground jutting out from the side of the cliff. You see that a pond is overflowing, part of its waters cascading down the cliff side and pooling in another flat below.

That same pattern repeats itself until the waters reach a level valley. You watch the falling waters eventually form a river that winds its way across the desert basin. Along the river has sprung up a variety of shade trees. All else appears brown and dry. Then in the far distance, hills grow into mountains. In the forefront arise huge columns of stone, cathedral-like, forming spires of varying shapes and heights. The colors vibrate with life, offering images of the blues and oranges and browns and beiges like those of Venetian palazzos when reflected in the waters of the Grand Canal.

In the far distance to the left stand even grander mountain ranges. Puffy clouds float slowly across the sky. You focus attention on a fire burning next to the pool, and you feel yourself being nudged there by the bear, nudged in a very persuasive way. Then, from behind the cougar lifts its front paws onto your shoulders, forcing you into a cross-legged, seated position before the campfire. Finally, all four animals form a semi-circle around you, from your left side, behind you, and to your right.

Looking at the animals quizzically, you notice that each is focusing on an object in the distance. Allowing your eyes to follow the path of theirs, see a bird of some kind flying directly at you, drawing nearer by the second. Its speed accelerates as it moves dart-like across the skies, aimed at your chest like an avian arrow. Yet you feel very calm.

As the bird approaches closer and closer, you extend your arms and, with the sides of your hands touching and your palms up, you form a landing area for the fowl. A raven, the bird of death that comes from the spiritual realm, now slows as it approaches even nearer. Why had you not made that association between spirit and death and this bird? It swoops upward to curb its flight and, with only a slight, backwards fluttering of wings, settles gently into your outstretched hands. The other fauna watch but do not react.

The bird stares at you, and you at the bird. You sense the bird drawing forth something from within you that is flowing out via your eyes and moving directly into the eyes of the bird. You watch as the bird leaves, but you feel as if you have left and that your mind has stayed behind. A second degree of separation you seem to detect.

The raven soars over the valley, flying high, then flying low, and then flying high again. Its spirit is high. Soon, it makes a direct course for the mountains, for it us driven to try to reach the mountaintop. You no longer watch from the cliff but see everything below through the eyes of the raven. After missing the mountaintop, the raven passes beyond and begins a fast descent toward an ocean which has come into view just after topping the peak. The raven begins to dive lower, and lower, and lower yet.

Suddenly, the spiritual exuberance of the high-flying raven seems to be unraveling into an imminent and deadly crash against the ocean's surface. Following a huge impact—one that you take to be the end of you—the waters first splash upwards from the collision and then fall back into the ocean. Ultimately, the waves settle, and the sea surface smoothes out to a mirror finish. Suddenly, a bird's head forcefully breaks the surface, but it is not the head of a raven. Instead, the head of a gull—the bird of ignorance—comes forth, gasping for air. You find that you are no longer observing the gull, but have transitioned into the gull. A third degree of separation from what you had left outside the arch, then by the pool, and now through the raven, has manifested.

The gull surfaces further and then begins flapping its wings. Leaving behind the cleansing, baptismal waters, you in the form of this gull fly and play and dart. You feel like a child again, flying high, until suddenly crashing into an eagle. More truthfully, you feel yourself merging into—maybe even dissolving into—the eagle. For a time, the eagle soars, glides, and mainly just witnesses. You feel the remnants of the gull; you sense the remains of a raven; you look at "you" seated at a fire and see only a mental image; you look through the arch and see the figment of a body imagined. Another degree of separation.

But now You the Eagle have no time to contemplate, for you feel yourself being pulled deeper into the universe through a clear-walled tunnel in the remotest part of the heavens. You feel yourself accelerating at the speed of light. In fact, at the end of the tunnel, you can see nothing other than light. Your speed now nearly doubles, and just as you reach that point of mach two, with the deafening sounds of the winds racing by your ears, you crash through a veil of sorts and find yourself in a mostly dark, crystal cave.

You stop abruptly and then are swooped into an upright position, floating near the ceiling of the cave. You feel at this moment as if you are exactly between nowhere and . . . nowhere. Never have you known such peace. Sensing yourself in only the vestige of a human-like form, you drift toward a lake below that covers most of the bottom of this huge cavern. You experience a fifth degree of separation—as if estranged from all illusionary roles, as if removed from a phony world left behind, as if moving closer to a degree of connection with the Real.

Your slow descent allows time to study the cave. Across the way a dome glows brightly, the source of the vivid light you'd seen through the arch and more recently at the end of the tunnel. A huge pipe organ sounds from the highest peak of a cliff on the far left side of the gigantic grotto. To your left and to your right drift millions of forms, and on closer inspection, You see that they are . . . You! Each looks to be a clone—maybe a transparent clone but a clone neverthe-less—of You!

As You near the water, You automatically pivot so that Your back faces the opposite shore. Sinking shoulder-deep into the water, You feel Your feet rise. Your entire body stiffens momentarily, Your feet rise further, You float onto Your back and then You bob on the surface of the water. Now relaxed, You begin to be moved along, gently propelled toward the opposite side of the cave. Your movements just happen, no effort on Your part required. The music of the organ—ethereal and heavenly—sounds softly, beautifully; the waters are now calm and warm.

You float with millions of Your likenesses, or so it seems, flowing toward gigantic, granite steps cut amphitheater-like into the opposite wall of the cave. Yet the likenesses aren't likenesses at all. They Really Are You! The steps ascend from underneath the waters, breaking the surface and then rising and narrowing upwards, converging on one point—at the door to the dome. As You near the steps, You feel Your body stiffen again. This time You rotate in the water so that You sail along face down.

Just before Your head might have bumped into the steps, You are stopped. Your feet begin to be lowered, and You find yourself in an upright position, standing on steps in chest-high water. You begin to ascend the steps, leaving the water behind. You, and millions of Yous, walk in exactly the same fashion, moving toward the narrowing peak that leads to the door of the dome. You wonder, How could so many be entering the dome? It really isn't that large, now that I can see it more clearly. It seems that much that You perceived as more is really…less.

But the nearer You All move toward the door, the more You witness a siphoning effect of sorts. As All near the door, All seem to dissolve into a form of light being drawn inside. As You approach, You feel the last remnants—remnants of whatever You had formerly thought yourself to be—gradually fading away. The dissolving seems to be occurring in slow motion, and you feel ecstatic. It's almost as if You are feeling blissful as your beingness seems to be dissolving into non-beingness.

Finally, You merge with the All, into the light, and it seems . . . it seems over. It seems as if everything is over, is finished, is very near complete. Then some degree of consciousness seems to linger after this additional degree of separation fades. Even without a physical body or an earthly mind or a spiritual body, a subtle body detects a series of chambers leading to other universes. All then fades into light. It is sensed that nothing represented in the vision is the Real. It is understood that only by peeling back all the layers of false identities—including the body, the mind, the spiritual identity, the child ignorance, the witness, even the True Self—could That Which One Really Is be known.

It is understood that what You Really Are Is That, That which is often removed from awareness through many degrees of separation. In the fading moments, as beingness transitions into non-beingness, You come to know that You Are That common building block of All in this universe, in All universes. No wonder some can say, "I don't even know who I am." You finally Realize how far removed most are from the knowledge of the original unicity as a result of conditioning, programming, and dogma.

Then, before fading into the perfect peace of rest in the Totality, Your last consciousness is of the process that had moved That Which You Are from the rest state in the Absolute, past the non-being and into being, and then into whatever that True Self was. You see how you came to witness, how the learned ignorance corrupted the pure consciousness of the child state, how spiritual and religious roles were assigned, how mental identities were accumulated, and how dominated the existence was by the physical body's fears and desires. You KNOW. And then, even that dissolves. THAT is all there is. [End vision]

Next, reflect on the content of the vision that reveals "The Seven Degrees of Separation from Reality"; then, take the "Spirit Journey" regularly until its truth is revealed, until it resonates throughout that "inner resource" that is available to you, until its truth becomes fixated at the very core of your being, until you become liberated from ego and false selves, until you are in conscious contact with Reality, and until you stabilize in an awareness of Your True Self and then revel in the bliss of full and final liberation.

FREEDOM FROM SHIFTING BETWEEN STATES OF HAPPINESS AND UNHAPPINESS

CHAPTER ONE

SATSANG (Satsanga) is defined thusly in Sanskrit: "sat = true and "sanga" = company). In Indian philosophy, the reference is to (1) "the company of the highest truth" or (2) "the company of a guru," or to being (3) "in company with an assembly of persons who listen to, talk about, and assimilate the truth."

Literally, therefore, satsang means "the company of truth" and refers to discourses about "the Knowledge." To tell someone about Knowledge in a gathering is called "giving Satsang."

Now the fact is that Truth can be known but not stated, but the point is made. Originally, in pre-electronic-technology days, seekers had to travel in order to be in the presence of a guru / teacher. Now, satsangs happen via Skype conferencing, via teleconferencing, and via electronic forums that allow for the free flow of statements or questions with a teacher offering replies. The content of this book contains the record of satsang exchanges that took place via one such forum.

In the loft of Sri Nisargadatta Maharaj, twenty seekers might have been present but some days, only a few entered into direct dialogue with Maharaj. Why allow more into the room than can participate?

It is known that pointers must be heard (or read), but they need not be spoken directly to a seeker for their meaning to "take hold." It matters not if the teacher is speaking directly to an "individual" because in Reality it is the consciousness that is speaking to the consciousness.

One speck of consciousness might be addressing another, but all specks that are present can receive the pointers to Truth that are being offered.

It will be seen in this book which will share the results of a series of satsangs that only a few entered into direct exchange with the teacher / author called "floyd," but many more specks of consciousness were "looking over the shoulder of the seekers" and receiving the message visa the exchange; in fact, seekers in over eighty different cities around the globe were participants.

The primary exchange being shared here was with "Louise from South Africa" who would eventually Realize Fully and become the co-host of the website at www.advaitavedantameditations.blogspot.com. She would report years later of that particular series of satsangs that will be shared in this volume:

"I remember that series well. It was such a turning point (clearing point?). All of the relative life, there had been the attempt to stabilize as 'good', 'spiritual', 'wise', 'abundant', 'happy', etc. That series somehow enabled me to see how fixation on one half of a dualistic pair simply kept me trapped on the roller coaster. What a breakthrough! Thank you."

The exchanges in that series of satsang sessions began with her sharing the following:

Louise:

There has been a temporary shift in the experience of consciousness expressing: very natural and easy experience - the mind quiet - with a kind of gentle ignoring of thoughts - through no effort on the part of a "louise" - who on investigation appeared quite empty - just experiencing without resistance - watching "louise" and experiencing what is happening without much involvement - and yet feeling vividly present in life happening at the same time. There is an absence of a memory stream from the past and no movement to plan a future - not so easy to explain in words.

Then suddenly - not even sure of the trigger - "louise" returns and is now able to reflect on the past. It appears that there was a short period of stepping out of the mind-body-personality construct. This has left a view of a different experience of reality.

What pointers do you have at this stage? I am continuing to gently ignore the mind stream and using the "I am". I am also reading "I Am That" and your blog and your book "From the I to the Absolute" as these texts seem to break the solidity of the mind-body-personality. Are these spiritual practices I should abandon? They seem helpful - in fact they are my only connection with pure reality and help me feel sane. I would be very grateful for any additional insights.

Floyd:

As usual, your comments provide an opportunity to offer some pointers that other seekers might find relevant, relatively speaking. The first part of what you shared is an accurate description of what a taste of AS IF living is like.

As for additional insights, You can now sit down to the full course in order to "feel full," chewing the teachings thoroughly, swallowing them in their entirety, digesting them during quiet contemplation, and then witnessing whatever follows, naturally and spontaneously, as it happens.

In your commenting, you actually identify why you've only tasted the sweetness, why you have not become fixed firmly in the beingness, and why you are once again supposedly "experiencing" a "temporary shift." What you (euphemistically) call a "different experience of reality" is actually "louise" shifting from the state of relaxation and beingness and peace to the notion that there is a "louise" and that "she" is "experiencing" no sense of relaxation, no sense of the mere beingness, and no sense of peace.

What is that which you have identified that shifted you away from the peaceful state? It is some illusion of "the past" which you think you are "reflecting" upon. To say erroneously that there is a "louise" who is "experiencing" something other than the peace is really to say that "perceiving is happening from the position of one or more assumed identities rather than via the pure consciousness."

This business of "reflecting on the past" is a happening that Advaitin teachers have long suggested being free of. In western cultures with their annual Christmas "season," persons begin to talk about their "sadness" or "loneliness" or "suffering." To use your word, the suffering is often said to have been "triggered" by a "memory" of times from "the past."

Much has been written in my books about the fact that "memories" invoke discontentment or unhappiness on one hand to extremes of misery and suffering on the other. The stage is set for such misery or suffering since billions on the planet dualistically label certain days as "The Holiday Season," a practice that convinces persons that certain days are "different from" or "better than" other days.

It is suspected that certain of your earlier days are being seen as different from your present days. That dualistic act of suggesting that some days are different from other days, and that some are actually "holidays"—that is, "holy days"—sets the stage for the kind of fluctuations you describe.

What happened to you a few weeks ago is that a prior illusion was brought forth from "the memory bank" in your brain and was upgraded…was perceived dualistically to be something "better" than it likely ever was and something better than "louise's current state." It's all fiction, but "louise's" perception seems quite real to her, does it not?

Similarly, the non-Realized—especially during "the holidays"—will upgrade their "memory-based" illusions: "I was a spouse" becomes upgraded to "the most wonderful spouse on earth has died and now I'm alone during _____ (fill-in-the blank) Deepawali, Thanksgiving, Ramadan, Advent, Bodhi Day, Christmas, Hanukkah, Eid-al-Adha, New Year's, Rosh Hashanah, Al-Hijra," etc.

Also during "holiday seasons," the tendency is to upgrade the illusion that "We were a family" to "we were a really happy family that showed love by sharing all our traditions" (at least before the divorce that revealed how erroneous the early perceptions were). Now, current perceptions are flawed as "the mind" typically "rewrites history" ... meaning, "idealizes," "normalizes," or upgrades illusions.

To those who talk about their "seasonal sadness," the suggestion is this: to call one day or season "holy" (or to label a parcel of land as being "holy land") will result not only in "individual" misery and a surge in suicide rates during the "holiday season" when people recall (in a distorted fashion) certain events or persons. Such differentiation will also get you some widespread misery, bombings, killings, and wars over who is to control all the "holy" things and over who knows the "right beliefs" to have about all things "holy."

In fact, the upgraded "memories," if thoroughly investigated, would reveal how distorted the current view is of the "past events" and the persons involved.

One man thought it was so sweet, the way he and wife and family traveled to a tree farm every year, cut a tree together, rode the hayride back to the entrance, loaded the tree into the truck, took it home to be decorated, and shared all of those "bonding experiences" with his kind and loving spouse.

Only later did she reveal to him that her holiday wish every year had been that he would die. Yet he still "misses the holidays and the family events that meant so much." Even after having been told that his perception of those events was a complete fraud, a total illusion, his "memories" beg to differ...and his illusions supersede clarity to the point that he has contemplated suicide during most of the holiday seasons since the divorce.

Thus the constant shiftings and fluctuations in moods and conditions among the non-Realized: happy as long as the dream is not proved to be a dream, miserable when it is.

For clarity, though, this pointer must be offered as well: would a Realized Advaitin suggest that you should not feel? Of course not. Yet a teacher / guru might suggest that you take the steps that can eliminate emotional intoxication.

Again, there are book-length discussions in various books where the difference in feelings as opposed to emotions are clarified. The short version is this: the former can be witnessed as they rise and fall while the latter, always associated with an ego-state, will generate emotional intoxication.

Feeling during the manifestation is not pre-empted by "Realization." What can happen until "The Experiencer" disappears completely is that feelings can be witnessed without attachment.

Then, the source of any "negative feeling" can be understood, the WHO that is supposedly feeling can be identified, the illusion of the WHO can be seen, and then that process that allows for peace to happen consistently can manifest.

CHAPTER TWO

Another visitor replied:

"I don't mind duality. I like the ups and downs you mentioned. It's all fun to me. It makes for a full life. If a person is mature, he can handle the good times and the bad times."

Floyd:

"Then your up's and down's shall surely continue, as will the co-dependencies that ego-states require in order to think they exist and in order to guarantee the continuation of such fluctuations. One woman was recently overhead to say that she loves to start arguments with her husband because "make up sex is better than regular sex."

Both you and that woman—preferring the unnatural to the natural—shall be guaranteed a relative existence marked by the unnatural, by turmoil, by instability, and by ever-changing moods, shifting between states of happiness and unhappiness.

The pointers here are for those who have had about as much of that type of "fun" as they can stand. The pointers here are for those who are seeking stability and sanity and reason and logic after an overdose of what you call the "fun" of instability and insanity as well as the unreasonable and the illogical.

The pointers are for those who have no ability to relax, or who cannot sustain a relaxed condition, but are seeking the relaxed state. The "no-desire, no-agenda state" here allows pointers to be offered with no attachment to outcome. Consider...or do not consider. Love up's and down's...or not. Argue...or not. Fight...or not. Let memories of loss confound and overwhelm you...or rejoice in memories of things "you" think you "had" that provide "good" memories. Go ahead and experience all of that duality.

Yet the question must be asked: "Why are you here, searching in place that can provide a means by which persons can be free of the instability generated by self-deceiving memories and by belief in dualistic falsehoods?" One Advaita teacher noted that, "A dual-minded man is unstable in all ways," so the instability you think is "fun" cannot be compartmentalized and will mark every aspect of your relative existence.

It might be that some basic background information about duality is called for at this point. It might be relevant to make clear why most are "set up" to accept duality and to experience, therefore, the constant shifts in moods and dispositions which do not characterize the relative existence of the Realized.

For those who would be free of the continual shifts between happiness and unhappiness, is it not clear that it is acceptance of duality and attachment to dualities that must be cast aside if one would stability into a state of happiness?

It should be contemplated why do so few ever find the "relief" they seek from the duality of shifting between the strum und drang vs. stabilization in a peaceful state.

It is partly because most accept the "up's and down's" as "just the way it is and there's nothing that can be done about it." It is also partly because, among the majority of those who do seek, their starting (and ending) point is organized religion which is steeped in duality.

Buddha spoke of impermanence (which eliminates the possibility of an everlasting soul) but according to some Hindus and some Advaitins, the Atma or soul is synonymous with God / Brahman. Followers of the teachings of the three religions of Abraham think that the soul is eternal as well and that it will know one element of duality or the other: either bliss or eternal suffering, either reward or eternal punishment, either everlasting heaven or hell. Members of those five religious groups alone account for nearly six billion "believers" on the globe... actually meaning "believers in duality while claiming "oneness."

Is it not clear how belief in such binary opposites generate all disharmony and suffering on the planet? Is it not clear that once a "mind" forms, it will make use of dualistic pairs to label all and to then generate egotism and "separation"?

Is it not clear that use of the "either-or reasoning fallacy" provides the means by which humans have long justified either the honoring of one member of the pair or the oppression of the other?

Jews vs. Christians
Christians vs. Muslims
Catholics vs. Protestants

Shi'a vs. Sunni

White-skinned vs. Brown-skinned

White-skinned vs. Red-skinned

White-skinned vs. Black-skinned

White-skinned vs. Yellow-skinned

Straight vs. Gay

Free men vs. Slaves

Anglo Saxon vs. non Anglo-Saxon

Men vs. Women

Red state vs. Blue state

Believers vs. Non-believers

Ad infinitum

If one studies history and sees the actual effects of humankind's belief in duality (namely, murder, torture, war, starvation, enslavement, slaughter, oppression, decimation, misery and suffering) the result is that those who are awake, aware, and conscious would not characterize any of the results as having been "fun."

And on an "individual" level, the shifts and instability being addressed in the response to Louise are not considered "fun" either, at least by those who have reached a point where they are seeking the peace and happiness that only come with freedom from duality and the resulting stabilization.

CHAPTER THREE

THE words of Louise describe a style of functioning that any sane and reasonable human would choose while traveling along the "path" to Full Realization, if choice were an option...which it is not: natural and easy, quiet, ignoring thoughts, no effort, quite empty, without resistance, watching without involvement, vividly present, absence of a memory stream from the past, and no movement to try to plan or control.

The problem is that programming and conditioning remove choice as an option because it drives persons to operate blindly on "auto pilot." If you could merely choose between that mode and the mode that followed, of course you would choose the mode described above.

But note this, Louise: because you were able to live in that AS IF style for a time shows that (a) it can happen and that (b) it can also happen with other seekers and that (C) it can happen with you again.

Then, your query is seen to be a sane and reasonable one, and a fairly simple one, actually. The basic question for all who have seemingly "gotten it," only to seemingly "lose it," is this: "How can these 'shifts' stop and how can I fixate in a natural and peaceful fashion of AS IF living for the remainder of the manifestation?"

Look to certain of your own words for the key to the answer:
"natural and easy experience"
The use of experience reveals vestiges of identification with the body-mind-personality triad. The consciousness is what is at this point. It can ONLY witness (or "watch" as you said). It cannot experience. I experience nothing. I do witness all.

"the mind quiet"
There is the second clue to explain the shifts from a state of happiness to a state of unhappiness. Understand that the "mind" has nothing to do with the consciousness. As has been noted in some of my books, "Consciousness is rooted

in the Absolute. The brain is rooted in the elements. The 'mind' is rooted in wrong programming and faulty conditioning and lies and concepts and ideas and superstitions and falsehoods."

Consider the point offered in the title of one of those books for its message might provide a relevant pointer for this part of your "journey": THERE IS NO SUCH THING AS "PEACE OF MIND" (There is Only Peace if You're Out of Your Mind.)

"with a kind of gentle ignoring of thoughts"

If you truly come to an understanding of what the "mind" is, and if you truly see the detriment to peace that it is, you would abandon it like an abusive mate, yet conditioning and programming and the influence of "the mind" can prevent persons from abandoning that which is abusive. Your "thoughts" are a major abuser that you must abandon if the "shifts" between states of happiness and unhappiness are to end.

"just experiencing without resistance - watching 'louise' and experiencing what is happening without much involvement"

Again, that word "experiencing." Do you now see what "the mind" is telling you? It is telling you that there is "someone" who is experiencing things. You are the consciousness which can witness. Peace happened when You "watched." Peace ended when you began to "do" again, thinking dualistically that there is some "do-er" or "experiencer" of "negative" experiences who is wanting "positive" experiences. See the duality there?

There is no "you" to experience what "the mind" is telling you that you are experiencing. You Are, but You Are not experiencing. Understand that and the misery-generating wanting and desiring will end, along with the misery-generating fear that you won't ever have what you want. I want nothing, can own nothing, can gain nothing, and can lose nothing.

A person can sign a contract and think he / she "has" a house. A judge with the stroke of a gavel can make very clear what an illusion it is to think that you own that home! But how could a quantity of energy, which is what the consciousness is, "have" or "own" or "lose" or "gain" anything? It cannot, and understanding that pointer can bring about an end to the happiness / unhappiness "shifts."

"absence of a memory stream from the past"

Again, you've imbedded the answer to your own question. The shift you describe is rooted in "memory," in the notion that (1) in the past you had something you desired but do not have it now and so you feel as if something is missing or (2) in the past you had a shot at attaining something but failed or (3) something in your past was so much better than what is now in your "present" (or what is not now in your present).

All memories are distortions, triggering unreasonable desires or misconceived fears. Illusions from the past are upgraded by the impure consciousness, so persons now deemed to be "missing from your life" are idealized by "the mind" into something far greater than was the case; or, memories of past offenses are exaggerated and assigned far greater significance than is the case. All memories are much ado about the nothing that they are.

Earlier, a pointer from a Realized teacher was mentioned: "A dual-minded person is unstable in all ways." If it is stability that you want, then dual-mindedness must go. That means your belief is duality must go and your belief in the validity of "your mind" must go.

If you would stabilize, then You must abide as the Absolute. Meaning? Meaning that the blockages that prevent the consciousness from seeing Reality and Truth must be completely removed so that the consciousness can once again function in its pre-manifested, no concept, non-dual "condition." That will remove those "problematic" delusions such as thoughts, experiences, and memories and will fix You firmly in touch with the stable, non-shifting Reality.

CHAPTER FOUR

ANOTHER visitor asked, "Why blame religion for duality?"
[The reply] That inquiry about duality and religion will be addressed along with the response to Louise's query since duality is also at the heart of the shift she described: happy vs. unhappy; OK vs. not OK; orderly vs. chaotic, etc.

(Note the way that all dualities foster a sense of separation and arrogance. The first of any binary pair is given preferred status by the non-Realized: "us vs. them"; "Christian vs. Jew"; "American vs. others." Even if ego-generating nonsense such as public declarations like "We are the greatest nation on earth" were not verbalized, believing that the message implied by any dualistic pair is true will automatically foster a "better-than" and "different-from" mindset.)

But to explicate the role that religions play (and have always played) in dreaming up dualities and then supporting them is not "blaming religion" as you have charged. It is explaining. Duality has become big business across the globe nowadays, so trace its history from "then" to "now" to see the role that religion has played:

The earliest persons living in darkness and in ignorance (joined by the earliest self-appointed priest, medicine man, or shaman) were the manufacturers of dualistic, supernatural explanations for naturally-occurring happenings.

From the past to the present, non-Realized persons believe duality-based statements if delivered by a supposedly "holy person," statements such as "An angry God - vs. a happy God - destroyed those people and their homes" or "Their bad karma - vs. the presence of good karma - caused Hurricane Katrina to devastate New Orleans, Louisiana," etc.)

Organized religion evolved and became the guardian of duality (teaching binary concepts such as good-bad, right-wrong, heaven-hell, punishment-reward, us-them, ad infinitum).

Today, the continuum of duality - and thus ignorance - flows thusly:

Churches and temples and mosques and synagogues are now the distribution centers of duality.

Those who are sleepwalking about the planet, believing with "faith" whatever they hear without any sane or sound inquiry, are the buyers of duality.

And now, governments and businesses and religions and many philosophies are the users of duality, using dualistic proclamations in order to control and manipulate the programmed masses to do whatever non-Realized persons want.

Next, note that here, the third step of the seven steps from identification with the false "I" to abidance as the Absolute is the religious or spiritual step. There is no recommendation here that religious or spiritual "works" or involvement be avoided. The step must happen, but it must also be transitioned if Full Realization is to happen.

From another visitor: "But doesn't 'abidance as the Absolute' prevent feeling?"

Floyd: That question has been addressed thoroughly in the writings over the years as the difference in emotions and feelings has been defined and clarified. The short version is as follows in regards to the "witnessing of feelings" vs. the "experiencing of emotions" as mentioned earlier to Louise:

It is only the latter (emotions)—generated by the assumption of ego-states as identities—that will lead to emotional intoxication and "actions" and "reactions" and misperceptions of shifting between the perceived duality of "happy vs. sad." Feelings, by contrast, can happen; however, the Realized merely witness them as they rise and as they fall. The do not shift the Realized from an uninterrupted state of happiness into either a momentary or extended lapse into unhappiness.

That said, never has any Realized teacher suggested that feelings must be repressed if AS IF living is to happen. If tears flow, they flow. If laughter happens, it happens. If seemingly incredible pleasure happens, it happens. Understanding I AM THAT does bring the I AM-ness to an immediate end. The understanding can, however, bring stability.

What does not continue post-Realization, and which is relevant to what Louise shared, is the emotional intoxication that is generated by deception-based memories.

It is Realization that results in freedom from instability when the dualistic roots of emotional reactions are seen, when the belief in illusions can be discarded, and when events inspired by delusions and emotional intoxication are transitioned with the abandonment of false identities that think they have been interfered with or hurt or threatened or harmed.

Since ego-states are not real, they will always generate a sense of insecurity in the "mind" that is assuming one or more roles. Persons are driven to think thoughts, say words, and take actions that preserve their images, but those images and false identities have no more substance or life-expectancy than any mirage that has ever appeared temporarily in a desert. Misery will accompany the belief in such illusions, and any sense of peace will be destroyed if an ego-state is assumed or if a former ego-state is recalled from "memory."

Thus, the peace that happened for a period with Louise will always be interrupted when the "mind" remembers some "past" ego-state that no longer exists or some "current" ego-state that is not receiving what it thinks it needs or desires at the moment. The "husband" that has "lost his wife" might be miserable during this "season," but if that event had been preceded by the understanding that "I am not 'husband,' but husbanding can happen...or not," then the current misery would not have manifested (and would not continue to manifest).

Full Realization can result in an end to misery-producing co-dependencies and can provide a means by which persons can be free of the instability generated by self-deceiving memories and by belief in dualistic falsehoods.

CHAPTER FIVE

FLOYD: So, Louise, the circumstance you describe is typical among the persons of the planet who "experience" moments of happiness or who enter into a peaceful position of neutrality, only to find that they are once again unhappy or taking "positions" that create disturbances.

"Positions" can only be taken by ego-states, by false identities, and will never allow peace to happen consistently. Why? Because before "positions" can be stated in words, they first manifest in the form of "thoughts," and thoughts are generated by the fictional (and always distorted) "mind" wherein is stored the false belief in all of those assumed identities which take "positions."

The prerequisite for peace is stability. The prerequisite for stability - for fixating in a state of happiness rather than constantly shifting between states of happiness and unhappiness - is fixation in the no-concept, non-duality Reality. In addition to those relative dynamics already discussed that interrupt peace and stability, there are other factors that should also be considered.

When a former ego-state was (a) assumed as an identity and (b) when the memory of that ego-state is recalled and (c) when it believes that it was interfered with or hurt or threatened or brought to an end by the actions of a former co-dependent that was helping to support the illusion of that identity, then peace and stability face another obstacle, namely, archetypal messaging.

Prior to Realization, "floyd" "experienced" that double challenge to peace and stability. "Husband's" emoting generated the thought, "She abandoned me." In the process, "Floyd the Homeowner" "died"; "Floyd the Family Man" "died"; "Floyd the Father" "died"; "Floyd the Lover" "died"; and if space permitted another dozen or more false identities could be catalogued.

The illusion, therefore, was not just that "I" was being killed but that "I" was being killed a dozen times over. What a hopeless and miserable mindset. To compound the perceived pain and "loss" and suffering, an archetypal message triggered another physical and mental and emotional response.

Archetypes are instinctive (genetically-transferred) roles that exist even prior to the assignment or acceptance of all of the other roles that persons take as a definition of "who they are." As a result of millions of years of such coding, some of the instinctive roles are the same as culturally-assigned roles, such as "partner," "father," "mother," etc.

Archetypes manifest as images which carry dualistic connotations, all rooted in the multi-million-year-totality of human experience. They are all based in what has—and has not—assisted in the survival of the species. Thus...

"up" is a "positive" archetype whereas "down" is a "negative" archetype; "dark" is a "negative" archetype while "light" is a "positive" archetype; and "together" is a "positive" archetype while "alone" is a concept stored at a genetic level that carries a "negative" connotation.

When a person said to "floyd," "I am leaving you," not only did those words trigger fear and / or anger among the dozens of assumed but false identities that imagined that they were being threatened. Those words also engaged a physical, mental, and emotional component that lies at the inherited core of every human.

Those components were as ancient as humankind, and they rose from a subconscious (subliminal) level into the (warped) conscious level and sent the message, "You are in immediate danger...your existence is being threatened ... so a "fight" response or a "flight" response (or even a "freeze" response) is called for."

And when identities believe that they are being threatened, the flight nor freeze responses are seldom the typical responses.

[See the content of the book CASTING LIGHT ON THE DARK SIDE OF RELATIONSHIPS for further discussion of this phenomenon and you'll understand why 59% of all murders of females in the U.S., and 41% of the murders of all males, happen during a "breakup." When the programming and archetypal perceptions combine to generate such levels of distortion that one believes she / he is being killed a dozen times over, you can understand why 50% of the time "flight" is not considered as an option and "fight to the death" becomes a typical reaction.]

Is it becoming clearer exactly what the non-Realized are "up against" in an effort to stabilize in a state of peace and harmony? Is it becoming obvious why the non-Realized are constantly shifting between states of happiness and unhappiness?

Is it becoming all the more obvious why those teachers (those specks of re-purified consciousness) that share the pointers which can end human suffering, propose that Realization is at the heart of being free of the distortions and illusions that perpetuate such high levels of unhappiness (or even misery) planet-wide?

Do you see now why Realized teachers suggest that, when peace and stability disappear, that you should ask, "WHO" (what persona or personas) thinks she / he is being hurt or was hurt? "WHO" thinks he / she was wronged? "WHO" is 'experiencing' the pain and suffering and misery that is being triggered by a memory rooted in distortion?"

When the "WHO" is seen to be an image (either of the archetypal type or the culturally-assigned type) then peace and stability can return as the focusing on "I am an abandoned husband" or "I am a wronged wife" fades from the (warped) consciousness and the "I AM ... only" becomes the focus once again.

CHAPTER SIX

ANOTHER contributor to unhappiness (and to instability, which assures that periods of happiness will be interrupted by periods of unhappiness) is a belief in the concept of "time." That concept plays a major role in generating illusions that result in unhappiness and instability because

(1) "linear time" is about division, separation, and the dualistic concepts of "this" being more special than "that" and "this day being better than that one" and "holy days being more important than other 'regular' days" and because (2) just as current distortions will be "future memories," so past distortions are your "current memories."

First, time. Consider how time is used to reinforce the dualistic concepts of "different from" and "better than" and "more special than" and "less special than."

For those arising to go to work, 5 AM or 6 AM or 7 AM might be considered a "bad" time when an alarm is heard. Later, "noon" might be "good" if a lunch break is available. 5 PM is "better" if works ends then. "Time" sets persons up to "experience" "up's" and "down's"—as well as periods of contentment and discontentment—throughout any "24-hour period."

Then, those days become weeks in the minds of persons tied to "time" concepts. According to some, therefore, "Mondays" are "bad" but "Wednesdays" are an improvement since they represent "Hump Day" and since the week is considered to be a downhill coast from there.

Fridays and Saturdays are "good," and "Sundays" are "holy" and "more special" than the other six days of the week. If programmed and conditioned with the typical Anglo-Saxon mentality, one day is for rest and relaxing and taking it easy, while six days are for working and not relaxing and not taking it easy.

He who is stabilized and who takes it easy - without interruption - is unacceptable or strange in cultures where instability and chaos are "minimized" and "normalized" with such conditioning statements as:

"Hey, life is all about ups and downs. Get used to it." Many modern cultures thus endorse instability and justify their chaos and disorder on an individual basis, on a national basis throughout the year, and on an international basis as well.

That will always result in "personal" instability; that will result in a nation that is often in disarray; and that will result in some international crises and wars, guaranteed. And it will all be considered "normal" and "acceptable" among a conditioned population.

The concept of "various months" also generates a sense of differentiation and thus mood instability: "Winters are too cold and dark and dreary, but summers are too hot."

Rather than enjoying uninterrupted stability (no matter what name someone gives to the time of the week or the time of the month or the time of the year) linear time distinctions guarantee a sense of separation and instability and shifting moods.

The result is a planet populated with self-absorbed persons who are trapped in "The Goldilocks Syndrome," so these types of "thoughts" and "words" become commonplace:

"This time of year is too hot but that time of year is too cold"; "this partner is too hot but that one was too cold"; and "you cooked this egg too hard but the one yesterday was too soft."

Trapped in such differentiation, only "perfection" is acceptable, but the concept of "perfect" - when applied to anything in the relative - is as bogus as all concepts; therefore, no consistent sense of satisfaction or acceptance or neutrality or joy will happen among the non-Realized who are trapped in concepts and time distinctions and beliefs about what constitutes "perfection" and what constitutes "not perfection."

Because "different" days and "different" months are assigned different levels of "goodness" or "badness," moods can become unstable as a result of nothing more than labeling. Next, the labeling of some days or weeks as "holidays" ("holy days") takes the instability to new heights as not only are "hours" and "days" given good or bad labels, but such dualistic labels are also applied to "months" and "seasons" and "years."

Even as they proclaim "I love this time of year," few are aware of how emotionally-intoxicated and completely unstable they become every year during the "holidays," be those celebrations called Deepawali, Thanksgiving, Ramadan,

Advent, Bodhi Day, Christmas, Hanukkah, Eid-al-Adhà, New Year's, Rosh Hashanah, Al-Hijra, or some other "special" event.

And how many of those few who might become aware of that annual pattern would be willing to abandon their seasonal going and doing and zooming in order to allow sanity and stability to manifest?

How much truth can be involved when some think something is "good" but others think it is "bad"? Consider "Thanksgiving" in the U.S.: most citizens believe that the concept on which the holiday is based is certainly "good": a "new nation" was founded that is based in Christian doctrine. ("A theocracy here is 'good' but a theocracy there would be 'bad'.")

If the 150,000,000 who were slaughtered in the conquest of "the Americas" had a voice, they might beg to differ about the noble connotation assigned by the masses to the U.S. "Thanksgiving holiday."

Non-Christians and people living on other parts of the globe might have no opinion about the holiday or might consider it nonsense. "Good" … "bad" … "indifferent"? Where is the stability?

Only the Realized, aware that it is all conceptual (and therefore all much ado about nothing) are free of being "swayed" by any emotionalism around events dreamed up by men and women. They are also free of any emotionally-intoxicating "memories" of events such as "past holidays" that were better because of "this" or "that" which is now "missing."

Similarly, two billion persons would claim that it is "good" to celebrate a virgin birth during "the Christmas holidays." Four billion non-Christians who claim affiliation with other religions, however, would consider the holiday to be a celebration of infidels or "wrong believers."

Some dismiss the celebration as one based in pagan-based fiction, Christianity having been the twenty-third religion (not the first) that was based on the belief that a savior was supposedly born of a virgin.

Is it clear that the concept of linear time sets the stage for "up's" and "down's," for instability, and for fluctuations between happiness and unhappiness to happen throughout the year, throughout the months, throughout any given week, throughout any given day, and even throughout any given hour?

Add in the physical, mental and intellectual fluctuations that occur throughout any given 30-day time-frame and the result is a very unstable population planet-wide. Are you beginning to see how multi-faceted the factors are that contribute to instability and to the subsequent shifting from various states of comfort and discomfort, from happiness to unhappiness?

Are you seeing that anything that is "multi-" in nature is a fraud and that peace and stability can only happen if fixated in the singularity of the non-dual, no-concept reality of the unicity? It is in abidance as the real and true unicity, which can be understood after abandoning belief in all fictionalized multiplicities, that peace and stability happen consistently throughout the manifestation.

Among the Realized, there is no time. There is no differentiation by second, minute, hour, day, month, season, year, decade, century, or millennium. There is only continuity and steadiness. What significance could I possibly give to a man-made concept such as "a season" when I have always been and always shall be? Understand that, and be at peace

CHAPTER SEVEN

IN the previous discussion, it was seen that the concept of "linear time" is based in duality, that it can generate a sense of division and separation, and that it can control the moods of persons (a.k.a., their "frame of mind") throughout what they see as "different hours and days and weeks and months and seasons." This pointer was offered as well:

Just as current distortions will be "future memories," so past distortions are your "current memories."

If persons know that they are not Fully Realized at this point, then they know that their present "thoughts" are distorted because those thoughts are being generated by a "mind" which is (1) an accumulation of concepts and ideas that are all based in untruths and which is (2) precisely what is blocking the pure consciousness from perceiving in a non-distorted fashion.

Thus, any (distorted) perception that is being formed right now will be filed away in the memory section of the brain for storage in either the short-term memory area or the long-term memory areas. At some point in the "future," that memory can be triggered (to use Louise's term) and thus retrieved, at which point it will be taken to be "an accurate view" rather than "a distorted perception that is being recalled from memory."

As for the accuracy of retrieved memories, it should be clear that the memory-functions of the brain are unreliable at best. Names of people met only the day before can be forgotten. An Advaitin pointer that was read and understood one day is not remembered the next.

Names of places or things can be erroneous: "Was that place where we ate called "Tom's Restaurant?" "No, it was called 'Tony's Restaurant'." "Was that in Minneapolis?" "No, it was in St. Paul."

Yet even though the faulty nature of memory is revealed on a regular basis, persons ignore that evidence and continue to believe that "past" events really were as they are being perceived in the present.

One woman was abused for years (mentally, emotionally, and physically) but after the funeral for her husband, her perceptions about their marriage began to be re-framed. Five holiday seasons later, the "bad" memories of her marriage were filtered, her "mind" told her that they had enjoyed a "good" marriage, and now she experiences misery and depression during every "holiday season," missing her abuser and regretting the fact that they are "not together during the holidays anymore."

The Realized understand that all of those classifications of "good" or "bad" are based in faulty perception and warped (or obscured) consciousness. The way that one especially candid seeker in a recent session described the relative phenomenon of "holiday delusions" was thusly:

"To spend an entire day with certain friends or family members that you only see once or twice a year is a clear reminder of why the occurrence of such visits happens with such infrequency."

Of course, all memory-based misery is experienced by some ego-state and not at all by You, the Pure Witnessing Consciousness; therefore, all memories are memories of mirages. Things "then" were not as perceived "then," so they certainly are not being seen "now" in any realistic fashion.

Right now [in 2007] among the non-Realized, misperceptions are being filed away in storage areas of the brain, and in "the future," some of them will be retrieved and taken to be an accurate recall of "the way things were back in 2007."

The person recalling 2007 happenings in future years will really believe that those memories are accurate memories of "the way things were." In fact, all memories being filed away right now among the non-Realized are distortions that will generate distorted memories at some point in "the future," will inspire some distorted belief, and will result in unhappiness or misery or suffering or depression or suicide.

Now some would label the state described by Louise as "a period of freedom from the bondage of ego" and the subsequent condition she described as "the result of the reconstruction of the ego." Of course both views are fallacious since they assume that the ego is real, but it is not. By definition, it is "the false 'I'."

The terminology above that some employ suggests that (1) a mirage could actually hold you in bondage and that (2) a mirage could reconstruct and determine the way that you think or believe or react or emote. Such could never happen in Reality and is only imagined to be real among persons who are not

Fully Realized and whose emotional states are being controlled by their erroneous belief in warped memories.

Freedom from mirage-generated misery manifests when a mirage is seen to be a mirage. The more accurate assessment of the conditions mentioned by Louise would be this: she described "a period during which no ego-state was being assumed as an identity" and then described the condition when "a memory of one or more ego-states which were assumed as identities in the past have once again been taken to be real."

CHAPTER EIGHT

FROM another visitor: "Teachers sometimes speak of 'impressions.' Are there not some impressions that are real or truthful in basis?"

The reply: Yes. There are two. They will be discussed during this series of satsangs, but the "time" and "memories" discussion will be completed first.

One result of discarding your belief in the concepts of "time" and "memories" is that emotional intoxication and instability—which are rooted in "time and memory" distortions and which inspire attachment—will end. Will non-attachment (and the discarding of all prior attachments) prevent "enjoyment" from happening? Of course not.

It is the means by which joy can happen with consistency, or the means by which whatever is happening can be witnessed without emotional intoxication, or the means by which a position of neutrality can be maintained in spite of the surrounding disorder and insanity that mark the relative existence.

Further, Realization will prevent the erroneous perception of "past distortions" as "current truth," eliminating the emotional intoxication that comes when ego-states seem to be impacted by delusions about "past" events.

More to the point, how could You possibly have a "past" when the flawed memories of that "past" were believed to have taken place in "this world" and were believed to have involved "other persons" in "this world"? You are not in the world, and You have never been in the world. To the contrary, the world is in you, specifically, in your "mind."

If what anyone takes to be "this world" is actually nothing more than a composite of millions of mirages that have been erroneously taken to be real, then "this world" can ultimately be nothing more than a mirage as well ... all a product of imaginings generated by the warped consciousness.

And if you are unhappy or angry or discontent as a result of the memory of "someone" and what he / she did, understand that persons are also nothing more than a figment of that same imagination - and of flawed perceiving - which have resulted in the concept of "this world."

Have there not been many instances when you thought you knew certain persons, only to find out that you did not know them at all, relatively speaking? You accepted the image they projected as being real and genuine; you formed your own image of them; and they clung privately to their "self"-image that they took to be real.

Images…images…images. And though they were all phony, they all combined to form "your mind." And in the absence of Full Realization, "your mind" will sustain the false belief in "them" and "the world you and they live in." Know that if you did not know them at all, relatively speaking, then you also did not know Them at all, absolutely speaking.

And if "you" are experiencing unhappiness, it is because the memory-sections of the brain stored those false beliefs and false images, and now current events are triggering false memories and flawed perceptions. You have formed co-dependencies with false memories and are allowing false beliefs and concepts to control your emotions.

If you are mourning some perceived "loss," the case is (speaking absolutely) that You cannot actually be missing "that" or "them"; you might, however, be missing what you thought "it" or "they" were. If so, mirages are determining your moods. Depression might be situational or organic. Consider the insanity of being immobilized by depression that is not rooted in organic factors but that is rooted in a "memory" about a mirage instead.

Consider this as well: can a speck of energy "miss" a speck of energy? Consciousness cannot "have" anything and cannot "lose" anything. The Consciousness can merely perceive accurately…or inaccurately. Misery and suffering are rooted in the warped perceiving that happens if the consciousness has been blocked in the way that "the required journey" is really all about. Only if that "journey" is completed can "clear seeing" happen.

So "mood swings" and "shifts from happiness to unhappiness" are all rooted in faulty perceptions, all based in concepts which are always dualistic (and there-fore always open to debate regarding whether something is "good" or "bad"), and are all supported by distortions called "memories" that are merely remembrances of mirages.

CHAPTER NINE

A visitor asked, "What do you mean by situational or organic depression? I am wondering if that might apply to me?"

The response to Louise will continue, but the question might be pertinent at this point in order to provide clarity and to ensure thoroughness in regards to the discussion of depression and instability and swings between happiness and unhappiness that happen among persons:

First, consider this disclaimer: no Realized Advaitin would suggest that she / he has a monopoly on treating depression or mood swings or personality disorders. Much of the suffering on the planet is rooted in body-mind-personality identification, but other contributing factors certainly exist, factors which cannot be addressed completely by Advaitin pointers.

Some depression might be situational and can be natural. For example, during the years spent in the forest, various animals were seen to be "grieving" as they inspected the fallen remains of a companion. Here's an example:

One spring, a buck and doe were observed while grazing in one of their regular feeding spots. Later in the fall, they were seen on several occasions while mating; then, at the beginning of the following summer, it was seen that a fawn had joined in their grazing sessions.

In late August or early September, gunshots rang out near a creek. After following one of the trails that led toward the water, the following was witnessed: the fawn had been shot and had run some distance from the creek before falling. The doe and the buck both seemed to be smelling it and nudging it, trying to encourage it to rise and run, but they eventually realized it was not going to happen. They stood still and witnessed.

Both spent some time there involved in what was clearly an instance of "situational depression." Their demeanor left no doubt that feelings were arising. Suddenly, two boys—hunting out of season—began making a great deal of noise as they approached.

It was seen that the feeling of grief being experienced by the deer was being replaced by a feeling of fear. They were torn, moving away from the fallen animal for a moment, then returning for a few moments in a final effort to check on the fawn.

Finally, the two boys appeared, but a shout went out at them regarding out-of-season hunting. They ran back toward the creek and the buck and doe bounded deeper into the forest.

Weeks later, both deer would be seen to have returned to their regular, daily routine ... grazing in one particular clearing during the morning hours or in another favorite feeding area in the afternoon. Their behavior with the fawn was an example of situational depression, and people can experience the same and behave the same ... functioning, feeling, moving on.

The Realized witness those feelings and do not deny them. They watch them rise and fall. The non-Realized are driven by emotions into a state of emotional intoxication, and what began as situational depression might become a chronic condition, which is unnatural.

For the sake of thoroughness, know also that on-going unhappiness or depression might be a result of a chemical imbalance in the body. Three very different body types exist among humans, and each requires a different food plan in order to optimize the functioning of organs.

One-third of the people on the planet will thrive on a vegetarian food plan; one-third can thrive on a balanced food plan; but one-third will function poorly on a balanced plan or an all-vegetable food plan. They are actually committing "suicide-by-diet" if they follow a vegetable-only food plan.

[For those who are eating only vegetables as part of their "spiritual journey," only one-third of you are providing what your organs require for maximized functioning. Two-thirds will pay a physical, mental, and emotional price, relatively speaking, by following a food plan that is not appropriate for your body type. Also, there is no need to write to this author to defend your practice since those letters will be disposed of. Instead of writing in protest, spend the time investigating the above and determining which food plan is best suited for your body type. In this discussion of mood swings and depression, understand that some instances are organic in basis.]

Next, some who make contact during "the holiday season" in order to describe their misery may be suffering Seasonal Affective Disorder, triggered by being exposed to too little light during the winter months. It is estimated, however, that only 4-6% of the people on the planet fall into that group.

On the other hand, it is known that nearly 99% on the planet are suffering from one or more personality disorders. With the odds being nearly twenty times greater that mood swings and unhappiness and suffering are the result of personality (rather than being situational or chemical or organic), the discussions here always begin with an invitation to sufferers to find "WHO" they think is suffering and to abandon belief in the personas that are triggering misery.

If that process brings no relief, then the other factors discussed above can all be addressed with health care professionals. So, to any who might experience depression during a particular "season":

If your efforts to stabilize via the Realization process should fail, you might seek out advice from trained professionals and explore the situational-chemical-organic possibilities. And as has been noted in the past, if anyone is feeling suicidal during any particular season, he / she might consider reporting immediately to an emergency room at the nearest hospital and sharing those thoughts at the intake desk.

That said, the satsang will continue by focusing on the depression and instability that is generated from personality, that is, from assuming false identities and allowing them to determine thoughts, words, and deeds.

CHAPTER TEN

I F organic and chemical and situational factors are not at the root of instability and mood swings, then personality can be considered as a source. All personality is rooted in duality, and one binary set that is rooted in duality and that will generate a sense of instability and mood swing is the "less vs. more" pair.

Persons / personas never have "enough," much less "plenty" or "too much." With that subconscious belief, how could anyone ever feel fulfilled, and in the absence of that, how could one ever assume a position of neutrality in place of an assumed identity?

The result is that persons live unnaturally or supernaturally in their quest to accumulate "more"; in their disparagement over not having "enough" or "something needed" or "that which once was but has been lost"; and in their endless longing for "continuity of personas" and for "continuity of body and mind."

The teacher of "Nisarga Yoga," which offers up natural living as an alternative to the above fiction-based existence, understands that there are times when it is natural for the deer to feel fear and / or anger and / or grief of sorts.

If someone were beating you and abusing you and you claimed that you had no fear or anger around that, your claims would not be evidence of "realization" as much as evidence of denial, as evidence of one or more personality disorders, and / or as evidence of insanity.

As far as the Advaita teachings are concerned, eliminating the relative consequences of the bastardized consciousness (and eliminating the subsequent human suffering during the manifestation) provide the sole rationale for attaining the understanding. That is one of the most basic elements of the Teachings.

Louise: Among seekers who have moved farther along the "path," (that is, beyond the assumption of religious and spiritual personas, which are adopted at the third of seven steps to Realization) it can be understood that spiritual practices are not helpful? Why?

Farther along the "journey," it becomes understood that there is no "one" to be helped and because "practices" merely reinforce a belief in newly-assumed ego-states, including "The Good Person," "The Religious One," or "The Spiritual Giant."

However, such practices can be used for a time if they involve (a) reading or hearing and then (b) considering in the silence the pointers which can lead to Realization. (If one cannot visit a teacher, as is often recommended, then one can read the words spoken or written when it is the re-purified consciousness that speaks.)

As for "religious or spiritual practices in general," they are not a connection with pure Reality since YOU Are That Pure Reality. To speak of "connection" is duality ("this" being connected to "that"). Also, such practices, if clung to, can become a source of insanity or discontentment since they can lead persons to believe that they are being "connected to" or "with" something rather than knowing the unicity that You Are...the unicity that All Is. Experience that, and then even "The Experiencer" can disappear.

In regards to spiritual exercises and work and practices, Maharaj offered the following pointer to those who had moved as far along the "path" as the third step: "Whatever you have tried to understand during your spiritual search will prove false."

In the end, it is seen that all concepts are false. It is seen that all personas (including the "bad" ones that might have been discarded as well as the "good" ones assumed in their place during the religious or spiritual phase) are based in lies and self-deception.

CHAPTER ELEVEN

TO help understand that sense of having "gotten it" for a period before there was a "shift" whereby "louise" returned, Maharaj explained why persons seem to grasp the understanding and then seemingly "lose" it: "You are so used to the support of concepts that when your concepts leave you, although it is your true state, you get frightened and try to cling to them again."

Regarding whether you should focus or refocus on your former traditional spiritual exercises, he said, "Whatever spiritual things you aspire to know are all happening in this objective world, in the illusion. All this is happening in the objective world. All is dishonesty. There is no truth in this fraud." It is suspected that you have done plenty of such exercises for many years, but where did those "disciplines" get you, in the end? Now, to some of Louise's other words:

Louise: "This has left a view of a different experience of reality."

Floyd: The next phase is to see that there is no experiencer. Be rid of "louise" once and for all and revel in the freedom of the non-attachment that happens when the subject-object witness merely observes all of the supposed happenings of "this world" and when the Pure Witness observes the Oneness.

At the point of Full Realization, it is understood that there is no "one" to be happy or sad and that there is only the consciousness that witnesses. The question then is, is the consciousness witnessing all exactly as it is, or has the pure consciousness been blocked from witnessing purely?

If the latter is the case, then all perceptions are in error and unhappiness is happening because (A) "they" fooled you first and now you are fooling yourself and because (B) they robbed you and now you are robbing yourself. Find whatever it is that you are fooling yourself about. Find the opportunity and the possibility that they took away from you by their programming, conditioning, acculturation, and domestication.

The result of the blocked consciousness is that persons (the non-Realized) are aware of nothing as it actually is. If the consciousness has been re-purified, it sees clearly (which then results in a sense of oneness and peace).

If the pure consciousness is "warped" or "blocked," then it will sense the misery of separation and aloneness. If it believes that false identities from the past were real, then persons will mourn "what was but no longer is."

Louise also asked: "What pointers do you have at this stage? I am continuing to gently ignore the mind stream and using the 'I am'. I am also reading "I AM THAT" and your blog and "FROM THE I TO THE ABSOLUTE" as these texts seem to break the solidity of the mind-body-personality. Are these spiritual practices I should abandon? They seem helpful - in fact they are my only connection with pure reality and help me feel sane."

Floyd: Of course if a seeker cannot visit a teacher, then the reading of the words as consciousness speaks—and then taking those into silent contemplation—is the alternative. Understand, however, that the process of considering pointers requires none of the common "religious" or "spiritual" practices that billions engage in regularly.

Regarding the words of "my teacher Maharaj," read I Am That if you like, but understand that those transcripts were from the early words spoken by that speck of consciousness called Maharaj. The later collections of pointers from that speck—especially the words uttered during the final months of that manifestation—are far more to the point and reveal a far higher degree of speaking coming from the totally unblocked consciousness.

(In the "I Am That" days, Maharaj was still hosting bhajans and sharing the types of spiritual talks that were being offered by his contemporaries rather than the type of sharings that came via the consciousness later on. Later, he would urge seekers to abandon their structured and rigid "spiritual living" and to abide in a spontaneous, natural - that is, nisarga - fashion only.)

In the end, he rejected all such game-playing and spoke far more purely and far more directly and far more unequivocally (even "abruptly" or "brusquely," some would claim). Yet those final talks are the ones that offer the greatest clarity and serve up the teachings in the most straightforward version of the Direct Path manner as the consciousness began to speak more from "an Advaita point" than from "a Vedanta point."

Further, note that the aim of his talks are the aim of the sharings here as well: to provide a means by which "human suffering" can end and a means by which a peaceful, happy, AS IF existence can happen for the remainder of the manifestation of any given speck of consciousness, ending those seeming "shifts" between the duality of "happiness" and "unhappiness."

CHAPTER TWELVE

FLOYD: It is natural to be stable, and it is unnatural to be unstable. It is also unnatural to try to live supernaturally. To contrast the ease of natural living with the toil of unnatural living and the effort required to try to live supernaturally, consider the following.

The case with both the space that is called "a deer" and with the space that is called "floyd" is this: since both are living in the natural fashion, not once during any given day does either ring a bell; not once does either burn scented sticks; not once does either hold a special rock or mineral; not once does either sprinkle water; not once does either wear special clothing; not once does either sport a special hair style.

Neither of those specks of consciousness shave off all hair as an act of spirituality; nor do they enter a special building, read a holy book, genuflect, attend meetings, sing praises, meditate, hum, chant, light candles, cheer, pledge, sit on a special rug, buy special accoutrements, adhere to a "holy" diet, wear a funny hat or robe, worship, or display crystals in a special arrangement.

Those specks of consciousness do not repeat a mantra, model any particular stance, accumulate, sit under a pyramid, face a particular direction on the compass, or participate in any nonsensical acts that are contrary to the ways of natural living.

Only one of those two (specifically, "floyd") tried some of the above practices and disciplines in a search for Self and peace and stability. As a result, movement along the path to Full Realization fixated at the third of seven steps and did not continue until all religious and spiritual roles were transcended.

Natural living happens spontaneously and automatically, as was the case for the millions of years prior to the last few millennia when controlling men dreamed up concepts and dogma and rituals and dualistic thinking.

For those fixated in religious or spiritual ego-states and who engage in any or all of the "religious" or "spiritual" practices delineated above, so it is. The

FLOYD HENDERSON

third step IS a step that must be taken, yet it must also be transitioned if Full Realization is to happen.

For those who eventually see that all of the activities and doings above have nothing to do with sane, normal, AS IF living, then the invitation to them is to relax and take it easy. When was that option lost? When shall you determine to reclaim it?

When Full Realization happens, energy is not focused on; the I AM is not focused on; the I AM THAT is not focused on; and no other concepts are focused on. "Focusing" and "practicing disciplines" ends; then, natural and spontaneous living merely happens.

Anything of "this world" that can be focused on is not real anyway. What passes before the consciousness can be witnessed, but nothing among the Realized is sought out to focus on or to occupy the "mind." The "mind" has ended. "But what of the True Self or the Pure Witness?" some ask at this point.

Pure witnessing just happens, and it happens from a position of neutrality because the belief in subjects and objects (which can oppose each other) no longer exists. Subject-object witnessing gives way to the Pure Witnessing of the unicity.

It should be realized that these states of waking, sensing presence, and sleeping are temporary states that came upon You but are not You. Understand that all suffering and misery among the non-Realized is founded in the programming and conditioning that block the consciousness and that inspires the belief the Is-ness involves "being this" or "being that" rather than merely being.

CHAPTER THIRTEEN

NOTICE the following:

Certain shifts throughout the month are natural to the degree that they deal with (a) the physical, (b) the intellectual and (c) the emotional aspects of the relative space.

Yet You are not the physical body. As pain happened when cancerous cells were growing in "floyd the plant food body," it was possible to witness those waves of pain as they rose and fell. During that event, I was not the body but the witnessing consciousness. Was treatment for the body's cancer refused as a result of not identifying with the body? No, but the doctors practicing traditional, mainstream medicine were fired and an alternative approach happened, which resulted in the elimination of the cancerous cells once and for all.

Too, the intellect, if functioning under the auspices "the mind," will hinder the happening of Full Realization.

Furthermore, all emotional intoxication is only believed to be a real experience by the blocked consciousness that allows the "mind" to take misidentify Self as one or more false identities (or roles, characters, images, ego-states) which have been hurt or interfered with or terminated as a result of the actions of a former co-dependent that was helping to sustain a false image / false identity.

Organic and chemical aspects (along with not following the food plan that is proper for your particular body type) can trigger mood swings and depression and anxiety and many personality disorders, yet You are not your personality.

Another factor that can result in instability is the belief in linear time. That can result in focusing on "past" roles that can no longer be played as a result of the absence of the other co-dependent player who had once made the playing of that role possible. It will cause a perceived but fictitious sense of differentiation in the times of days, months, seasons and years. Dualistically, some seasons will be considered "the most wonderful time of the year" and others will be considered "bad seasons or days or months or years."

Instability and mood swings can result when it is not understood that whatever gives you pleasure in the relative existence will eventually give you pain and that whatever gives you the greatest pleasure will eventually give you the greatest pain (be that booze, a role being played, a partner in the co-dependency games that persons play, drugs, nicotine … whatever). Nothing in the relative will be permanent, and the illusion that something in the relative can be permanent will cause suffering and misery when it ends.

You will be miserable and will suffer instability or alternating periods of happiness and unhappiness if you do not see the typical pattern of dualistic "relationships" (wherein "this" is believed to be relating to "that"). In fact, the pattern of role-playing in "relationships" is always shifting and in flux, moving from "OK" to "not OK" as the roles being played will shift (in the majority of instances now) from "stranger" to "acquaintance" to "friend" to "best friend" to "lover" to "spouse" to "one's beloved" to, eventually, "an irritating and disappointing spouse," and then back to "stranger" (as in, "I don't even know who you are anymore") and then to "enemy," to "ex-spouse," and to "mortal enemy."

Unhappiness will happen (a) as long as "others" are seen as persons (rather than as contaminated specks of consciousness) and (b) as long as one's own assumed personas take themselves to be real … or to have been real in "the past." Consider one case when a woman claimed that "Mike" had "treated her worst than anyone in her life." Her take: "I just can't get past the horrible things that Mike said and did when we were married, the things he stole from me, the things he destroyed that were so precious."

In that regard, the answers to the following questions can move one along the "path" to Realization and therefore to freedom and happiness:

"WHO" is this "Mike" you mention? Peace comes when you realize that there is no such thing as "Mike." (Relatively speaking, might he be considered by many persons to be one of the grander jerks of all times? Possibly, but peace will never be found as long as that relative assessment prevails and as long as the absolute reality is not seen.)

What is taken to be "Mike" is nothing more than a composite of images: the one he had of himself; the one he showed you; and the one you formed of him (without basis).

Yet the problem lies not in the phony images which he developed and which he worked to sustain. The problem can be revealed by finding the answer to these questions: Which of your personas believes that it was your real identity? Which believes that it was destroyed? Which now believes that it makes sense to be angry with a plant food body called "Mike" about the fact that one of your false ego-states ... one of your false identities ... came to an end?

Which of your personas believes that it is real (or was real) and that it makes sense to be angry with a fictional "mind" that resulted when a speck of consciousness that is called "Mike" was programmed and conditioned by warped specks of consciousness called "his family" and warped specks of consciousness that are called "his society" and "his culture?

Which of your personas believes it is real (or was real) and is now angry with another fictional persona? And which of your personas feels as if it were threatened or hurt or interfered with or terminated by that which you call "Mike"?

In every case, nothing is happening except that the consciousness that You Are and that is engaged in object witnessing is deluded ... is perceiving inaccurately. You—the Consciousness—is not "bothered." What is "bothered" is a fictional "mind" and several fictional personas that thought they were real, that still think they were real, and that think they were not treated in the manner expected or deserved.

Were the consciousness to be re-purified, it would perceive the facts behind the questions above and it would stabilize in the peace and joy and freedom ... freedom from being jerked around by false beliefs and false perceptions and phony images of what "was" or what "could have been" or "what should have been."

CHAPTER FOURTEEN

CONSIDER also:
"Goodbye Sadness" must be preceded by "Hello Clarity." If clarity (per Realization) does not happen, continued sadness shall happen. Periods of relief might be interspersed, but a lack of clarity guarantees instability.

Instability is also guaranteed if one believes in dualistic concepts such as "gain vs. loss." The related concept of "missed opportunities" can generate a sense of frustration, as if there is something other than the consciousness … as if there is "someone" who might have gained but did not or as if there is "someone" who gained but then lost.

Too, desires and fears will generate alternating periods of happiness and unhappiness because some desires might be fulfilled, some desires will never be fulfilled, and some that were fulfilled will not remain fulfilled forever. Meanwhile, the fear of never receiving all that is desired, or the fear of losing what has been "attained," will also manifest.

Mood swings will also happen if a person takes the objective world to be real and engages in subject-object witnessing (which still involves duality) rather than pure witnessing. Subject-object witnessing can generate a thought such as "He / She (subject) hurt me (object) by saying the most vicious and vile words imaginable." Pure Witnessing sees no "he" or "she" but can merely witness with non-attachment any blocked speck of consciousness in motion.

Freedom from lingering resentments comes when it is understood that, as a result of that warping, some person / persona thought and spoke and acted on "auto-pilot. "Auto" means "self," so persons operating on "self-pilot" (taking self to be real), work to fabricate and maintain the image of self and attack any who seemingly threaten their (false) self-image. By contrast, the Realized function in a spontaneous fashion which might sound similar to "auto-pilot," but in the case of the Realized there is no self that is taken to be real.

Thinking will generate instability. Thoughts are produced as "the mind" is in constant motion, generating current distortions or recalling past distortions.

Current "memories" are a recalling of past distortions and, when recalled, become current distortions.

Current distortions are being generated as a result of distorted programming and conditioning and will become "memories" at some point in the "future." All thoughts, marked by egotism since they are generated by the belief in ego-states, spawn views that are the 180-degree opposite of reality: "I'm going to tell the boss to take this job and shove it." Opposite view: "It would be reasonable to put the ego on hold and find another job before quitting this one."

"I was ripped off in that relationship. I did not get what I deserved." Opposite view: Did you deserve what you did get that you only thought was "good"? Did you deserve what you did get, which most would have considered "bad"? The very concept of "relationship" (see "relative" in the name?) is dualistic.

To believe that "this" can be "related" to "that" preempts any possibility of understanding the unicity, and if the unicity is not understood, how could any notions about what "Love" is be understood?

"Hurricane Rita did great damage in our area—God is trying to tell us something" (to quote a resident of West Texas). Opposite view: Is it possible that hurricanes happen, that any meteorologist can explain why, that there is no god who sends messages via weather systems, that there is no god controlling weather patterns, and that there is no god at all?

"Hurricane Katrina hit New Orleans because of the bad karma of the people there" (to quote the Dalai Lama). Opposite view: "Is it possible there is no good karma, no bad karma, no 'Karma Record Keeper and Karma Balancer in the Sky,' and no karma at all?"

"I'm unhappy because of him, her, what happened, what was taken, what I never got that I should have gotten, what I don't have, what I do have, the lack of fairness in the world, the inequities that life has handed me, the way people have treated me, the things taken from me, ad infinitum." Opposite view: "There is no 'I' to experience any of that. All of those beliefs are figments of the imagination, generated by 'the mind.'

"Furthermore, 'the mind' is a just collection of the figments of the imaginings of other programmed persons who were told lies that they took to be truth and then passed on. I Am a speck of consciousness that is temporarily manifested. I cannot "have," "gain," "lose," be treated unfairly, or experience. I can only witness with clarity ... or without."

Similarly, ego-states generate egotism, egotism generates a sense of entitlement, and entitlement will generate a sense of anger or disappointment. Why? Because the ego can never be satisfied since it never believes that it is getting everything it deserves, as expressed in these types of statements or thoughts:

"I'm entitled to have what I want but don't have."

I'm entitled to be taken care of, but I'm not being taken care of."

"I'm entitled to be treated like a prince or princess, but I'm not being treated that well."

"How dare you not honor me!" or "How dare you not show me proper respect!"

Instability will manifest when persons (the non-Realized) are driven to live unnaturally or supernaturally. Both of those styles of living involve body-mind-personality identification. Stability manifests when a natural AS IF style of living happens, devoid of identification and personal attributes.

The deer lives naturally because it does not have any body or mind or personality identification, and the result of living naturally and without any body-mind-personality identification is that the deer passes each day and night of its relative existence in a stable fashion. The same is true for the Realized. To know what nisarga (natural) living is like, look to nature for models ... not to your family or your culture or other cultures.

Sanity, reason and stability are evidenced during the relative manifestation only if abidance happens without concepts and without belief in any dualities. Only the no-concept, non-dual reality exists, and to believe that anything pertaining to the relative existence is based in truth is to be insane, is to function without reason and logic, and is to be unstable. And to be unstable is to constantly shift between states of happiness and unhappiness. Peace and Light.

WHY YOU MUST BE EMPTY IF YOU WOULD BE FULL

CHAPTER ONE

A reminder of this pointer came recently: Advaitins speak of "the drop dissolving into the ocean." Govinda, however, (influenced by Buddhists, the Gelug-pa sect members, Advaitins, et. al.) spoke of the next step: "the ocean slipping into the drop."

Suppose that you typically have a cup of coffee with sugar and cream each morning. Suppose that the cream you add to the coffee one morning is curdled and instead of blending in with the coffee it actually clumps up and ruins the taste with its sourness.

Would you believe that you could extract all of the curdled cream from the cup of coffee, that you could thereby return the cup of coffee to its original state, and that you could then add some fresh cream to the newly-cleaned coffee and then enjoy its taste? Of course not. Yet that is what seekers attempt to do, usually for the entirety of their search.

Most try to take their corrupted "mind" and just add some new ideas and new thoughts and new beliefs to it, filtering out or abandoning some former concepts, thinking they then have a pure "mind," and then believing that they can just add some new concepts to replace the old.

Such efforts will always prove to be futile. The entire contents of the cup must be discarded if you would fill the cup with that which can bring you something with a taste that can be enjoyed. There is no other way than the way of emptiness first, fullness second…no other way than the way of de-accumulation, period. Why?

Because you have been filled with curdled concepts. Ingredients have been added that formed a "mind" with contaminates which block the taste of sweetness and which guarantee that the relative experience will be marked by more and more sourness.

Using denial ("I love my life") or spinning the truth ("My parents did a great job and never taught me anything that has not proven to be true") or even being blinded by dissociation will not change the facts that are observable to an objective witness. Yet so many want to hang onto their contaminated cup of coffee (and their contaminated "mind" and their contaminated existence) wanting to improve it, change it, make it the way they want it.

If you follow the path of reason, can you possibly keep the original cup of coffee and do anything to it that can make it enjoyable? No. It must tossed completely. Then, something with a taste of sweetness can come. When all learned ignorance is tossed, then everything that also accompanies ignorance will go. At that point, You will know that You Are as a drop dissolving into the ocean. You are At One with all.

You will have returned to your original nature…Your original state…merging into that ocean of awareness without awareness of. Call the effect "bliss" if you like, but that is not a state of bliss. A state of bliss is a state in which the bliss is known…is felt.

That can only happen NOW, not "later"…only "here," not "there." At the point when You begin to abide as that original state, then nothing is needed, nothing is desired, and the nothingness is relished. You will have tasted the sweet taste of the nectar of immortality; You will have been healed via the ultimate medicine; You will have returned to that state prior to consciousness; You will have found the source of the seeds of consciousness; and You will abide as That Which Is What Can Make Stability Possible rather than as the consciousness which guarantees fluctuations and instability, dualistic up's and down's, and yes, even chaos.

Maharaj said that you cannot "imagine the taste of pure water; you can only discover it by abandoning all flavorings." What is "flavoring" the relative existence among the non-Realized? Lies, concepts, false beliefs, attitudes, and all of the effects of programming and conditioning and learned ignorance.

The flavoring also includes hatred; entrapment in the illusion of things thought to be personal; the false but unsavory sense of separation and emptiness with nothing to provide a manifestation of fullness; fears; unmet desires; anger; judgment; unmet expectations; fighting; war; arrogance; and—relatively speaking—the breaking of relationships. In short, concepts and duality.

The essence is that which is "the root, the foundation, the timeless and spaceless possibly" of what is called during the manifestation "all experience." What seekers would taste is the sweetness of the essence, but they are trying to taste it indirectly by clinging either to body-mind-personality identification or to religious or spiritual personas or to some elevated notions about the value of consciousness.

Maharaj taught that the natural and original state as understood by the Realized "tastes of the pure, uncaused, undiluted bliss." He pointed out that to know the sweetness, You must taste it. Its sweetness cannot be otherwise understood. Here, the circumstance is not unlike that of a tour guide taking you to a vineyard for a wine tasting.

Here, You Are guided to "The Vineyard of the Absolute" where the sweetest tastings take place. Here, if you complete a seven-step "journey," the tour will end with a savoring of the only nectar that is Real. Few can complete the "trip" alone since they are blocked by the obstacles of distortion and delusions and illusions.

To that end, M. spoke of the "distortions and impurities" of the mind. He did not say they need to be replaced with something else. He said they must be "removed." Just as the coffee is ruined by the impurities of the cream, so the relative existence is ruined by the impurities of the mind. In each case, the impurities block the enjoyment of the tasting.

The ruined cup of coffee must be discarded in order for the cup to be filled with that which can provide the taste that would be tasted; similarly, the mind must be discarded if any sweet taste to the relative existence is to added...if the ocean is to enter the drop.

Currently, the taste is being ruined by impurities. The cup that You Are must be emptied first if it is ever to be filled with all that provides the taste of sweetness that is possible during the manifestation.

To solve either the problem with the ruined coffee or the problem with the ruined existence, all must be tossed so that the original state of emptiness can return and so that a pleasant fullness can happen. Empty, the coffee cup can be filled with that which brings joy. Empty, the person can be filled with the Realization that brings joy. Empty, the ocean can slip into the drop.

In Advaitin terms, allowing the drop to dissolve into the ocean results when (A) the sense of separation goes, when (B) the awareness of the unicity comes, and when (C) the sense of being "different from" and "more special than" goes. Then the fullness of the essence slips in, along with the perfect and unshakable understanding of the "I AM THAT; I AM." Why?

Because at that point, the essence and the substance will have combined. The eternal and the transitory are ironically (but nevertheless surely) One. Even as the Am-ness continues, it knows it is THAT and it abides as THAT.

Suddenly the senseless "world" makes sense in that its senselessness no longer triggers any surprise regarding the fact that it is senseless or regarding the fact that the adult masses really do live as if six years old.

No longer does a witnessing of the evidence prompt any shock at the degree of widespread insanity, so no longer in there entrapment in judgment when the results of ignorance are seen to manifest over and over and over again. There is witnessing and understanding.

Suddenly, all of the ignorance and nonsense and immaturity and insanity make sense in light of the ignorant and nonsensical and immature and insane ways that persons are exposed to via cultures and programmers and conditioners and domesticators. Peace, therefore, manifests as beauty is seen beyond the abject darkness and the pervasive ignorance.

CHAPTER TWO

MAYBE the drop has dissolved into the ocean, but has the ocean yet rushed into the drop?

Seekers become seekers because they have a sense that "something is missing." They lack a sense of "fullness" and "wholeness" or, in some cases, are dominated by a sense of emptiness; thus, they set out to seek that which might "fill them up."

However, few will ever seek because early conditioning places the six billion "Religious Persons" on the planet in a mindset that their religion has all the answers and will fill them up if they just follow the dogma and doctrines and rules. Even when it never happens, denial or dissociation will prevent seeking outside the venue in which they were programmed and conditioned.

I tell You, however, "seek not to be full and fulfilled. Seek first to be empty." All that you have been filled with is exactly what has resulted in a sense of emptiness. Now the task if to be emptied of that which has left you feeling empty.

Only then can you truly be filled with that which will manifest as a sense of completion and wholeness and true fullness. [Ironically, I will later move You to the Void...to the Nothingness, but one step at a time for now.]

Only if you empty yourself of all that was placed inside your "mind" during the acculturation and domestication process can the ocean rush into the drop.

Before continuing the discussion, please see what else can be understood via the coffee cup metaphor used earlier. What was the condition of the coffee cup when it manifested as a cup that was made from the elements? It was empty, yes? Then what happened?

A person desired. Specifically, a person desired to taste an appealing "flavoring"...with a sweetness...with a smoothness. So because of personal desires and agendas, the cup was filled and things went along rather smoothly for a time.

Then, the very same component that had been providing the smoothness and the sweetness turned. It interrupted the smoothness and the sweetness. What had once given pleasure suddenly robbed the relative experience of its pleasure.

It was thought that what brought happiness would always provide the same taste of sweetness, but it suddenly turned and brought a taste that was most sour. So it is in the relative.

The cup was still filled, but it could no longer provide any pleasure. The essence of sweetness no longer manifested. The source of sweetness and smoothness was seen to be unpredictable, sometimes giving pleasure…sometimes pain.

The wise will see from that example that all relative pleasures are the same way—fleeting—so the question becomes how to avoid attachment to the relative…how to find a continuous source of joy; how to stop reacting when the cream goes sour; how to stop being irritated or disappointed or stressed when "other people and other things" disturb the smoothness and take away the sweetness; and how to enjoy the Am-ness and the THAT-ness simultaneously.

Re-consider these points: Suddenly, all of the ignorance and nonsense and immaturity and insanity make sense in light of the ignorant and nonsensical and immature and insane ways that persons are exposed to via cultures and programmers and conditioners and domesticators. Peace, therefore, manifests as beauty is seen beyond the abject darkness and the pervasive ignorance.

Thus it has been asked, "So do you just forgive them? Is that how you stay at peace? Is the answer to follow the old advice, 'forgive them for they know not what they do'?" Forgiveness only happens when one has first judged, found "wrong," assumed the role of a god, and determined in a "noble" fashion that forgiveness shall be handed down as if from on high.

When Christians and Hindus and Muslims (as well as others who have been programmed with religious dogma) send e-mails and declare that they forgive me for denying the existence of their god or gods, the response is, "Keep your forgiveness, but give up your attachment to fiction if you would ever know truth."

Next, as difficult as it is among persons (the non-Realized) to understand pointers regarding emptiness, even mention of the notion of being "empty" is anathema. To speak of de-accumulation to accumulators almost always falls on deaf ears.

It has taken a global depression (yes, depression) to rein in acts that are rooted in financial insanity and in being programmed to accumulate. That pattern is marked by buying things not needed with money not available, often to impress persons not even known.

Of course nothing in the relative lasts, but the historical evidence shows that cultures based in accumulation are guaranteed to hasten their own "coming apart." Nations have shared a "buy-it-up-and-fill-it-up" mentality because that mentality characterizes the non-Realized masses who populate those cultures of accumulation.

They fill up their surroundings with stuff, and they fill up their bodies and "minds" with stuff. When they hear talk of their being full of them "selves"— filled as they are with false pride about their false identities—they generally deem the message to be what is empty.

What they do not realize is this: if a fist in raised above one's head, it displaces the air where it is located, but if the fist is lowered, the air rushes back into that spot. There is no vacuum in the relative; nothing is lost and nothing is diminished. But the fist must be removed for the air to rush in and fill the space.

Consider the fist to be a metaphor for the "impurities" that Maharaj said must be removed. Once removed, that which is pure will rush into consciousness, recognized by the pure consciousness ItSelf. (That is, in fact, the only worth of that consciousness which, beyond that, is the root of all suffering.)

So what must happen if the ocean is to rush into the drop, and what are the impurities that must be emptied out in order that the pure can be known? The discussion of the impurities will follow.

CHAPTER THREE

MAYBE the drop has dissolved into the ocean, but has the ocean yet rushed into the drop? If so, then the next question must be: after the drop dissolved into the ocean and after the ocean rushed into the drop, did both the ocean and the drop eventually dissolve as well?

Earlier you were invited to consider this: "What must happen if the ocean is to rush into the drop, and what are the impurities that must be emptied out in order that the pure can be known?"

This invitation to become empty is almost unique to the Advaitin approach. You need not be filled with more knowledge, more information, more learning; instead, the invitation here is merely to "unlearn it all."

The paradox is that—by unlearning all that you have been taught during the relative existence—you will come to understand the functioning of the totality. To that end, Maharaj said that if You would taste That Which is ultimately Pure, then you must abandon all "flavorings" as well as all distortions and all "impurities."

What are the flavorings that are distorting the relative existence and preventing it from happening spontaneously in a natural fashion? What are the impurities that result in thoughts tainted with a caustic flavor, in words seasoned with sour distastefulness, in deeds marred by a caustic, corrosive taste?

All of those flavorings were added via programming and acculturation and conditioning and domestication, and—along with certain other influences that will be discussed as well—make up the host of impurities that Maharaj mentioned. These must be removed if the ocean is to flow into the drop that You Are.

THE IMPURITY OF EGO AND EGOTISM

First, what must be removed if you would be filled by the rushing of the ocean into the drop is that which separates you from the ocean as much as any other factor, namely, the ego.

Take that to include personality and personas, roles, assumed identities, and their triggering of the ego-defense mechanisms that result in the breaking of relationships during the relative existence.

If the ego and its egotism were to dissolve, if body-mind-personality identification were to disappear, if being full of self were to end, if all sense of separation and differentiation were to be cast aside, then what would rush in to fill the void for the remainder of the relative existence?

In other words, what is that "ocean"? It is a sense of peace, of independence, of freedom, of contentment, of the unicity, of at-one-ment, of Oneness. In a word, it is Love. What is the opposite of Love? Some say, "Hate." No, the opposite of Love is Untruth, manifesting as belief in a personal self, as belief in separation, as belief in better-than-ness, as belief in ego and egotism.

As a result of the impurity of ego (the false "I") then the ocean of Truth/Love will never rush in to fill you. You will be plagued with the emptiness of hate and by a false sense of separation and by your belief in lies and myths and superstitions and ideologies and dogma. You will have no choice so you will have no freedom? Why no choice? It's quite simple:

If you adopt the persona of "Christian," then you will think and feel and behave as instructed by others who have adopted that phony identity before you. If you adopt the persona of "Muslim," then you will think and feel and behave as instructed by others who have adopted the phony identity before you. If you adopt the persona of "Jew," then you will think and feel and behave as instructed by others who have adopted the phony identity before you.

If you adopt the persona of "A Recovering Alcoholic," then you will think and feel and behave as instructed by others who have adopted the phony identity before you. If you adopt the persona of "The Super Spouse," then you will think and feel and behave in the ways that you have witnessed others playing that role (though what they let you see is nowhere close to what they are hiding.)

If you would be the Oneness, allow yourself (or selves) to dissolve in the ocean of All. If you would be filled with bliss and Love and gentleness and peace, allow the ocean to rush into you.

CHAPTER FOUR

MAYBE the drop has dissolved into the ocean, but has the ocean yet rushed into the drop? If so, then the next question must be: after the drop dissolved into the ocean and after the ocean rushed into the drop, did both the ocean and the drop eventually dissolve as well?

A visitor asked: So I think I got the drop in the ocean and I'm getting the ocean in the drop, but the next part you added makes no sense. If I understand rightly, the ocean in Advaita usually refers to the ocean of the Absolute. The drop is me, moving from the manifestation to the unmanifest. So how could the ocean and drop dissolve (or the Absolute not be and how could what is unmanifested not be?)

If you view the first three titles in Advanced Seeker's Package, you might then consider the implications of the titles: First, the "shift" is FROM THE I TO THE ABSOLUTE; then, the understanding involves distinguishing between CONSCIOUSNESS and AWARENESS and understanding THE NATURE OF REALITY BEYOND SELF-REALIZATION. But that state of awareness-without-awareness-of is not the "end." Finally comes the "shift" FROM THE ABSOLUTE TO THE NOTHINGNESS.

Consider those three titles and then see if You might be able to answer your question YourSelf. That said, your question is mentioned at this point because it relates to the next impurity that must be removed if You would feel full now:

THE IMPURITY OF BELIEF IN AN EXPERIENCER "NOW" OR IN ANY IDENTITY "LATER"

There is nothing personal; there is no "one"; thus, there is no one to experience...either now or "later." The closest to any experience happening during the relative manifestation is when the consciousness "experiences" itself.

In fact, that is all that is happening during the manifestation. In only a few instances will the consciousness also fully "experience" ItSelf—that is, come to know ItSelf fully.

All of that is offered with an asterisk attached since when Full Realization happens, the experience, the experiencer, and all other identities (including the so-called phenomenal ones and the so-called noumenal ones) will disappear.

If you believe in the person and the personal, you will find that you will take things personally all day long, every day. What a miserable way to pass through this relative existence. Does that suggest that a cold, robotic existence is the only alternative?

Only to those who have not understood the steps that can bring joy and happiness and bliss to the relative even as abidance is happening as the care-free natural state. When the essence and the substance become as One (when the Am-ness and THAT are One and are known to be One) then there is unrestrained delight in the unchecked joys of the relative.

There is also, post-Realization, an unbridling of previously-subdued pleasures which can come (and which can come without the alternate, dualistic pain that shows up when not Realized) because events—though substantive—are no longer strapped with relative "flavorings" but are saturated with the sweetness of the bliss-heightening essence.

The result: the acts which the non-Realized see as pleasure-providing and which they fear would be stripped away by Realization are understood by the Realized to have higher dimensions of delight than ever imagined by the non-Realized.

When essence and substance become as One (and when the THAT-ness is overlaid on the Am-ness) then the resultant bliss and amusement—and yes, even fun—take on the same limitless and boundless and infinite qualities of the Absolute.

[NOTE: Seekers have e-mailed periodically—along with two most recently—to ask if the approach used here recommends celibacy...as required by their gurus. If they understood the nisarga natural yoga, how could that question even arise? The topic is seldom discussed here because the natural is regularly advocated. Since the queries have been raised, however, this will be offered:

Would it be natural for the deer to be celibate? Those gurus making such a demand of protégés are advocating duality, ignoring the fact that Reality can be overlaid on the relative...that the essence and the substance can function as One. If the cloak of celibacy is worn comfortably, so it is, but should that not be a conscious choice rather than a subconscious constraint or a guru or priest-imposed restraint?

It is only after The Understanding happens that Love and love can be understood to be One. How inane to promote any deprivation that prevents the overlaying of Reality upon the relative or that would block in any way the awareness of the "not-two-ness" of the Am-ness and THAT, even during the manifestation. In fact, is that not the "aim" of the "journey"?

If that not-two-ness is understood, then those of you suffering exposure to spiritual advisers, gurus, religious leaders, and cult founders who demand that you remain celibate will understand that such a restriction will prevent the ocean from rushing into the drop and will assure that the essence and the substance shall never be known to be One.

Is that a contradiction of the "desire not" message offered here? No. Is that an invitation to engage in the promiscuity that has been a standard part of retreats that have been conducted over the last decades at certain "ashrams"? No.

Is that to say that the "forest-dweller-take-a-break-from-chasing-the-phys-ical-in-order-to-focus-on-the-non-physical-journey"-stage has never served to allow some seekers to advance along the "path" by remaining focused on the Self rather than the self? No.

Is that to say that sex addicts should not take a break from practicing their addiction and their destructive behavior (relatively speaking) in order to seek The Understanding and liberation? No. But at the end of the "path" discussed here, the relative happens naturally, not in an unnatural fashion and not in a pseudo-supernatural fashion.

Realize fully, find Truth, and then relish the sweetness of the essence-coated substance while the manifestation lasts. Post-Realization, no one will be empow-ered to influence you to abandon the natural for their unnatural and myth-based supernatural ways.

Once freedom manifests, there is no one to be told what he/she can do or cannot do, should do or should not do. Realized, no one will have the ability to overlay their abnormal restrictions and limitations and duality-based neuroses on You.

You Are That Which Is boundless and limitless, and abidance as your orig-inal, natural state (even as the consciousness is yet manifested) will provide the only chance for you and You to know bliss.]

CHAPTER FIVE

MAYBE the drop has dissolved into the ocean, but has the ocean yet rushed into the drop? If so, then the next question must be: after the drop dissolved into the ocean and after the ocean rushed into the drop, did both the ocean and the drop eventually dissolve as well?

THE IMPURITY OF GIVING LIP SERVICE TO PEACE WHEN THE SWORD IS STILL REQUIRED

It has been noted how few will ever seek. It has also been noted how few who seek will ever find. That is the case because, typically, at the third of the seven steps to Realization, even if seekers begin to understand that the roles assigned by cultures are false, they nevertheless assume new roles such as "The Religious One" or "The Spiritual One."

What the latter is really involved in is kindergarten spirituality, certain that he/she has reached the end of the "journey" and has "arrived" (though not yet even to the halfway point along the "path").

At the point of adopting those "new and lofty roles," they often claim that nowadays they only carry an olive branch, moving through the existence as if "The Dove of Peace." In fact, since they have not yet completed even half of the "journey," the olive branch needs to be set aside.

The call is to take the sword in hand and completely eliminate all that must go if the ocean is to rush into the drop (and if the ocean and drop are eventually to disappear as well).

Possibly the sword was used for a time to hack away at egotism-generating identities such as the "The Saint" or to eliminate guilt-and-shame-generating identities such as "The Bastard" or "The Whore"; however, if additional roles have been adopted such as "The Religious One" or "The Spiritual One"— thought to be of the "new and improved variety"—then the sword should not yet be placed in storage.

Two thousand years ago, a man who had been totally-programmed and totally conditioned with Jewish dogma heard some of the Advaita teachings and began to speak afterwards of the need for the sword. He had spent years quoting sections of the Torah. He became called "Rabbi" (meaning "Teacher"). He became called "The Son of God."

Eventually, he was exposed to a variety of different teachings, including some teachings from members of a group called Gnostics, some teachings from members of various cults in the Middle East, and finally some teachings from an Advaitin.

Contrary to the teachings of his followers today that he was "a man of peace," he was quoted as having said after hearing certain Advaitin pointers, "Do not think that I came to bring peace on the earth; I did not come to bring the peace. I came to bring the sword."

His modern-day "followers" understand that no more than they understand how it is that "heaven and earth shall fade away"; how "no one will ever see heaven since it is within"; or how the claim that "before Abraham was, I AM" could be an expression of anything other than nonsense.

Among the religious of his day, the initial reaction to his words after his exposure to Advaita was to kill him. Such reactions could hardly be said to have brought peace. The government feared that he would incite riots…hardly a peaceful event, either.

And even his "followers" were upset when he instructed, "Do not call me the 'Son of God.' I am the 'son of man'." In the end, he even rejected that label, saying, "When you speak of me, speak of Me as I AM."

Too, there was no peace generated from his comment that "I came to turn a man against his father, a daughter against her mother, and a daughter-in-law against her mother-in-law." Of course, the pointer was an invitation to reject all of the culturally-assigned labels that were resulting in agenda-driven personas which, in turn, were causing the relative existence chaos in their lives (a point as applicable now as "then.")

The sword is actually the sword of truth which allows false identities to be seen; once seen, then the sword of truth can be used to eliminate belief in those personas. To set aside the sword too early on the "journey" is to guarantee that the remainder of the relative existence will happen via "a person that feels empty inside."

To feign peacefulness when the actual driving force is either (a) passive-aggressive thinking or (b) denial or (c) dissociation from the way one truly feels is nothing even close to true peace. The invitation is this: set not the sword of truth aside until all beliefs and all concepts have been eliminated.

CHAPTER SIX

MAYBE the drop has dissolved into the ocean, but has the ocean yet rushed into the drop? If so, then the next question must be: after the drop dissolved into the ocean and after the ocean rushed into the drop, did both the ocean and the drop eventually dissolve as well?

THE IMPURITY OF ATTACHMENT TO THE UNNATURAL AND THE MAGICAL (SUPERNATURAL)

In the late 1960's, Aretha Franklin released a song entitled, "You Make Me Feel Like A Natural Woman." Close, but no cigar. Here, no one can be made to feel like a man or a woman, though all seekers can come to understand the natural (nisarga) yoga and thereafter function in a natural fashion for the remainder of the manifestation.

Here, when The Understanding manifests, there is neither woman nor man, neither being nor non-being, neither a You nor a you. When the understanding manifests, then the remainder of the relative existence all happens in an AS IF fashion.

Here, the response might be, "Having Realized, the relative existence is unfolding in a natural and spontaneous manner, without attachments." Here, the response might be, "What I AM for the remainder of the relative will function in a totally natural manner.

"There is not an iota of the unnatural (including personality disorders, insanity, identity, conceptualizations, duality, beliefs, ideas, or attachment). Also, there is not an iota of the magical thinking that results from being programmed and conditioned to believe in things supernatural (including a god; gods; angels; guardian angels; demons; divine intervention; creation and creationism;

"heaven; hell; an afterlife; a prior life; rebirth; resurrection; prayers answered; prayers ignored; a god said to love unconditionally who simultaneously destroys and punishes eternally; holy cannibalism and holy vampirism, a.k.a., 'body and blood communion'; duality; trinities; and multiplicities.)"

The impurities of programming and conditioning that involve dogma are a key source of dualistic beliefs and ideas and concepts, and all beliefs and ideas and concepts block the consciousness from seeing truth...even from seeing ItSelf.

The impurities of the fictional personality, as well as the subsequent personality disorders that manifest with the fictional personality, will function alongside the fiction-filled "mind." That combination of belief in personas and in the content of the "mind" will then lead to most unnatural thoughts and words and deeds.

Realized, thoughts vanish because the "mind" vanishes; words are used less and less as the silence becomes the norm more and more; and deeds happen less often as alignment with the beingness (and eventually with the non-being-ness and beyond) eliminates the do-er and the doingness and the going and the zooming.

Then, even if surrounded by the insanity and disorder and chaos of the relative, non-attached witnessing happens. The Pure Witness knows it is All and also knows that It Is nothing. And while that might sound contradictory, it is not so.

Once the Reality is overlaid upon the relative, belief in any duality or trinities or multiplicities ends because no belief in anything remains. Paradoxically, when all beliefs are forfeited, the door is opened to an understanding of the functioning of the totality, including the no-concept, non-dual Reality.

CHAPTER SEVEN

MAYBE the drop has dissolved into the ocean, but has the ocean yet rushed into the drop? If so, then the next question must be: after the drop dissolved into the ocean and after the ocean rushed into the drop, did both the ocean and the drop eventually dissolve as well?

[The discussion of the impurities that must be eliminated if the remainder of the relative existence is to be marked by a sense of wholeness and fulfillment will continue after responding to an e-mail since it partly relates to today's subject matter]:

A visitor asked: What is the difference between action and reaction? Rajesh

The reply: Hello Rejesh. Because your question provides no evidence of "where along the path" You might be, the question will be addressed as follows: the answer varies, depending on whether Realization has happened or not.

An action among the Realized is what happens spontaneously with no belief whatsoever in an "actor" or a "do-er" and with no attachment to outcome. As far as reaction, there is no such thing among the Realized.

An action among the non-Realized is what happens as a result of entrapment in body and mind and personality identification combined with a belief in an "actor" or a "do-er" and with attachment to outcome.

As far as "reaction" is concerned, a reaction is what happens during the manifestation among non-Realized persons as a result of a persona thinking it has been interfered with or hurt or threatened, after which emotional intoxication will inspire activities/reactions intended to protect what is actually nothing more than a false identity. Thx for the question. Regards.

THE IMPURITY OF ATTACHMENT TO ANY IDENTITY, PART A

Truth cannot be stated. The knower and the known and the knowing shall all fade away. Even "consciousness knowing ItSelf" is duality (is it not?) so that too cannot be Truth. (Do not confuse that pointer about consciousness with "Awareness that is not aware of," which is the "not two.")

Since truth cannot be stated, then it is impossible to state truth when making claims about "Who you are" or even about "Who You Are." Pointers to truth can be used as a thorn can be used to remove a thorn—after which all thorns are tossed; however, pointers are not Truth…just pointers to Truth.

Since Truth cannot be stated, there is no you or You that can tell anyone Who or What You Are. Even that which knows is temporary, so even that knowing is not the ultimate Truth.

It is also impossible to state truth when making claims about "self," "Self," "self-ness," "Selfness," or "True Self." For example, suppose the pictures taken of a body/space/form during schooling, such as during the thirteen years from kindergarten to high school, were gathered and then shuffled with the thirteen pictures of one-hundred other students.

No one who did not spend those thirteen years with that body/space/form could separate out in exact sequence the thirteen pictures of that particular body because both its "appearance" and its elemental and conscious-energy substance would have undergone near total change.

Why could the thirteen pictures not be found among the 1313 photographs? To answer, "Because the looks of people change over the years, especially during the early years" would be incomplete. The fact is that the thirteen pictures are assumed to be of the one, same body, but that is a distortion.

The cellular structure of that supposed body actually changed daily. The body that a person takes to be "his/her body" at the beginning of the month is not the same body at the end of the month, so of course it will "look different" over a period of time.

Also, the consciousness involved with the plant food body is constantly coming and going as well. As pointed out recently, there is no continuous consciousness manifested in one particular space, so to assume the identity of "the consciousness" is false as well.

When there is talk of an "I" or an "i" during the relative, it is the consciousness speaking, yes. But it is not the exact same quantity of consciousness that spoke earlier. The consciousness speaking today is not the same exact consciousness that was present yesterday.

(Read the transcripts of talks by Maharaj in chronological order and you will see a tremendous variation in the message, the level of the seeker being responded to notwithstanding. Some called that "an evolution of consciousness." Not true.

The fact is that it is only Awareness that allows the Understanding to seem to have continuity via one space. The consciousness is ever moving, ever shifting.)

Realize fully and then an understanding of the no-concept, no-identity, non-dual, original, natural state will manifest. Only then will belief in the drop and in the ocean and in any identity also dissolve.

CHAPTER EIGHT

MAYBE the drop has dissolved into the ocean, but has the ocean yet rushed into the drop? If so, then the next question must be: after the drop dissolved into the ocean and after the ocean rushed into the drop, did both the ocean and the drop eventually dissolve as well?

THE IMPURITY OF ATTACHMENT TO ANY IDENTITY, PART B

Cultures and their institutions are at the core of maintaining belief in duality, including the assignment of false identities, but note the relative impact. If there were no identity, WHO could be considered "good" or "bad"? Moral or immoral? Happy or unhappy? Upset or content?

Joyful or joyless? Peace-less or peaceful? Bothered or untroubled? Stable or unstable? Subjected to the slings and arrows of the relative existence or non-attached to what persons take to be "this world" and its events? Concerned with living or with dying? With birth and with rebirths?

With keeping a god or gods happy or with fearing when the god or gods are angry (which is also an excellent metaphor for parent-child-role-reversal where the child tries to be the therapist to the adult and to restore peace to a co-dependent adult...or god). Concerned with the temporarily manifested consciousness or even with abiding as the natural state?

Yet persons (the non-Realized) are so attached to the consciousness that they desire its continuity, and most cultures are more than happy to suggest that such continuity is possible...if only you think and talk and believe and behave as the leaders say.

Presently, nearly 6.5 billion persons are convinced not only that their religious beliefs and religious practices can assure such continuity but also that they can be guaranteed pleasure rather than pain after they "die" (another misconceived concept itself).

They would be in for quite a surprise if it were possible for the consciousness to know anything post-manifestation, but they will not be surprised since there will be no one to know what fools they were to unquestioningly accept what they were told by ignorant persons with agendas.

As for the belief that "Well, at least I'm the energy that cannot be destroyed. As energy, I've always been in this universe and always will be," it can be asked, "How well does that identity hold up when it is understood that there was at one point a no-energy, no-matter void 'in' the space that is now called this universe?"

More to the point, though, is the fact that—while various forms of energy do have certain attributes—none of the attributes include any "I-ness" or "i"-ness or any "Self-ness" or "self-ness."

So there is really nothing that can be pointed to as an identity or Identity of any type. The ego will hate that; the unblocked consciousness will love it since that awareness allows Love to manifest for now and allows the search for self/Self to end and allows freedom to manifest along with total peace and independence for the remainder of the manifestation.

Thus, nothing that is claimed as an identifier, now or "later," is true. To cast aside the supposedly "ignoble" identities and to claim even a "noble" one or "the noble ones" is delusion. No freedom can happen, and no spontaneous happenings can happen, as long as any identity is assumed.

Teachers suggest to those seekers just beginning the search to "find first all that You are not." That is an appropriate pointer for a beginner, and what an amazing shift would occur, relatively speaking, if only persons could find that much.

For a few seekers, however, The Understanding manifests. It happens where you or You shout "Eureka" over "the new and most recent insight or awareness," but then pause and finally admit, "OK, wait a second...I am not that either, there being no such thing as an 'I' or an 'i' and no such thing as any identity."

How will that set with the community of "noble seekers"? How willing will they be to accept those pointers and admit that the Truth cannot be stated and can only be known (and only for a finite period at that)? Not well. But what is the relative "price" for such attachment to an "Identity" or to "identities"? Arrogance, instability; dependence; entrapment; delusion; subjugation to influences and influencers; a sense of separation; a sense of inferiority or a sense of superiority or fluctuations between both; the drive to believe in illusions and then upgrade some while downgrading others; ignorance; personality disorders; insanity; chaos; ad infinitum.

That said, most will never reach the final understanding. No problem. Find who you are not and find all that you are not, and leave it be. For those who understand the no-concept, non-dual, no-identity and no-Identity Reality, then at that point "You're" truly done and "you're" truly done. Then, the remainder of the relative existence will happen spontaneously and effortlessly and naturally.

And when the relative existence unfolds naturally, then there is no more attachment to any identity than there is among the naturally-living deer, than among the naturally-living fish, than among the naturally-living birds.

Specifically, there is no identity assumed by fauna or fish or fowl, so they experience far most peace than humans. A visitor reflected on a consideration heard some time back which he only now accepts: "You really grossed me out when you said that a roach was better off than I…was more at peace than I."

Such peace can only come when there is no identity assumed, as happens among the Fully Realized. At that point, the incredible lightness of being results in a mode of moving through the relative existence that is almost like…floating.

Chapter Nine

MAYBE the drop has dissolved into the ocean, but has the ocean yet rushed into the drop? If so, then the next question must be: after the drop dissolved into the ocean and after the ocean rushed into the drop, did both the ocean and the drop eventually dissolve as well?

A visitor hearing these pointers said: There has been a big impact from the pointers in some mysterious, entirely unfathomable way. There is a powerful inner response here – even as "the i" doesn't know or understand why. I am just reading the words and allowing them to have their effect. The insight came for why the trust is necessary: that the limited or flawed view of "me" must be relinquished, even while it feels "true," and replaced with true understanding – which requires a leap of faith that is only possible with infallible trust. This insight was affirmed instantly with the spiraling and spontaneous tears.

The reply: It is appropriate to cry at "your" own funeral if the tears are tears of joy which indicate that total independence from entrapment in the relative has finally happened and which indicate that the ultimate freedom has finally come (even as the manifestation continues).

Now, the continuation of the discussion of the impurities that must be eliminated if the remainder of the relative existence is to be marked by a sense of wholeness and fulfillment:

THE IMPURITY OF MOVING INTO AND OUT OF

The Non-Realized identify with the body and mind and personality only; the practically Realized identify with the consciousness even as they continue to abide "in the world"; the Fully Realized abide as awareness that is not even aware…abide as the natural, original state.

Sometimes, seekers on the "journey" may no longer be judging others as often but continue to judge and berate and abuse themselves when they believe for a time that they "have it" and then prove later in the day or week or month that they have seemingly "lost it."

Abiding as the body and mind and personality will guarantee instability and fluctuation and even chaos. Abiding as the consciousness can never provide consistent stability either, the consciousness being ever in motion.

Yet that is no cause for self-judgment or self-punishment during the period when the focus is on the dissolution of the self. Moving into or out of consciousness or awareness is often a part of the process, and the persistence of the obstacles that block Full Realization should not be underestimated.

Many seekers nearing the end of the "journey" will step into the Absolute, look about, enjoy what is seen, but occasionally be pulled back by the gravitational force of the conscious-energy. Last April, there was a move from one side of the lake to the other. Some items were brought along to the new house, some were cleaned out and thrown away.

Some additional time was spent in the former residence before moving permanently into the new home because the move spanned several days, unfolding at a very leisurely pace. Even after having moved into the new location, however, there were even more items that were seen to be unnecessary and best thrown away or given away.

You understand the comparison, yes? In this regard, the following exchange happened:

A visitor said: It's so frustrating that even though i can come to more and more understanding.....on the same day i can go out and the body's old conditioning and responses to things fire up and offer a similar experience as if the understanding never was.

The reply: This is a sign of living as the consciousness rather than the awareness. The fluctuations will come until stabilization as the natural state happens. In the meantime, enjoy the results of the continuing "journey." There is no scoring on "the path" or during this dance. Peace and Light

Also, this was shared after a seeker read of the book CONSCIOUSNESS / AWARENESS):

"Floyd, this book is awesome...I loved it. Again, you did a great job and I want to thank you for helping me understand things more clearly. I could just abide in the peace and let it all go by. You've come in like a fireman and carried us out of the burning house as we "scream for help." I suppose it's like after you put us down on the ground outside you point us back in the direction of the house and nothing's there and you say you really aren't a fireman and there was no burning house. Holy Crap!"

Indeed, so much of the crap being taught and learned is of the holy variety, but it also comes in spiritual varieties and is often dressed up in all sorts of other cloaks and disguises. To be free of all such nonsense and to be free and joyous during the manifestation, then abidance must stabilize as the original, natural state.

Until that happens, judge not your self (or selves) for moving two steps forward and one step backward along the "path." Take the pointers in the readings into quiet consideration and the full and final understanding may manifest, or not.

Know, though, that if the "path" leads you to seeing much of what you are not and seeing more clearly all that "the world" is not, then additional levels of freedom will nevertheless begin to manifest with each ego-state that dissolves.

Chapter Ten

MAYBE the drop has dissolved into the ocean, but has the ocean yet rushed into the drop? If so, then the next question must be: after the drop dissolved into the ocean and after the ocean rushed into the drop, did both the ocean and the drop eventually dissolve as well?

THE IMPURITY OF CLINGING TO THE MIND, PART A

From a visitor: There have been longer periods of seeing the mind stuff as just old thought patterns, conditioning, programming and all the things you have taught. It's like someone else made the analogy of the movie a beautiful mind - when he realizes that those images aren't real and he sees them but isn't bothered by them anymore because he knows they aren't real.

My question to you is, will the mind stop reacting in those old ways? There is much peace in laughing at the thoughts that still come up but I was wondering if the ego will get tired of not being taken seriously and give up.

Thank you again for introducing me to this teaching. It's funny to think of the things i used to do before 2001 when you started to dismantle my old belief systems. I used to beat my self up because I felt my inventories weren't good enough or my prayer life wasn't strong enough. It's all bullshit. Thanks again, Walter

The reply: Hello again, Walter. The mind is the seat of the ego, and you understand as well as—or better than—most that each ego-state will (a) fight for its "life," will (b) tolerate intolerable abuse and nonsense, and will (c) employ words and deeds to try to convince itself and others to believe that it's real.

To your specific question, as long as the "mind" is there, it will not stop reacting in the old ways because it is also the seat of emotional intoxication (a state that manifests when a persona imagines that it has been interfered with or threatened or hurt, which happens constantly when attached to false identities).

Try to list some things that you were really attached to in the past, or things you thought you really loved and needed, but that you eventually "saw through" and discarded without paying a bit of attention to those things anymore.

The content of the "mind" can eventually be devalued in the same fashion if You truly see that the beliefs stored in the "mind" are what would have you remain attached to abuse and nonsense and non-truths and, as you said, BS. The beliefs and concepts and attitudes stored therein also want "you" to react and to believe in needs and to mistake false love for Real Love.

Also, for the "mind" to be devalued, You would have to admit that there is no such thing as "your mind" but that you are presently operating under the influence of that which is "their mind." "They" made it; it's "theirs"; and via what is "theirs," "they" continue to control your every thought and word and action.

Some of "them" may be considered "dead and long gone," but "they" are as surely in charge of you as if "they" were standing behind you at this instant and holding a gun to your head and dictating unilaterally the way you feel and think and behave.

"They" planted in that "mind" everything that is there; those were "their" seeds of ignorance that took root; "they" continued to heap on more and more BS which only served to fertilized what was growing into a larger crop daily.

What you did not know is that the seeds they planted were not the seeds of consciousness but were seeds of learned ignorance. Further, you did not know that they had applied poisonous pesticides.

Thus, when you were old enough to go forth and harvest according to what they had planted, you began to spread the contaminants they had sown and began to experience the relative consequences which you have been reaping ever since.

And all of your consequences evolved from "their mind" which was nothing more than the storehouse of "their" concepts, "their" ideas, and "their" beliefs, all of which you unquestioningly assumed to be your own. It is as if they had been carrying about a huge collection of garbage on their shoulders and as if they removed part of the content and placed it on your shoulders.

How proud the ego wants to be of the legacy handed down from its ancestors and parents and leaders and heroes and relatives, totally trapped in delusion while showing off smugly what any clear-seeing witness would recognize as rubbish.

And you have continued to carry that garbage about on your shoulders (specifically, in the part of the brain called the "mind"). Understand that the "mind" is a part of the brain that human-like beings have only had for a tiny fraction of the fourteen million years during which they have walked about on the surface of the planet.

Prior to the brain having evolved from its long-standing one-cup size to its more recent three-and-a-half-cups size, and prior to the brain having developed an area for storing information and an area that can retrieve parts of that stored information, human-like beings lived naturally under the auspices of the mindless brain.

The same is still happening with the deer and the birds and the fish and the insects, so they have no means by which to attach to (and be impacted by) the nonsense and disorders and learned ignorance that have come to plague the relative existence of humans.

If you would be free of living under the influence of that which is the seat of every lie you believe (which is to say, is the seat of every belief that is a lie) then you must be done with giving any credibility to the content of the "mind." For that to happen is neither as impossible nor as difficult as some assume.

CHAPTER ELEVEN

MAYBE the drop has dissolved into the ocean, but has the ocean yet rushed into the drop? If so, then the next question must be: after the drop dissolved into the ocean and after the ocean rushed into the drop, did both the ocean and the drop eventually dissolve as well?

THE IMPURITY OF CLINGING TO THE MIND, PART B

A man who came recently to a retreat finally understood why he has been stuck for decades at the point of trying to be rid of the "mind" and the ideas and concepts and beliefs stored therein. He had spent most of his adult years researching one piece of dogma or ideology or concept after another.

For example, when he found the truth that disproved one of the church's teachings, he'd discard belief in that single teaching and then move on to the next to be considered and studied and researched. He employed the same method as he studied the tales told during the decades of his life by politicians and parents and teachers and revisionist historians.

He was shown at the retreat that his method could never lead to Realization and freedom because he could not possibly live long enough to question each teaching individually and disprove one concept or belief at a time.

He was told: "You have found scores and scores of instances where the words of your priest and your culture have been shown to be false; you have found scores of examples where the scriptures in the book he called 'special and holy and one-of-a-kind' were shown to have been plagiarized from pagan and mythological works; "you have seen how the gray-haired, white-bearded Zeus and the multiple gods of creation and the multiple gods of sustenance and the multiple gods of destruction were all morphed into 'the one god of Abraham'; "you have seen other instances where your priest's supposedly unique scriptures were merely lifted from ancient fables which had become tales that were widely-shared as oral traditions for centuries before being purloined and written and eventually printed; "you have seen thousands of lies told by politicians and parents, and you saw how your so-called self-help program with its dozen steps failed to address your real problems as the persons there encouraged you to employ magical, supernatural thinking to treat issues that actually required the skills of professionals rather than amateurs; "you have found time and again examples of supposed 'truths' that were later seen to have been false or inaccurate or nonsensical. So the question now is, 'How many more examples are going to be required in order for you to conclude once and for all that those scriptures are all purloined twaddle and that the words heard from leaders in your culture are claptrap and that the teachings from other cultures are drivel'?"

Now, since you asked about being free of the reactions inspired by the content of "your mind," the next consideration for you is this: "Are you willing to rake through a bag of garbage just before the collectors come, thinking that there might be at least one useful thing in the trash that would be worth keeping, or is it possible that you really do need to toss all of the garbage and be done with it once and for all?

"And if you search through the trash bag and find its contents truly are nothing more than valueless garbage, and if you determine that the proper course of action would be to toss the valueless garbage, then why would you decide not only to keep the fouled garbage bag but also to honor it as well?"

Is it not time to be done with both the "mind" and its content? Many have asked, "But floyd, how can anyone survive nowadays without a mind?" The fact is, everything that is currently surviving right now on the planet is doing so without a mind, all except non-Realized persons. "But isn't a mind required for "survival" or "success"?

A basic fact about "survival and success" on planet earth is this: if every human were struck down today, life on the planet would prosper as a result of the contributions that mindless insects make to plant sustenance and, as a result, to the continuing cycling of consciousness; however, if every insect were struck down today, human life would end abruptly. Why? Plant life would end without the contribution made by insects to the growth cycles; the cycling of consciousness among humans would therefore end; and the end of all human existence would follow, not matter how mind-full and knowledgeable those humans might be.

Humans with their "minds" and their accumulated knowledge (a.k.a., learned ignorance) are rendered less effective and less adaptable than bugs. When considering the worth of "the mind," or lack thereof, contrast the value of what bugs provide to events on the planet as opposed to the worthlessness of what is generated from "the minds" of humans.

Both historically and currently the mindless insects have thrived and are thriving; they would continue to thrive even more in the absence of humans with "minds." As a matter of fact, the planet did quite well without people for billions of years but has not fared so well now that it is experiencing the effects of "mind-driven beings."

[Recall the humility-inspiring pointer mentioned recently when a seeker finally admitted that the roaches that occasionally visit his house are functioning in a far more logical manner than the persons in that home...and those roaches are totally mind-less while the people there are completely mind-full.]

The conundrum for most persons who would be free of the effects of the content of the "mind" is that the ego is seated in the "mind" and it is the ego that values itself without limit; as a result, the ego values its abode (the "mind") as well. To set out to be rid of ego only but not to be rid of every concept and belief will still leave "the mind."

Thus, to answer your question in that regard, no, the "mind" will never tire. The body can be so tired that it cannot rise from a bed, but the "mind" will not tire; instead, it will work and churn and toss and turn without pause. Thus, for as long as you continue to tolerate it, it will always continue to support assumed ego-states or will generate new ego-states to replace any that disappear.

"The Husband" disappears? "The Ex" appears, along with "The Hunter of a Replacement Spouse" or "The New Lover" or "The One Who Wants to Die," ad infinitum. If you witness how consistently the "mind" malfunctions, and if you witness the malfunctioning and its effects objectively, then you should reach the conclusion that the "mind" is not only useless but is actually a major detriment as well.

To set out to be rid of it, however, will trigger every possible ego-defense mechanism imaginable, and all of the assumed ego-states that are fed by the concepts and beliefs stored in the "mind" will, without fail, continue to be a source of delusion, illusion, distortion, and obstacles that block the consciousness from seeing truth.

No piecemeal efforts will produce the result being sought. To toss the garbage but to keep the putrid bag and to show respect for that which stored the garbage—or to toss the putrid bag but to still accumulate more garbage—will leave you nonetheless in the polluted presence of rubbish that can eventually debilitate you completely.

Your history is that, prior to 2001, you sought far and wide via multiple venues, and in each venue you were taught new garbage. You were never once invited to be rid of your own garbage and their garbage too. Only via these Advaita teachings were you told, "I have nothing for you. There is nothing you need to learn from Me. There is, however, much that must be unlearned."

In all of your years of trying to confront and be rid of ego, do you now see how those venues actually just reinforced the ego and in the end generated belief in even more ego-states? And which venue alone invited you to end belief in the ego and ego-states without telling you that "you must believe what I believe if you would be sane and free"?

Was it not ironic and even contradictory that in at least one of those venues you were told that your main problem "centers in the mind" but it was never suggested that you be rid of the main problem and the place where it is centered? Is it not ironic that they taught you that magical, supernatural thinking would address...your thinking problem? Thinking is not the antidote for thinking.

Why not find the place where the main problem is centered and be rid of it? If the doctors had eliminated only select parts of "floyd's" cancerous growths, the results would have been nil. All of the contents of the "mind" are a cancer on your relative existence. Remove it all.

Chapter Twelve

MAYBE the drop has dissolved into the ocean, but has the ocean yet rushed into the drop? If so, then the next question must be: after the drop dissolved into the ocean and after the ocean rushed into the drop, did both the ocean and the drop eventually dissolve as well?

THE IMPURITY OF CLINGING TO THE MIND, PART C, The Conclusion

In an earlier example, the pointer which was offered to one seeker that attended a retreat applies to all: of all of the ideas and concepts and beliefs that form the "mind," it is impossible to question one belief or concept or idea at a time if You would Realize.

The "Eureka," peripetia moment must happen, after which it is suddenly understood once and for all that it is all nonsense, all non-truth, all to be discarded. The truth cannot be stated, so to seek a version of truth that can be put into words is futile.

In the 50's as a child, the two days of the week when milk would be delivered to the front door of the home were anticipated. The homogenized milk came in tall bottles with several inches of heavy cream floating atop the milk.

Sometimes the cream would be poured over blackberries that had been gathered from along the sides of a nearby creek. Other times, the cream would be whipped, sugar would be added, and the whipped cream would be used as a topping on cake or ice cream that was served on rare occasions.

In every case, though, a separator was used to skim the cream and separate it from the milk, though both were to be kept and used. Similarly, the farmers in the family would have to separate the grains they grew from the chaff.

The grain would be kept and used while the chaff might be plowed into the soil to increase nutrients or might be used as fodder for their livestock. Those farmers also separated the hens from the rooster and the products from the hens was kept and used.

They churned their own butter and when drawn butter was occasionally called for, they used a separator to keep what they wanted to keep and to divide it away from the rest. When making a gravy, they also used a separator to split off the fat. Time and again, things were separated and one or both parts were kept and used.

The problem that is encountered by most seekers who begin this "journey" is that they will try to use the same approach at the second of seven steps although they have been invited to purge all of the contents of the "mind"; instead, they will cling to the belief that "surely the contents of the mind should be separated into two groups and that some parts are to be kept and used while others parts are to be selectively separated and discarded."

They believe that, as in the cases mentioned above, they can use a filter or a separator when it comes to "the mind," convinced that surely some parts are worthy or worthwhile and should be kept and used.

Unlike the cases dealing with milk and cream, grains and chaff, as well as gravy and fat or butter, there are no parts of the "mind" that should be kept and used after other parts have been separated out and discarded.

If the contents of the "mind" were likened to the items mentioned above, all of the content of your "mind" have soured and must be tossed; all of the content amounts to nothing more than chaff; all of the content is fat instead of gravy. There is nothing to be kept and used.

If the discarding of belief in all concepts has not been accomplished fully, then it explains why many believe that they are farther along the "path" than they truly are. They believe they have Realized or have almost Realized but they are really still at the second of seven steps. Then, they complain about "having it" but then "losing it."

To reject belief in what you know to be a lie is sound and sane and logical and reasonable. But the "Catch-22" is this: if "the mind" remains, it will prevent being sound and sane and logical and reasonable.

It will prevent differentiation between the true and the false because it filters or separates out everything that is heard which is contrary to its contents—to what it believes.

So with that restriction, what possible chance is there to be free of the "mind"? The key lies in this Advaitin pointer which is shared with some other teachings such as the Dao De Jing (Tao Te Ching) as well: the truth cannot be stated. Truth can be known during the manifestation, but it cannot be told.

That means that everything you have ever been told, which includes specifically all of the concepts and ideas and beliefs that currently form your/"their" fiction-filled "mind" must be false. Everything that you have ever been told that was said to be the truth really forms a large body of non-truths.

Some things told can point You toward the truth, but nothing told can be the truth; therefore, if you would be free, You must Realize that. If You discard all of the contents of the "mind," then You might also Realize THAT.

CHAPTER THIRTEEN

MAYBE the drop has dissolved into the ocean, but has the ocean yet rushed into the drop? If so, then the next question must be: after the drop dissolved into the ocean and after the ocean rushed into the drop, did both the ocean and the drop eventually dissolve as well?

THE IMPURITY OF FOLLOWING THE "I AM" WITH ANY WORD, Part A

A visitor said: People should be told that there should be no rush to Realize. The fact that I am patient ended up being valuable. Edward

FROM ONE WOMAN OVERHEARD IN A STORE: "I'm suffering right now but we're praying more than ever. All of this seems to have opened us up more to receive God." The response from the woman she was talking to: "Hang in there. Your suffering now is going to earn you a big reward later on."

HEARD IN SATSANG: My suffering was all worthwhile 'cause now I am helpful to others who are suffering."

FROM A VISITOR: I must be doing something right. I am more peaceful than I've ever been in my life.

FROM A MAN ATTENDING A WORKSHOP ON PERSONALITY: I think my personality is an asset...I am an achiever because of it."

At a certain point, Advaitin seekers might be admonished to focus on the "I AM" only. As long as the "mind" is the most influential factor during the relative existence of the non-Realized, then thoughts will drive words and words will drive deeds.

To think, "I am [insert a noun]" or to think, "I am [insert an adjective]" then the "mind" and thoughts and personas behind those thoughts and words will assure that Realization cannot happen.

In the early stages of "the journey," of course the seeker that says he/she has no peace will hear about peace; seekers feeling trapped will hear about freedom;

the seeker trapped in self-criticism for not fixating in the natural state but fluctuating throughout the day instead might be urged to be patient.

But none of that has anything to do with Truth. In the statements above, WHO is reporting on certain relative conditions? WHO (that is, what false persona) is being reinforced, often by the extolling of his/her "virtues")? WHO is, in effect, making the claims that…"I am a patient person," "I am a sufferer," "I am a helper," "I am a peaceful person," or "I am an achiever"? To the seeker that "found Advaita a few days ago" and asks, "Are you peaceful—can I be peaceful too," the answer at that point can be in the affirmative.

Later, as that same seeker nears the end of "the path," a level-appropriate question might result in a different understanding by the seeker. At that point, the seeker might be asked, "WHO (that is, which ego-state) is making a claim that she/he is peaceful?"

Can energy be at peace as long as there is any identification with the consciousness or with an assumed role? If seekers hear one extolling "the high level of peacefulness that he/she has attained," is it not obvious that some ego-state has been assumed and that there is a thought that is generating those words? And mustn't the thought have something to do with that braggart's "self-concept"?

If one is touting the level of patience attained, is not some identity instigating that claim? Of course Edward is far from alone in touting self and concepts and thus self-concepts. It happens trillions of times per day on the planet. In the East, many tout as an asset the concept of naixim or Nai Xim to use one Chinese word for "patience." Yet "assets" and "liabilities" are merely aspects of personality.

Here, there is no one who has any assets; nor is there anyone here who has liabilities. Yes, persons or seekers who come here speak of the peacefulness, of feeling comfortable, of this or that. But in effect, there is no one here to be peaceful or not, comfortable or not, a helper or not, a hope-giver or not. There is just the beingness for now, but abidance is not even happening as the beingness.

"Surely," it has been asked in satsang sessions, "you are not going to devalue the notion of patience, are you?" The answer is, "Yes." Look at the effects of making claims about being peaceful or helpful or patient:

Ancient dogma taught in the Mideast asserted that "The lord is wonderfully good to those who wait for him and seek him" which served as the basis of a proverb, "Good things come to those who wait";

Of course, that concept is part of the programming and dogma disseminated by organized religions that leave billions of persons each day in a "waiting mode," waiting for their prayers to be answered…and waiting…and waiting… and waiting.

All misery and suffering is associated in one way or another with a fear or a desire, specifically a fear or a desire taken to be real by a persona. Patience does not eliminate either fears or desires. Patience perpetuates wanting and, therefore, perpetuates a sense of longing or disappointment or dread or suffering.

Patience will keep persons from questioning and from seeking other possibilities. Patience will trap them in the ego-states that result after being programmed to wait and being conditioned to "just be patient."

In the West, patience is given lip service, especially among Christians and members of "self-help" groups…patience being a concept which the personas claiming membership in those groups often endorse but rarely practice. The Truth cannot be stated, so anything given lip service is most assuredly false.

All notions and concepts will be devalued here. Patience is merely one-half of a dualistic pair, namely, patient : impatient. It is not unlike asset : liability. It is not unlike virtuous : debauched. It is not unlike peaceful : anxious. It's all duality, and it all traps persons in identifying with one or more assumed identities.

If you are claiming certain "positive traits" as a result of your religious or spiritual efforts and practices and disciplines, then the question to ask is "WHO is making such claims?"

CHAPTER FOURTEEN

MAYBE the drop has dissolved into the ocean, but has the ocean yet rushed into the drop? If so, then the next question must be: after the drop dissolved into the ocean and after the ocean rushed into the drop, did both the ocean and the drop eventually dissolve as well

THE IMPURITY OF FOLLOWING THE "I AM" WITH ANY WORD, Part B

Review: If you are claiming certain "positive traits" as a result of your religious or spiritual efforts and practices and disciplines, then the question to ask is "WHO is making such claims?"

A visitor asked: Peaceful – does that count?

The reply: Peaceful counts relatively speaking (yet have You considered this: in the end, WHO is peaceful vs. who is anxious)?

The visitor: So who? The Advaitin. The One Without Attachments. The Wise One. The One Who is Unruffled by Events in the Relative – including deadlines. The Recluse. Yes – so here is a Someone with an Attribute: peacefulness.

[Note how "peaceful" follows the "I am" construct. Note too the way she realizes that "peaceful" is a descriptor, a trait, a characteristic and sees that descriptors are all personal…all about a person and not at all applicable to a quantity of energy.] She continues: If I look more closely at the "peacefulness," I see it masks a variety of old programmed "anxious" behaviours: nail biting, forgetfulness, over-eating. Usual deadline pressure stuff.

In fact is this really peaceful at all? Is it just that irritability, panic, self-criticism, self-pity and being reactive with others under stress (old anxious behaviours that seldom show up any longer) are absent from the mix? It "feels" peaceful, but perhaps what I call "peacefulness" could actually be described as "anxiety". Just depends what benchmark is used.

I am starting to "get" that non-duality means … um … well …. non duality. Why then, do You talk about joy or sweetness – aren't these dualistic terms?

The reply: Excellent question, and yes, those are dualistic terms, level-appropriate for some seekers; now, it is time for You to move on beyond that level. Understand that the pointers in Your case are now being offered at a different "level," fitting for seekers that are as far along the "path" as You.

Conditions or states (sweetness, peace, patience, joy) are all attributes that can only (1) be thought to have been "experienced" by persons or that can (2) be known by a knower. And in either case, that is happening only during the relative manifestation. Too, they often inspire denial, such as, "I'm so advanced along the 'path to peace' that none of this is affecting me."

"The Religious One" and/or "The Spiritual One" ego-states can generate misery while inspiring a claim that their dogma or practices are providing peace, thinking their "journey" into the (day) light has led them to noontime when it is really only dawn for them.

Seekers seek sweetness and peace and patience and joy and some few find them, but what they have found is all a part of the relative, and what is known is known via the manifested consciousness. Since the consciousness is ever-moving, then the seeker that knows sweetness and peace and patience and joy at times will also know bitterness, disharmony, impatience, and misery at other times.

A visitor said: You're wrong about the mind and you're wrong about seeking pleasure. Maharaj asked what's wrong with the mind seeking the pleasant and avoiding the unpleasant. He said "Between the banks of pain and pleasure the river of life flows." Michael

No disputing that Maharaj said that to one particular seeker, Michael; however, if you read the entire transcript of that talk, rather than one extracted quote, you would see that Maharaj eventually offered a different set of pointers to that same seeker.

You would see that the same seeker's questions and comments revealed that he might be ready for an understanding available to those farther along the "path" then Maharaj's first assessment. If you review the transcript, you would see that M.'s later pointers changed from the one that you are quoting. He said, "Desire is the memory of pleasure, and fear is the memory of pain. Both make the mind restless. Moments of pleasure are merely gaps in the stream of pain. How can the mind be happy?" Later, he added, "…Joy is joy only against a background of pain."

Then, even later he pointed out that "…pleasure and pain are all in the mind. The Self stands beyond the mind, aware, but unconcerned." In due course, he taught: "Pain is the background of all your pleasures. You want them because you suffer. On the other hand, the very search for pleasure is the cause of pain. It is a vicious circle."

You have been told here that whatever gives pleasure will surely give pain. You have been told that whatever gives the greatest pleasure will surely give the greatest pain. Many persons believe that is enough…that it is worth putting up with such fluctuations and tolerating pain in order to have some pleasure. So it is. Others will minimize the frustration of constant seeking and flux and chaos, even justifying the "negative" by upgrading the "positive."

Some have written here to say the nisarga yoga is all wrong, that their yoga is right for it has led to bliss now and will assure eternal bliss as well. Though Easterners, their belief systems have a rather Baptist or Presbyterian ring to them.

It matters not if your "god of bliss" is imagined to look like a corpulent elephant or like old man Zeus, the key word here is "imagined." The reality is that neither bliss nor misery will be known post-manifestation. The unmanifested consciousness will merely be absorbed into the pool of awareness that is not aware of anything. There will be neither bliss nor misery, neither reward not punishment.

Furthermore, the paradox is that those states of peace and joy and sweetness—once known—are (A) fleeting and thus frustrating and (B) are capable of making the opposite, former states all the more miserable when revisited. Then, seekers write to complain, "I'm sick of all of this 'I've got it—I've lost it—I've got it—I've lost it' cycling."

Only being free of the knowing, the known, and the knower does the fluctuating end. Persons/the non-Realized will never know sweetness, peace, patience, joy; some seekers will know those, and will then take those as indicators that they have reached the end of the "path"; yet they will still experience the annoying fluctuations if not abiding as the natural, original state. In that awareness that is not aware of abidance, then happenings associated with "the Am-ness mode" will actually be rooted in "the THAT-ness mode." Then, there will be no claims about any attributes or traits or characteristics—all of which are aligned with personality.

Now, all that said, the paradox is that when Reality is overlaid on the Am-ness, joy or pleasure can happen NOW without any notion that there is an

experiencer, without any of the constant fluctuations that mark the manifestation, and without any return to the no-joy misery state—an all-relative state that
cannot be registered in the awareness that is not aware of state.

The stability of the THAT state becomes overlaid on the otherwise unstable
Am-ness state. Further, just because Reality is overlaid on the Am-ness does not
mean that I—this consciousness—am not at One with your pain, with your
suffering, with the anguish and affliction that mark the existence of so many
persons on the planet.

This awareness after the At-one-ment is understood and after Real Love
manifests is what moves this space to take the morning's cup of cappuccino to an
in-house office each morning, is what moves this space to sit before a screen, and
is what determines which keys are spontaneously struck.

And if you should reach a point along the "path" before Full Realization
happens, and if at that point you write (as many seekers do) to describe a level of
freedom that has, in turn, generated what most certainly seems to be a sense of
joy or bliss, then this space will nod…yes.

Chapter Fifteen

MAYBE the drop has dissolved into the ocean, but has the ocean yet rushed into the drop? If so, then the next question must be: after the drop dissolved into the ocean and after the ocean rushed into the drop, did both the ocean and the drop eventually dissolve as well?

THE IMPURITY OF FOLLOWING THE "I AM" WITH ANY WORD, Part C

A visitor said: I'm finally understanding my mom's behavior to some degree. She is in her late sixties, dating a man with a history of abusing women. She admires him because he is a preacher, even though he recently put her in the hospital. Now, she has gone back to him. I looked at what you've written about personality and see she's a type two who thinks she HAS to be in a relationship – has always been searching for love. I know what you say about pain and pleasure is right on. And you are also right in that she is willing to accept all the pain to get a little pleasure. I might try to discuss this with her, but I doubt she'd change. Thanks at least for helping me and my sisters to understand a little more about why she is doing what she is doing.

The reply: One of your references is evidently to the pointer offered earlier that most of the non-Realized believe "…it is worth putting up with such fluctuations and tolerating pain in order to have some pleasure." Your mother's behavior illustrates the pointer exactly. Driven by personality, she will tolerate a hundred pounds of pain to receive an ounce of pleasure. That is common among the non-Realized, in fact, typical. Many will conclude that she is insane, but what she is doing is more likely the result of personality and its subsequent personality disorders. You have provided visitors with a concrete example of the way that these "supposedly theoretical" teachings really do reflect what is happening in the relative when personality is directing the play. Now, the discussion of the concept of "patience" will continue, even as the visitor above also provides a pointer about patience as well, the woman being quite patient with her abusive partner.

If you claim "I am patient," you will be impatient at times as well. Why? Because a person (meaning one with a belief in a "personal I") is guaranteed to be in a constant state of flux.

When one is in a constant state of flux and also claiming that she/he is patient, then impatience will be guaranteed to follow. As noted in other postings, to be patient is to be waiting, and to be waiting is to be wanting or expecting; and to be wanting or expecting will trigger periods of being impatient.

The concept of "being patient" also results in ignoring the only "real time" there is (NOW) and causes non-Realized persons to give credibility to the illusory "future." As a result, no peace or contentment can happen. Consider this specific example:

During a seminar with employees of a business that uses enneagram results for hiring and for development of staff, it was seen that seven of the employees were Personality Type Threes.

Threes focus on success and achievement, historically ignoring the now and concentrating instead on their long-range financial goals, which they can always express in exact, concrete amounts of currency.

When asked about the amount, a Three will not require so much as a second for contemplation since they have already determined the exact amount of money that, once accumulated, will be evidence of having achieved "success" in their "minds."

When each Three was told, "Your type always has a specific dollar amount in mind, an amount that you believe will indicate you are a success and which will allow you to finally enjoy your life. What is your amount"?

Without a second's hesitation, the numbers came: "$1,000,000; $10,000,000; $12,000,000; $50,000,000; $100,000,000; $500,000,000; and $900,000,000." (The latter explained, proudly touting his humility, that "only arrogant people would say they have to be 'a billionaire' to be happy." Yes, that is an example of distortion, sleepwalking, delusion, and many other factors that mark the relative existence of persons.) When asked about the odds of ever accumulating such sums, they all spoke of "being patient" and of "persevering" (though Three's are one of the least patient of the nine basic personas).

Interestingly, nearly three years ago, the man who cited "$12,000,000" as his magic number had reported that $1,000,000 was the goal. When asked about the change, he said that he "was getting close to a million and that he always raises his goals and sets new ones if he is about to reach an old goal."

Do you see the trap among those assuming the ego-state of "The Super Achiever" and among other persons with the same thought-life, claiming "patience" and "perseverance" until they reach their goal someday?

First, they are removed from living in the now. Secondly, if they achieve their goal, then their identity of "The Achiever" would end since there would be nothing more to achieve, so their goals and magic number must always be a moving target...always being moved out of reach.

Note the Catch-22: if they are to sustain the false identity of "The Achiever" or "The Performer," they must never achieve their goals. The most that can happen in this scenario is they "get close to" a goal. In the process, therefore, they guarantee that they will never experience a sense of fulfillment.

Their "patience," which drives them to keep plugging away day in and day out (and to keep waiting for their goals to be met someday with their belief that "all good things come to those who wait") assures that they will always feel the frustration of unmet desires; of unreachable goals and expectations; of a constantly-increasing sense of self-worth and an overly-inflated value of self; and the subsequent arrogance that shows up often with that type.

Another contradiction with that paradigm is that freedom becomes dependent. Its manifestation depends on giving up any and all concepts, including the ones that some cultures teach are the "good" ones (such as "patience") because they are a setup for duality—which is, in turn, a setup for feeling empty, incomplete or confused.

To accept the concept of patience as truth is to suggest that there is someone who can be patient. For every "asset" that persons assume, they reinforce a sense of separation; they believe they recognize the opposing "liability" in others; and that bolsters a sense of better-than-ness.

It's all duality, and all duality is false.

Chapter Sixteen

MAYBE the drop has dissolved into the ocean, but has the ocean yet rushed into the drop? If so, then the next question must be: after the drop dissolved into the ocean and after the ocean rushed into the drop, did both the ocean and the drop eventually dissolve as well?

THE IMPURITY OF FOLLOWING THE "I AM" WITH ANY WORD, Part D

ONE WOMAN OVERHEARD IN A STORE: "I'm suffering right now but we're praying more than ever. All of this seems to have opened us up more to receive God." The response from the woman she was talking to: "Hang in there. Your suffering now is going to earn you a big reward later on."

The non-Realized attach to the liabilities generated by their personalities. Seekers who have completed a part of the "journey" and have assumed identities such as "The Religious One" or "The Very Spiritual One" attach to the assets associated with those roles.

Yet all liabilities and assets are nothing more than personality traits and are therefore illusions. The Fully Realized, freed from all personal identity, make no claims about assets or liabilities.

You might as well lean across a countertop in your kitchen, put your mouth near an electrical outlet, and ask the energy if it was "good" or "bad" yesterday, if it has been "patient" or "impatient" today, if it plans on being "moral" or "immoral" tomorrow.

You might as well whisper into the wall outlet and tell the energy that you think it has been very helpful, the way it participated in preparing pancakes that morning by operating the mixer. In fact, the energy is merely being. There is no do-er that is deciding to do or not do anything. The energy did not "think through" a set of options and make a decision to operate a mixer or not.

If certain actions by persons on the planet resulted in that energy being involved with some event (such as functioning with a coffee pot in the morning and with a blender later in the day) it all happened spontaneously, without thought on the part of the energy.

Thoughts can only happen if a "mind" has been formed. If those thoughts are expressed via words, then soon they will generate some action. In the process, a person thought some thought, a persona expressed the words, and then the persona became convinced that it is real and that it is a do-er and that it is doing something and that it choose to do that.

In fact, it has been shared often that everything labeled a "problem" is centered in the "mind." The "mind" is no more a benefit than any of the "asset traits" assumed by personas.

A visitor said: Way back, You told me that if I knew what the mind was actually like, I would abandon it like an abusive spouse. That was a "tough love" pointer for "me" – it felt like having ice water dumped over my head – it was such a dramatic shock.

That pointer is occasionally recalled, and of course is now known to be completely true. The mind and mind-generated personas are so toxic, it seems unbelievable that the mind-body-personality construct was once called home – and was even believed to be remotely habitable. Interestingly, with this under-standing there is simply no possibility of going back. It is useful to witness the personality under stress simply for this verification I guess.

With a "mind" generating (always distorted) thoughts and with the prac-tice among the non-Realized of following the I AM with nouns and adjectives, then it is understandable (though totally illogical) that some persons have been programmed and conditioned to believe that "suffering" can be noble or beneficial.

Another visitor inquired about "floyd's" pre-Realization days, including behaviors and "relationships" and miseries and delusions and mind-generated suffering. This exchanged followed:

She: So much suffering. Exhausting. Do you agree with the idea that "suffering works"? Would you have been as intensely focused on the "search" if the ex had a more benign personality and there was greater relative calm and you had stayed together? Is there a sense - post-realization - that it had to be this way for "floyd"?

Floyd: No, suffering does not work, it being nothing more than a totally-unnecessary consequence of ego and egotism. As for anything hastening the movement along the path, the focus was there from "floyd's" very early days, even prior to elementary school. The tendency to question illogical nonsense was automatic after the basic personality was formed.

No external impetus is required for one "wired" to seek the Authentic Self. [Note: Among the few that will seek that Authentic Self, they will be miserable if It is not found, and they can be at perfect peace if It is. How many on the planet develop during childhood the personality type that automatically seeks Self? One-half of one percent.]

Nor did it have to be the way it was, but it was that way as a result of programming and acculturation. As for still being together with the "ex," we never were together. It was all image and distortion, and all over the world tonight, people claiming to be "married to each other" or "in a relationship together" will actually share only a roof in common; therefore, they will be very much alone, and the few that understand that can have all the company imaginable, along with solitude and peace. It has been noted: 'Tis better to be alone and free than to be in prison with company.

In that regard, Thoreau (who spoke of a "unity beyond the multiplicity," who was "wired" to seek the Authentic Self, and who—even though not fully Realized—did have considerable pieces of the understanding) said something that many seekers will understand completely: "I have a great deal of company in the house, especially in the morning when nobody calls."

That said, did all of that misery and suffering allow the manifestation of an understanding of the roots of suffering as well as an empathy for seekers? Sure.

There is no one lost in personality that is not understood from "floyd's experiences"; the most asleep visitor here is no more asleep than was "floyd"; and no one that is so lost in the distortions of his/her culture that they reach a point where they can no longer tolerate their very existence are any sicker than "floyd" was, relatively speaking.

Does that mean some "good" came of the suffering? No. Does it mean anyone is being helped ultimately? No. There are no "ones" to help. There is merely the spontaneous flow that determines what is shared.

And that sharing happens, without agenda or motive or hope, but with an awareness that maybe the suffering of persons might be slightly mitigated for the time that all those specks are manifested and trying to negotiate the relative existence.

But it's all just happening naturally, just as with the deer that came and went last night when "floyd" was out of corn and just as the deer will come tonight and eat...now that the corn is restocked.

(And last night they had no thoughts about "floyd being inconsiderate" and tonight there will be no thoughts about "floyd actually being a really nice guy after all. " Their peace happens because of their mind-less, thought-less condition which preempts any ability to think or judge or separate from or cling to.)

Too, suffering is only optional for those about the Realize. Once Realized, suffering cannot manifest since it can only happen when the prerequisites for suffering (namely, body, mind, and personality identification) are assumed.

For all persons (the non-Realized), suffering is mandatory. For those programmed with dogma, they will actually upgrade the concept of "suffering" and "put a spin on the facts" (that is, distort the facts involved with their relative existence).

As a result, they will assign value to suffering, will expect to be reward eternally "later on" for their suffering, will ennoble their suffering, and will even claim that they are now able to be "The Helper"—almost immediately upgraded to "The Super Helper"—as a result of their suffering. And it is those who have adopted a religious and/or spiritual persona that most often engage in such distortion.

CHAPTER SEVENTEEN

MAYBE the drop has dissolved into the ocean, but has the ocean yet rushed into the drop? If so, then the next question must be: after the drop dissolved into the ocean and after the ocean rushed into the drop, did both the ocean and the drop eventually dissolve as well?

THE IMPURITY OF FOLLOWING THE "I AM" WITH ANY WORD, Part D, Conclusion

Reconsider: For those programmed with dogma, they will actually upgrade the concept of "suffering" and "put a spin on the facts" (that is, distort the facts involved with their relative existence).

Suffering is held in high esteem by billions of non-Realized, religious persons on the planet. The religious endorse suffering, suggesting that it should only be seen in the most "positive" light. Advaitins, by contrast, offer a "path" by which much of it can end.

Not only is suffering tolerated by the billions of religious and ideological persons but it is also elevated in status alongside certain other dogma-based concepts such as "obedience" and "bending to god's will" and "making sacrifices of time and money and service in order to please god."

That which is tolerated will continue, and that which is held in esteem by persons will most assuredly persist. So how has it evolved that the concept of suffering can be considered a "positive thing" and believed by the masses to be something to not only endure but to also be seen as "lofty"?

It's easy to understand once it is seen that, currently, billions of persons unquestionably accept the concepts and beliefs that are spread via the three sky cults that evolved from the words of Abraham and that, historically, trillions have done the same. The Jews assigned positive connotations to suffering; Christianity, with its Judaeo roots and continuing attachment to Jewish teachings, elevated suffering (via their "Passion of the Christ" tale) to a level of worth that will likely never be surpassed; and the Muslims add physical suffering to their mental and emotional suffering during their parades when self-flagellating men pick up maces and chains and metal spikes and beat themselves until the blood flows.

All three sky cults, in fact, are preoccupied not only with mental-emotional suffering but with blood-letting as well since their roots are in the pagan cults that cut the beating hearts from virgins and drank the blood and ate the body in order to appease the angry gods. "Sacrifice" and "suffer" are the marching orders for the members of all three cults.

So the Jews pushed the concepts of cutting the throats of sheep and of making sacrifice and of spreading blood above doorways to prevent a stopover by the angel of death; the Christians display their Christ with blood streaming from the head and hands and sides and feet and they drink weekly what they claim is his blood; and Muslims shed their own blood as some among them are also bent on shedding the blood of "infidels."

Is it any wonder that a Google search of "Jews" + "suffering" results in 4,700,000 hits? Is it any wonder that Christians—modeling themselves after "the one who suffered more than any other…and all for us"—now give suffering such eminence? Here are some quotes from a Christian site that reinforces the value of suffering for its followers:

"An important part of Christian living and spiritual growth is suffering"; "It is a startling fact that part of God's plan for every human being includes a certain amount of suffering"; "Suffering of some kind is part of God's Plan of Grace, if you can imagine that"; "God intends, as part of His Plan, for suffering to awaken the unbeliever to the reality of the existence of God";

"Whatever the immediate cause of his suffering, the ultimate reason is that of directing his attention to the person of Jesus Christ"; and "Only He can decide what combination of blessing and suffering is the best recipe for encouraging a person to become a Christian."

What sane and sound and logical adult would be attracted to such teachings? Is it understood why most now claiming membership in those cults had to have been enrolled and indoctrinated during childhood…before any ability to question "authority" or nonsense could manifest?

Is it any wonder, then, that so many on the globe not only tolerate suffering but also elevate its status? Expanding the widespread acceptance of suffering are those sleepwalkers whose ego and egotism inspire the claim that "my past suffering has been given great value now since it empowers me to help others who are suffering."

I tell you, and invite You to realize, that to follow the I AM with the word "suffering" (or to spin the facts and suggest dualistically that suffering is a "good" thing) is no different from any other distortion that is rooted in the nonsense of duality.

You need not suffer, but you most assuredly will unless you reject belief in any and all of the many illogical and insane concepts that are so widely esteemed among the non-Realized masses.

CHAPTER EIGHTEEN

MAYBE the drop has dissolved into the ocean, but has the ocean yet rushed into the drop? If so, then the next question must be: after the drop dissolved into the ocean and after the ocean rushed into the drop, did both the ocean and the drop eventually dissolve as well?

THE IMPURITY OF ALLOWING THE DECEIVED MIND TO BLOCK NISARGA (NATURAL) LIVING, Part A

In the book "The Creative Magician's Handbook," Marvin Kaye wrote: "The expert magician seeks to deceive the mind, rather than the eye."

It could also be said, "The experts at controlling seek to deceive the mind, rather than the eye." Have you considered how many persons during your childhood, and now how many during your adulthood, could be said to have that role as a job description..."Expert at Control over you"?

Parents, teachers, relatives, police, judges, friends, spouses, politicians, an imaginary god or gods...the list is endless, but of all who want to control every facet of every person's life—including control over every relative thought that is thought and over every word spoken and over every deed done—none can compare with those involved in religious and spiritual movements.

Cults have always been led by those claiming magical powers: "I can make it rain" or "I can assure that you'll receive an eternal reward and eternal life" or "I can say some magic words and via an act of transubstantiation, I can really make this wine turn into blood and I can really make this bread turn into human body" (though which body part is being eaten during that ceremony has never been identified).

Magic. Bread or crackers to human flesh. Magic. Water to wine, wine to blood, blood to drink, and around and around and around the wheel of nonsense turns. Magic. All of their claims are magical, and magicians would deceive your mind rather than your eye. So the eye is not deceived in their magical acts, including transubstantiation.

The "newly-created blood" still looks like wine to the eye; the "newly-created" body still looks like bread or crackers to the eye. No, it is the case among believers that what is really deceived is the "mind." That is why the Realized Advaitin makes clear that all beliefs must go. They are all deceptions, stored now in your "mind."

Admitting that no one has ever seen their god or gods, then, of course, they cannot deceive by the eye. They must deceive the mind, and to deceive the mind, they must assign magical (a.k.a., "supernatural") significance to natural or unnatural relative events. In that manner, they can actually convince people that they are seeing a miracle unfold, that they are seeing the hand of god at work, etc. Yet even that is a deception rooted in the "mind."

Some examples can be offered from recent visitors. One illustration offered was a comment made to a father whose child was killed the week before by a drunk driver: "There's some reason god had for taking your little angel."

In that case, a magical explanation was overlaid on the relative event, suggesting to a grieving father that "his daughter was killed by supernatural means rather than by a unnatural event" which is played out regularly in a culture that assigns more value to the right to drink (and drive) than the right to live.

Another example was provided via a quotation from the Dalai Lama in regards to why hurricanes (which are naturally-occurring events) follow the paths that they follow. According to his belief system, "Katrina hit New Orleans because of the bad karma of the people there."

The path had nothing to do with water temperatures, wind patterns, other weather systems, etc. It went where it went because some power in the universe had targeted for destruction a specific city and all of its bad-karma residents, so he would have you believe.

When the truly wise speak, wisdom can be recognized by the fact that only a small part of the population will ever understand their words. When the truly ignorant speak, their nonsense can be recognized by the fact that the masses will agree.

So, it has been seen that—in order to give their tales even more cred-ibility—it is the goal of the magician-minister-priest-imam-rabbi to try to make persons believe that they have indeed "seen" something magical or spiritual or supernatural.

When two women in a Texas church both had strokes that week, the "prayer chain" was activated. That means one member would call ten and say, "Mrs. X just had a stroke. Pray for her. Pass it on." Then, those ten would call ten and within an hour, hundreds would be praying for Mrs. X" or, as in this case, "the Mesdames X's."

The following Sunday, the minister stood before the congregation and tried to convince the members that they had indeed seen a miracle that week—had seen magic performed right there in the church.

"As a result of the prayer chain that I established when I first came here," he bragged, "Mrs. X"(#1) is on her way to a full recovery. You have seen the power of prayer." He did not mention that "Mrs. X"(#2) had died on Tuesday and that he had officiated at her funeral on Friday, the benefits of his prayer chain having manifested only at a rate of 50%.

Like the people who heard those words and nodded their heads in agreement with nonsense, most persons worldwide show up regularly at what they take to be "special services" or "special meetings" in order to have their conditioning and programming reinforced.

Yet, really, a person once programmed and conditioned and acculturated and domesticated does not require such weekly reinforcement to cling to magical thinking processes. The ego—supported by a host of ego-defense mechanisms—will function on auto-pilot to block any chance of knowing Truth.

A few persons, beaten down as a result of (A) a host of self-destructive and self-defeating acts that are driven by personality disorders or as a result of (B) being re-programmed by a "self-help" group, might come to an admission that "I am powerless."

If they remain under the influence of those new programmers, they will even conclude, "OK—now I'm close to god so I really do have power." Only the few that complete the "journey" to Full Realization come to understand that…

…there is no one who can have power; that…

…there is no one, once Realized, that has the slightest concern about power; that…

…there is no such thing as a person so there is no personal power; that…

…there is no other-world power that would control your thoughts and words and deeds; that…

…there is no power that has a list of things you must not do if you would avoid eternal agony; and that…

FLOYD HENDERSON

...there is no personal god so...

...there is no such thing as supernatural power or magical happenings or cases where the hand of a god can be seen to insert himself/herself into any relative happening.

All is merely happening, and it will either happen naturally if Realized or will unfold unnaturally or magically if still functioning under the auspices of those who deceived your "mind."

If that is understood, then the discussion tomorrow might point a twenty-six year old man to a place of freedom that lies beyond the angst that is now manifesting because a priest deceived his "mind."

How? A priest told him as a lad that a totally natural happening is really "an unnatural act that so displeases his god that the activity will assure that he shall be sent into the flames of hell for eternity if he does not avoid touching himself... forever."

Again, once programmed, especially with dogma, the mess can last for an entire manifestation without any reinforcement from anything other than a deceived "mind."

CHAPTER NINETEEN

MAYBE the drop has dissolved into the ocean, but has the ocean yet rushed into the drop? If so, then the next question must be: after the drop dissolved into the ocean and after the ocean rushed into the drop, did both the ocean and the drop eventually dissolve as well?

THE IMPURITY OF ALLOWING THE DECEIVED MIND TO BLOCK NISARGA (NATURAL) LIVING, Part B

Please review this which was offered earlier: In the book "The Creative Magician's Handbook," Marvin Kaye wrote: "The expert magician seeks to deceive the mind, rather than the eye." It could also be said, "The experts at controlling seek to deceive the mind, rather than the eye."

To see a mirage as a mirage and to discount it because it is nothing more than a mirage is to avoid being deceived by the eye. To know a mirage is a mirage is sane and sound and logical. To realize that anyone claiming that she/he has magical/supernatural powers and to realize that the claim is just an attempt to deceive the mind, then realizing that, too, is sane and sound and logical.

For a mind to be formed during childhood years and to be deceived in a way that it believes all of the magical, supernatural nonsense that is unquestioningly accepted as truth by billions on the planet is understandable; for an adult to continue to believe in childish, supernatural magical things is not sane or sound or logical.

Clinging to the "mind"—which is "their mind," really—is also insane, unsound and illogical. "Because I told you so" or "Because god said so" are the least rational reasons to accept any statements as being statements of truth. Be not deceived via the mind or the eyes. Question. Awake. See Reality.

Know the Truth that cannot be stated, and know that would-be magicians who would deceive your mind assume a variety of roles and labels, including "a priest," "a preacher," "a spiritual guide," "a medicine man," "a rabbi," "a sponsor," "a self-proclaimed guru," or "a teacher."

Then understand that if any of those role-players / magicians tell you that they can express in words the truth (or any number of truths) then You will know that they are trying to use their magical thinking and their supernatural (that is, "not-natural") teachings to try to deceive your mind. And they are most adept at what they do because they actually believe some of what they say.

Fall under the spell of their magical thinking and their supernatural (that is, "not-natural") teachings and the relative existence will unfold in a most unnatural way for you, as is the circumstance with the young man who wrote and revealed that he is totally frustrated and confused and uptight and repressed. (That is his circumstance because his priest deceived his mind).

Now at the age of twenty-six, he is seeking some view that is contrary to the one he has accepted from the priest/magician in his life who has told him that he will go to hell if he engages in such natural acts as masturbation or sexual relations or if he uses any protection against AIDS that would result in the mortal sin, in the suffer-in-hell-for-life-guaranteeing-sin, of "wasting the seed."

So that priest would rather the young man have unprotected sex and die than use protection that would "waste the seed" but allow him to live. And all the while, billions listen to talk about "not wasting the seed" without seeing that the driving force behind that institution's teachings in this regard is really to not waste any opportunity to increase their membership and income.

His magician has deceived his mind to such a degree that he now mistakes the natural for the unnatural. First, he was assured by My reply that he will have far more seeds than he'll ever be able to use. Next, it was suggested that in his case—as ready to explode as he is—that the wasting of a few seeds would not only be natural but that it just might also be freeing…but maybe not.

That "maybe not" is why it was also suggested that he may require professional counseling to get free of the plethora of anxiety-provoking beliefs which he has accepted from those who have deceived his mind and convinced him that the natural is unnatural and that the natural is prohibited by supernatural law.

Finally, it was suggested that he ask an impartial, non-judgmental counselor why he is still being driven by the mind that they deceived instead of asking, "Why am I told that I am supposed to actually eat his body but I am not supposed to even so much as touch my own."

Then, I as The Witness sat back after sending the reply to that young man and reflected on the relative circumstances of a male so young that is also so para-noid, so anxiety-driven, so fear-based, so brainwashed, so restricted, so limited, so imprisoned. Thus, the evidence has come again, and it serves once more as a reminder of how many among the masses have been made into fools by those who deceive the mind rather than the eye.

The focus here would be on inviting persons to reject belief in all of the concepts that imprison them; the focus here would be on inviting persons to take seven-steps to Full Realization and to know freedom...now; instead, the focus has been shifted to having to discuss one of the most basic and natural acts because magician-priests would have all believe that it is an unnatural act. May all of the nonsense that they dream up be damned.

Somewhat amazing, is it not, that a discussion of de-accumulation or non-identification or awareness or other topics must be set aside to tell a twenty-six-old man that he has permission to touch himself and that it would be quite natural if he were to do so?

Then, just when some might shout, "What in the hell have these discussions come to?!" a visitor named Ginny offered a reminder that freedom comes in stages and at varied levels and that this chap at twenty-six is as deserving of being free of the prison he's trapped in as "The Forty-Five Year Old Ex-Husband Who Wants to Die"; as "The Woman Whose Husband Brought Home an Incurable Disease" who wrote to ask how she can possibly go on; and as "The Investor Whose Savings Have All Been Stolen."

These teachings based in the nisarga (natural) yoga that speak of the freedom of the Nothingness and the no-concept, non-dual Reality are pulled back on occasion to address instead the most basic relative issues. Why?

Because of the lingering effects of the lies being presented as Truth by all those magician-priests-preachers-rabbis-imans-ayatollahs out there. (And most absurdly, it is one among that group of Catholic priests, with all of their abomi-nable history, who has the audacity to discuss who, or what, can or cannot be touched.)

Thus, so it is in the insane realm of the relative, but so it does not have to continue to be for the visitors here. Break those concept-chains that bind you... be free...enjoy...grab the bliss and guard it and relish it during the one and only instance in which you can...NOW.

Indeed, "a wave is happening." It is the wave being ridden by ginny, by louise, by andy, by dan, by andrew, and yes, by raja, too. And though seekers are making contact here from various locales and from every continent on the globe, they invite You to ride that one, same wave as well and to revel in the Oneness and the Love and the Bliss…now.

CHAPTER TWENTY

MAYBE the drop has dissolved into the ocean, but has the ocean yet rushed into the drop? If so, then the next question must be: after the drop dissolved into the ocean and after the ocean rushed into the drop, did both the ocean and the drop eventually dissolve as well?

THE IMPURITY OF ALLOWING THE DECEIVED MIND TO BLOCK NISARGA (NATURAL) LIVING, Part C, Conclusion

Several conclusions can be drawn from the information in Parts "A" and "B" of this topic: (1) the experts at controlling seek to deceive the mind, rather than the eye; (2) occasionally, however, they even try to deceive the eye, reporting that via this happening or that happening, you have actually "seen a miracle"; (3) to paraphrase Churchill, "Never in the field of human deception has so much been passed on to so many by so few" as has happened via religion and spirituality; (4) the ignorant, would-be controllers assign supernatural cause to natural events and the ignorant masses accept their explanations unquestioningly...the Dalai Lama not likely to have lost even one follower after claiming that it was bad karma which directed the path of Hurricane Katrina to New Orleans; (5) millions of persons are walking about who are totally frustrated and confused and uptight and repressed as a result of what they have been taught by religious or spiritual leaders; (6) most that will eventually seek Truth do not begin that journey until their forties, but occasionally one as young as twenty-six might reach such a point of misery that he is driven to undertake the quest; but more typically, (7) if you begin programming persons at a young enough age, they may never even consider questioning what they have accepted all along by faith alone.

Bill Maher, in his movie "Religulous," (a compression of "religion" and "ridiculous") says: "I'm here promoting doubt—that's my product. The other guys are selling certainty. Not me. I'm on the corner with doubt."

While not a student of the Advaita philosophy, his "path" has brought him at least to the point on the seven-step path to where he has transitioned the 3rd step as far as assumption of religious or spiritual roles are concerned.

However, the extreme pieties and moral convictions of the magician-priest class, when presented to so susceptible an audience as persons who are seeking continuity of body and mind and personality, are accepted as "the price that must be paid for salvation." Nonsense.

Yet the message offered by the magician-priest class or by their peers who are playing the role of "Spiritual Leaders," when served up with such ideological firmness and unfounded certainty, can most assuredly have a ring of validity for wishful, hopeful persons who are wanting and desiring the reward of eternal life and eternal bliss that those "leaders" promise.

Maharaj taught, "You have created a god because you want to beg from somebody and that is what you call spirituality." He said, "People worship so many gods, but these gods are only concepts which have occurred to the mind."

But how many billions are walking about with their hang-ups, refusing to enjoy the natural happenings that can be enjoyed because of priestly indoctrination or parental expectations? How many are being robbed, not just of 10% of their earnings but more significantly—relatively speaking—of Pleasure.

It was explained recently to a visitor that there are those pleasures that are sure to lead to pain, but once Love and Bliss and Joy manifest via Full Realization, there is a Pleasure that has no counterpart. The lies about "love" are rejected, (Real) Love is understood, Reality can be overlaid on the Am-ness, and unbounded Pleasures can happen.

Those will be the only opportunities for any bliss to be known. Post-manifestation, there will be no one to know or to enjoy (or to suffer) anything. Such Pleasure can manifest when Love is understood, when Love is Shown as Reality is overlaid on the Am-ness, and when the Noumenal Oneness is thereafter adumbrated in acts of phenomenal oneness.

Further, these Sense-of-Being-Filled-Happenings can also occur while standing on a mountaintop and knowing the sensation of ecstasy generated by the beauty of a sunset that is bathing the entire horizon with Fall-like colors; when a group of Advaitins Realize fully and then dance this dance as One; or when they ride as One upon the wave of Unicity and Bliss and Joy.

Note, though, that none of that can be understood and none of that can manifest unless the last vestige of the effects of "their" programming and conditioning and acculturation and domestication are discarded. If not removed, then those effects will guarantee a relative existence that is marked by an inability to "let loose" completely; by an incapacity to be truly free; by a failure to have understood prior to the Unmanifestation the unlimited and unreserved and unrestricted No-Counterpart Bliss; and by a lack of ability to be free of the last barrier resulting from programming, the barrier that blocks the ability to share the deepest Intimacy and intimacy that is shared among the Realized when Reality is overlaid onto happenings during their Is-ness.

There are those who would tell you to deny yourself, even though they, in their closeted lives, deny themselves nothing. There are those who will fill your mind with dreams of immortality and who will tell you that it can be achieved if you will but sacrifice for, and beg of, their god or gods.

There are those who will inspire you to stop the seven-step "journey" to Full Realization and abide at the third level as "The Religious One," "The Saint," "The Purest One," or "The Spiritual One." They will program and condition you to "worship so many gods" while blinding you to the fact that those gods "are only concepts which have occurred to the mind."

They will leave you totally frustrated and confused and uptight and repressed and deprived unless you question it all, unless You see their lies as lies, unless You see the resultant deprivation and limitations as they mark and mar your relative existence, and unless You cast it all aside.

This is your invitation to begin the "journey" to full freedom and Love and Bliss by undertaking the pre-step to the first of seven steps. That pre-step is a willingness to question objectively all of the magical thinking that has been required for you to buy into their magical (a.k.a., supernatural) explanations and tales and teachings.

To be able to take the pre-step, the ego-states and egotism that have convinced you that you "know" and that you are too intelligent to have been fooled must be discarded. What you know is learned ignorance. What you can know is within, but you must remove the barriers that block the consciousness from knowing what You know and have always known.

Then, the "attachment" to the content of the "mind" that was filled with deceptions by the magician-controllers with all of those false teachings can be discarded and you can then move along the "path" and eventually realize the Truth that You have always known.

CHAPTER TWENTY-ONE

MAYBE the drop has dissolved into the ocean, but has the ocean yet rushed into the drop? If so, then the next question must be: after the drop dissolved into the ocean and after the ocean rushed into the drop, did both the ocean and the drop eventually dissolve as well?

THE IMPURITY OF BELIEVING ANY BELIEF, INCLUDING THE BELIEF THAT YOU WERE BORN AND WILL DIE, Part A

[Caution: If you are among those who believe your parents must have been pretty damn effective and pretty damn wise—looking, of course, at the way you turned out—then you'll either want to avoid reading this section or at least buckle your seat belt to prepare for might be a rocky ride of some ego-states.]

Did your parents ever celebrate your birthday? Then they do not know that you were not born and they do not know that you were not created and they do not have a clue about how elements took on the appearance of "you."

They do not know how babies are "made" or what the process is whereby elements are transformed from plant cells into other type cells. They do not understand that an act of friction is merely transferring energy and cells from one locale to another. They do not have a clue about the facts surrounding "transformed energy," "transferred cells," or "cell division."

No wonder so many parents who were asked, "Where did I come from" answered "The stork brought you." They might not have believed that, but they could not explain the facts in this regard even if they had wanted to.

They have no clue about how non-usable energy is transformed via plants into energy that is usable by humans and other plant-eating forms. Nor do they have a clue about the simplicity of "transference" (as in the transference of elemental, transformed plant cells from one location, such as "in a male," to another location, such as "into a female"); nor do they have a clue about cell division which follows the transfer. Eighty-four percent in the U.S. now report that they believe that there are "supernatural, god-guided aspects" that are also involved in the process of "making babies" in addition to "the parents' part."

If you question these pointers instead of the tales they told you during childhood and even today, then put these statements to the test. If they are available, ask them. Ask them to explain how it is that energy transformation, cell transfer, and cell division all happen spontaneously. Ask them how those are the only aspects involved in what they call "making babies."

Ask them how it is that that process, and nothing else, results in certain elements taking on a different appearance. Ask how it can be that energy can be transformed via plants and how it is that elements and energy are transferred via the eating of plants. Ask them to explain how it was that you were not "created"— how it was that nothing was "created" in the entire process—and how, therefore, you were not "born." They won't have a clue.

They do not know the least bit about what is involved in the simple, natural process whereby some elements can take on the appearance of "a baby" while in other cases the same elements might take on the appearance of "a fledgling" or "a fawn."

Since they cannot explain so simple a process as the breeding process, then should you not ask why you have assumed that they know anything about the cosmos, about how this universe "began," about how anything in this universe has assumed its appearance (including you) or about the functioning of the totality?

Billions will tell you that they know that creation is real because Moses described the "creation of the world" in the book of Genesis, but which version of creation are they talking about? They'll not know what that means, either. They will not know that he included in Genesis both of the creation myths that were circulating in his day.

They will not know that there are two versions of creation in that one book; nor will they know that one version contradicts the other. Do you know why? Because 99% or more of those claiming to be Christians have never read the book which they claim is their guide for life.

They cannot tell you that there are two contradictory versions of creation in the first book of their "holy scriptures," proving that they have not even read the very first book of their "guide for life" (or that they were asleep if they did read it).

So why would you assume that their beliefs about a god or gods are true? Why would you assume that they have even the slightest clue about what they are talking about in regards to any subject, including birth, life, death, judgment, eternity, heaven, or hell?

Why would you give validity to anything else written in a book that offers as the truth two different versions of creation? Why would you believe anything written therein about god or the functioning in the universe? There is no need for anyone to contradict those scriptures. They contradict themselves.

Trillions have been told over the years that there is a Santa, only to be told later by the liars that they were lying. After that, why would you believe anything else you hear from an admitted liar? Are you being offended by these words? Then that is evidence of your ego and the egotism that is used to defend it.

Surely, since you believe you are a product of their loins, those parents must have been quite special—maybe even damn-near-perfect in fact, looking at what they supposedly produced, yes? What arrogant claptrap.

I tell you that you should ignore anything that they told you (and anything that they tell you if they are still offering advice and information). I tell you that you were not born and that you cannot die, but the difference is this: I do not ask you to believe Me, as they expect and as they demanded.

"But, floyd, they are so intelligent," some say. This is not about their being intelligent or not. Some of the most intelligent persons on the planet are totally ignorant as a result of programming and conditioning and acculturation and as a result of never questioning the nonsense that they were taught.

I tell you that if you would be filled with Joy and Bliss and Love and Awareness of Truth, then You must empty yourself of all that "they" told you and tap into what You know but do not yet know that You know.

CHAPTER TWENTY-TWO

MAYBE the drop has dissolved into the ocean, but has the ocean yet rushed into the drop? If so, then the next question must be: after the drop dissolved into the ocean and after the ocean rushed into the drop, did both the ocean and the drop eventually dissolve as well?

THE IMPURITY OF BELIEVING ANY BELIEF, INCLUDING THE BELIEF THAT YOU WERE BORN AND WILL DIE, Part B

After Margaret Meade studied the culture of the Trobriand Islanders and reported that brothers and uncles and grandfathers often assumed the role of "father" to children because the islanders made no connection between a sex act nine months removed from its "consequence," many persons in the U.S. mocked their ignorance.

But the fact is that 99% of the persons in the U.S. today can no more explain the actual process involved with what they call "conception" and "birth" than they can explain how the first astronauts to reach the moon did so in a spacecraft guided by a computer that had only 2K of RAM and 36K of hard-wired memory.

As mentioned earlier, the odds are that your own parents do not even understand the most fundamental procedures involved in one of the most basic of biological processes. Though many are that ignorant, many presented themselves as experts on how the universe began, how it works now, and what the future holds for eternity.

Understand that this is not to say that the persons who taught you nonsense are "bad." That would be a dualistic concept. It is to say, however, that they did not (or still do not) know what the hell they are talking about. When eighty-four percent of the hundreds of millions living in a nation believe that it takes a male and a female and a god to "make a baby," then ignorance is not bliss but it certainly is widespread.

Of course they (and your programmers) merely repeat the nonsense that they heard from ignorant or controlling people before them. Now, "their" nonsense, which became your nonsense, prevents you from knowing that there was no creation so there is no creator; furthermore, it blocks you from admitting that there are also no gods of sustenance and that there are no gods of destruction, either.

It blocks some from realizing that there are no gods with multiple arms nor gods shaped like elephants nor a god with white hair and a long beard. It prevents them from knowing that scriptures are not sacred, cows are not sacred, bulls are not sacred.

It allows persons to normalize streets covered with germ-infested defecation because of "holy" or "spiritual" beliefs. It allows persons to normalize cannibalism and vampirism as they "eat body" and "drink blood" weekly and teach their children to do the same.

It is ignorant to tolerate any nonsense simply because adults for generations before you have tolerated nonsense. It is ignorant to give outlandish beliefs and claims and concepts a "free-ride to complete acceptance" simply because they are presented as "religious or spiritual teachings" or as "long-held views."

Whether you are walking about with (a) cow manure on your sandals and feet or walking about with (b) a belief that "unconditional love" and "a willingness to burn you in fire forever" can be logical and compatible and loving, you are proving that you must be emptied of nonsense and falsehoods before there is the slightest chance that You might understand the Truth of the Functioning of the Totality.

[Note: If young persons are programmed to believe that god loves them but that he readily punishes them now and that he is willing to torment them forever if they break his rules, then imagine the warped behavior in the name of "love" that will be tolerated during the relative. The tolerance for abuse that is generated by placing such nonsense into a "mind" will be transferred, so the woman who was beaten to a pulp by a man last week will return to him this week and will excuse his behavior with, "Well, I know he loves me." Consider the childhood roots: "Yes, god will allow me to suffer and to be miserable now, and he will burn me for eternity, but he does love me." Hogwash. Yet you cannot compartmentalize "warped thinking." It will manifest in all ways, or as the Advaitin Jesus said, "A dual-minded person is unstable in all ways."]

Furthermore, there are no saviors or wise men that were born in a virginal, non-vaginal manner (and that includes Buddha, Christ, and Krishna and the twenty-two "saviors" before Christ who were said to have been born of virgins. Not only were they not born of virgins…they were not born at all).

Again, though, understand this: neither I nor any Realized Advaitin will ever suggest you believe any words stated here. That is the difference in Advaitins and your programmers. Your programmers demanded that you believe them, that you never question them, and that you believe everything they said (or still say) with unquestioning faith.

To the contrary, I invite you to stop listening to either of us and to accept this invitation to tap into that inner resource, into that inner guru, and test these pointers. Do not accept anything said here as truth.

But do not continue to blindly accept anything said "there" as truth, either. As Maharaj would say, "Hang Jesus, hang Krishna. Tell me what You know!"

Accept as truth only what is deep within you. Let those nagging doubts emerge and have the courage to challenge nonsensical teachings.

This does not mean you must resent or hate your earlier teachers because they passed on their ignorance to you, but it does mean that You must question all you have been told and find the awareness that is within if You would be in touch with Reality and know Truth.

It also means that it is time for you to doubt…to suspect…to question. If you begin to see that what "they" taught you is false, then you might understand that all of the concepts related to "being born" and "dying" are also false, including:

A Creator
A Sustainer God
The need to christen
Guardian angels
A god (or gods) of Punishment and Destruction
or
Hundreds and hundreds of other gods of specialization
Parenthood
Limbo (to handle infant "deaths")
The need to be "good" so that, post-"death," you'll get a reward
The need to avoid being "bad" so that, post-"death," you'll avoid punish-

ment (leading, therefore, to hang-ups; repression; guilt, shame; being anal; being rigid; being frigid, being fearful, ad infinitum)
"Bad" and "good"
"Reward" and "punishment"
"Moral" and "immoral"
"Right" and "wrong"
A body and mind and personality that can last forever
Eating body
Drinking blood
Spilling blood
Shedding blood
Self-flagellation (physically, mentally, or emotionally)
Fighting with, or even killing, those whose dogma differs from your own
Separation
The aggrandizement of suffering
The aggrandizement of sacrifice
The aggrandizement of giving away your earnings and assets
Believing that virgins can remain virgins even if they become pregnant and give birth

And the list could go on and on. How much of "their" stories are you still willing to believe? Do you never have some doubts? If you do, do you have even the slightest clue about why your doubts generate fear and why you sweep away those doubts so quickly when they arise?

Do you understand that only a fool would claim that he has never been fooled?

What are you waiting for? Doubt. Suspect. Question. Why would you not? Because they told you that if you do, there's a god that you'll make angry. So you have the power to determine the mood of the Power you worship? Your Power is that co-dependent, that vulnerable, that susceptible to mood swings?

Doubt. Suspect. Question. Why would you not? Because "they" told you that you will burn in hell forever if you do not have unwavering faith in what "they" have told you or because "they" convinced you that you cannot enjoy bliss now without believing and worshiping and praying and sacrificing. Yet again you are invited here to doubt. To suspect. To question. To wake up.

Chapter Twenty-Three

MAYBE the drop has dissolved into the ocean, but has the ocean yet rushed into the drop? If so, then the next question must be: after the drop dissolved into the ocean and after the ocean rushed into the drop, did both the ocean and the drop eventually dissolve as well?

THE IMPURITY OF ASSUMING ANY IDENTITY OR NAME, Part A

The drop dissolves into the ocean when the Oneness is understood, and it drops into the ocean at the point of unmanifestation. The ocean rushes into the drop when, among other things, the emptiness is replaced by an understanding of Love and a sense of the Fullness (which can only be known during the manifestation). At that point, it is truly realized that One is All and All is One.

In that instant, Love fills the void left after all dualistic beliefs about "love" and "hate" end. Recently, it was explained that "love" is totally relative and totally false, not to be confused with what can be pointed to with the terms True Love or Real Love.

Since "love" is relative and therefore fleeting, it can—and does—quite readily give way to "hate." Conversely, there is no counterpart to Love; however, even Love can only be understood during the manifestation.

During the "journey," there are typically many instances where the claim "Now I have it!" is made. One early instance of that occurs when seekers reach the third step and assume their "good and lofty" personas which they believe are replacements for their "bad and base" personas from the past. Another instance occurs when The Pure Witness level is reached.

Another occurs when belief in a past or a future are cast aside and "The now" is touted as the only real time. They will explain that they see that what is called "the past" is nothing more than memories, and since the way things were seen then was distorted, then the memories of those things are distortions.

They will explain that "the future" is merely imagined and therefore conclude that—since neither the past nor the future are real—then "only NOW is real." Fine for those at a certain point.

Yet in "the end," seekers that complete the "journey" and reach the final understanding know that that even "Now" is false. Why? By the time the knower of "no past" and "no future" speaks "NOW!" and identifies it as real, "Now" is "then" and is also a memory.

Nothing in consciousness will ever provide a steady-enough target to ever hit the bull's eye. Still another "Now I have it!" moment occurs when the focus turns from seeing the "Oneness of All" to seeing the Absolute beyond the beingness.

At that point, all sorts of identities will have been discarded, but some remain: "THAT"; "The Infinite Self"; "The No-Name Speck" (which is a name); "The Impersonal, Nameless Self" (which is a name), and that list can go on and on.

With certain elements of non-duality, the teachings of Taoism note that there is "no name" that can apply, either to "the path" or to "the way" or to anything else. Ho Yen reported that non-being (wu-wei) is nameless and is beyond forms and words, yet non-being (wu-wei) is a name.

To report that "Black and white obtain names but Tao has no name" is to have a name, so "Tao" is not real, either. To report that "Truthfully it has no name, but I call it Tao," is fine, as long as the seeker does not then believe that Tao is real, as many Taoists do.

Similarly, Advaitins uses the word "THAT" as a pointer to refer to what can be understood but cannot be named, so Advaitin seekers believe THAT is real. But when the Final Understanding happens, then the drop and the ocean both dissolve and there is no point, no pointer, and nothing being pointed to except nothing (and even that is a name).

When it is understood that the drop and the ocean dissolve with the Final Understanding, then this reply to a visitor can also be understood:

Seeker: "You really can't be ruffled, can you? I mean, there is no one and there is no thing that can bother you, is there? That is what I want."

The reply: "As long as something is wanted, then there will seem to be a want-er, and as long as there is believed to be a want-er, you will be ruffled. But how could persons possibly bother Me? They do not have even the slightest clue about where I truly live. Only a few on the entire planet called "earth" have a clue. Some might enter what is called 'floyd's house' or 'floyd's home,' but that is not where I live; in fact, 'where' I live has nothing to do with a 'where' at all. In this regard, there is actually only the 'how.' 'How' I abide is as the awareness, as the original state, as the natural state which has no boundaries, which has no defining traits, and which does not change. 'How' I abide is without conditions or conditioning, without qualifications, and without limitations. I can seem to be 'here' one second and 'there' the next, but that is about 'how-ness,' not any actual 'here-ness' or 'there-ness.' I am not confined to a space or form; furthermore, I can enter other spaces and forms, and do so regularly (as might happen the instant You read these words). Abiding beyond consciousness and beyond beingness and beyond non-being-ness, I can span the globe...I can span the universe...I have spanned all universes. Yet such 'while manifested' spannings seldom happen anymore, requiring far more energy than is worth the effort, and it most assuredly need not happen with You. As for Me, abidance will continue to happen in a whole and unadulterated and unambiguous manner until the consciousness unmanifests. Until that happens, then abidance will happen as Reality is overlaid on the relative without exception. When the consciousness unmanifests, then the drop shall enter the ocean and will span the Absolute; Awareness shall be, but aware of-ness shall not. Later, other universes might be spanned as well, or might not. Yet all of that is stated, so it, too, cannot be the Truth which You know but do not yet know that You know. Tap into the source and know Truth, but even then, do not suppose that You will be able to express Truth. You might invite seekers to tap into the same source as well, but that is all."

Chapter Twenty-Four

MAYBE the drop has dissolved into the ocean, but has the ocean yet rushed into the drop? If so, then the next question must be: after the drop dissolved into the ocean and after the ocean rushed into the drop, did both the ocean and the drop eventually dissolve as well?

THE IMPURITY OF ASSUMING ANY IDENTITY OR NAME, Part B

Why do Advaitins, as a "practical" matter—relatively speaking—suggest elimination of all identification, including body, mind, personality, "something beyond," or even "something beyond the beyond"?

Because all accumulation, all distortion, all desire, all fear, all sense of separation, all conflict, all chaos, all unnatural behavior, and all emotional intoxication are rooted in identification.

Because of identification, persons believe they are who or what they are not. They eventually accumulate a host of identities or ego-states and distortion takes hold. In an effort to fulfill the desires of their personas, to avoid the fears of their personas, and to sustain their personas when challenged, a sense of separation comes. When a sense of separation comes, conflict follows.

When conflict manifests, chaos follows. When chaos manifests, unnatural behaviors and emotional intoxication follows. Natural (nisarga) living is abandoned and an unnatural or a supernatural "lifestyle" is sought.

Consider this in regards to identities: assumed personas are false, so anything they inspire is therefore false and not natural...is unnatural or "supernatural." With thoughts being driven by assumed personas, then words are false and deeds become unnatural.

That is a direct result of the fact that every ego-state has its own hidden agenda, but more than anything, each wants to last, and to last forever. That is a formula for misery in itself. Are shock waves occurring as a result of these words?

Is there some sense that if all identification is abandoned that there will be some great loss?

I tell you, when "floyd" dissolved, there was no loss at all. There was—following the short, micro-second void—a subsequent rush as the ocean did indeed fill the brief emptiness. Reflecting on the happening and the ensuing effect, nothing has ever been so willingly forfeited.

Yet why do billions not as readily abandon all identity? Again, the discussion must review the role that magicians (priests, ministers, etc.) play in convincing persons that they are special, are "A Child of God," "A Gift from God."

Persons buying into their magic will also want to cling to their "positive identities" because the magicians have convinced persons that not only are they "something" rather than "nothing" but also that what they are "can be forever." The ego, with its attachment to the self and the selves and what ego takes to be an Infinite Self, finds the message of the magicians far more appealing then these no-identity talks by an Advaitin.

They have said, "What could this Advaitin possibly know, already admitting that he is not a power and that he has no power and that he wants no power? And who would want 'no power'?

"There is no comparison between that Advaitin and the ones I listen to, namely those who have the magical powers to make flesh from bread and blood from wine; who can make a cremated or decayed body resurrect and become its former self and have its former body with all its parts and nerve endings that can feel pain or pleasure forever; who can teach me a way to think and talk and behave that will insure that my body and mind and personality shall last forever; that I am blessed and shall be blessed.

"Who would possibly want to buy into his message that promises nothing when my mentors' magic has demonstrated that their power and knowledge have something to give? They promise something...not nothing."

How have the magicians been able for thousands of years to convince even intelligent people to believe in their magic and to mimic their magical thinking? S.H. Sharp's words provide insight:

"To be a great magician, one must be able to present an illusion in such a way that people are not only puzzled, but deeply moved."

To be "deeply moved" is to be emotionally intoxicated, and that is why the Advaita message is diametrically opposite from that which the magicians preach and teach: where the Advaitin invites persons to employ logic and reason and common sense and to remain non-attached to all that is illusory, the magicians are skilled at "deeply moving" persons…emotionally, illogically, unreasonably, and senselessly. Note, however, that a play or a movie can do the same, yet they are also fiction.

Realization is about de-accumulation, and that is not limited to things and roles and concepts only. At the level of the Final Understanding, de-accumulation (dissolution) is total, including not only concepts and beliefs but also any and all identities.

In the end, the question must be asked, "WHO wants to know a 'WHO'? WHO is there to know a 'WHO'? And even if the belief in the "WHO-ness" has dissolved, WHO still wants to know the 'WHAT-ness' or the 'THAT-ness'?" To be done with the personal is to be done with the "WHO-ness" and the "stuff" of the "WHO-ness," and to be done with the "stuff" of the "WHO-ness" is to be done with…

> … beliefs, for by WHOM could they be believed if the believer has dissolved?
> … thoughts, for by WHOM could thoughts be thought if the thinker has dissolved?
> … the search for the understanding, for by WHOM could the understanding be sought if the seeker has dissolved?
> … samadhi, for WHO could go into or come out of anything if "The Spiritual One" has dissolved and if all fluctuating has ended?
> … appearances, for by WHOM could anything be seen if the seer has dissolved?
> … continuous talk and continuous noise, for WHO could talk and make noise continuously if the talker and noisemaker have dissolved?
> … enlightenment, for WHO could be enlightened is all WHO-ness has dissolved?
> … and, yes, even Realization, for WHO could Realize if all WHO-ness has dissolved?

Are You seeing how, in the end, there is a transcendence beyond all of the futile efforts to know? Do you see why Krishna said that he is beyond both being-ness and non-beingness? Consider that: NON-BEINGNESS.

Are You understanding why You are told that all knowledge is "learned

FLOYD HENDERSON

ignorance"? When the drop and the ocean both dissolve—even during this manifestation—then there is nothing known; therefore, there is no knower and no knowledge and no knowing.

Now, here, there is awareness that is not aware of. Post-manifestation, there shall be Awareness that is not aware of; however, even awareness and Awareness are names. So is it understood why there is nothing that can be said to be real... to be "what you are," or to be "What You Are?"

A written question was left at the end of the day during one retreat. The question and response follow:

> Questioner: "You said that everything in 'this universe' originated with the manifestation of one atom in what was previously a vacuum. In that case, then at least it can be said that 'I'm an atom or atoms or energy,' right?"
>
> The reply: Since Truth cannot be 'said,' obviously not. Further, even if Truth could be said, the 'you-are-an-atom theory' or the 'you-are-energy' identity can be assumed at some point along the 'path' in order to facilitate movement to the next step. Yet at the end of the 'path,' it is to be understood that before the atom, there was nothing, as far as this universe is concerned. The 'atom' identity theory and even the 'energy' identity theory are eventually cast aside when it is asked, 'But what of all universes, and what of all the voids prior to an atom manifesting in what had been called "this void prior to this universe"? What of that void which was before the spontaneous appearance of an atom and energy? And what of the voids before that? You want to trace some 'eternal lineage.' You would to know every limb and branch on some 'cosmic family tree.' You want to know your 'celestial ancestry' and be able as a result to label some 'infinite heritage' that you would pass on. Your ego would likely upgrade that to 'your legacy.' Along the 'path,' this 'You' might be pointed to with various names, but before this retreat ends, you and 'You' must dissolve, the labeler must dissolve, the labeled must dissolve. There is still some 'one' that has come here to try to get something when you were told all along that I have nothing to give but much to take away. The invitation here is to discard, then dissolve."

To understand that reply is to understand why Truth cannot be spoken and why there is nothing to name. Seekers want peace. What is more peaceful than nothing? What is more Fulfilling than emptiness? The answer:

Nothing is more peaceful than something, and nothing is more peaceful than nothing. The emptiness is more fulfilling than fullness, The Fullness is more Fulfilling than the emptiness, and The Emptiness is the most peaceful of all.

CHAPTER TWENTY-FIVE,
THE CONCLUSION

MAYBE the drop has dissolved into the ocean, but has the ocean yet rushed into the drop? If so, then the next question must be: after the drop dissolved into the ocean and after the ocean rushed into the drop, did both the ocean and the drop eventually dissolve as well?

THE IMPURITY OF ASSUMING ANY IDENTITY OR NAME, Part C

Now, steel ThySelf, for You are about to be offered a level of understanding (a) that few have ever grasped during the manifestation; (b) that will be a guide for the dissolution; (c) that will provide what might be Your most thorough understanding yet of what "non-duality" really means; and (d) that has been understood by no more than a fraction of all seekers throughout all of the ages in which the Advaita teachings have been offered.

Thus, the Final Understanding is that—in the "end"—there should not be even a sense of "THAT-ness" in terms of identity. To understand the functioning of the totality requires no labels or names. That which is understood via the inner resource or the inner guru is understood but is not "nameable."

After reading the earlier points—which were provided in order to serve as the groundwork for building an understanding of what some seekers have found to be "the more obscure teachings of Maharaj"—it should now be possible to comprehend the "end of the 'path'" teachings which include this:

Maharaj said, "I am beyond the mind, whatever its state, pure or impure. Awareness is my nature; ultimately I am beyond being and non-being."

Yet there is something to be understood beyond that pointer which was expressed on another occasion by Maharaj: "When you go beyond awareness, there is a state of non-duality, in which there is no cognition, only pure being, which may be as well called non-being, if by being you mean being something in particular."

See, you are not anything in particular. Further, You Are not anything in particular. Whether pondering the relative, the Absolute, the beyond, the being-ness, or the non-beingness, neither you nor You are anything.

Maharaj said on another occasion, "Just like ice turns to water and water to vapour, and vapour dissolves in air and disappears in space, so does the body dissolve into pure awareness (chidakash), then into pure being (paramakash), which is beyond all existence and non-existence."

1. Take "paramakash" to point to "the great expanse, the timeless and spaceless Reality"
2. The term's roots begin with "param"
3. "param" means "highest," "most distant," and "greatest"
4. Then "param" is combined with "akash"
5. "akash" means "the void"

Now, review the earlier pointers about this void and the voids before and the voids before that, all the way back to "the most distant" + "void" (that is, all the way back to "the most distant void"). Do you now understand the point offered earlier about all voids?

Now continue, please. Maharaj later said: "To be a living being is not the ulti-mate state; there is something beyond, much more wonderful, which is neither being nor non-being, neither living nor not living. It is a state of pure awareness, beyond the limitations of space and time. Once the illusion that the body-mind is oneself is abandoned, death loses its terror. It becomes a part of living."

Allow the "WHO-ness" to dissolve and play around with the "THAT-ness" for a spell, but eventually see that even contemplating THAT is doingness. To be—without being "this" or "that" or "This" or "THAT" or anything—is the closest You'll come to Bliss. Dissolve and know that of which My Teacher spoke. Know "something beyond" that is "much more wonderful." Dissolve.

Next, in regards to such dissolution, Maharaj also said: "Reality is the ulti-mate destroyer. All separation, every kind of estrangement and alienation is false. All is one—this is the ultimate solution of every conflict."

He said at another point: "Non-identification, when natural and sponta-neous, is liberation. You need not know what you are. Enough to know what you are not. What you are you will never know for every discovery reveals new dimensions to conquer. The unknown has no limits." Non-identification.

One seeker attending satsang years ago when the term was employed in a talk said, "Non-identification? I've read every transcript of every talk your teacher offered—some many times—but that's the first time the term has really registered."

Yes, non-identification. Be satisfied and relax into the comfort of those words that invite you to an awareness of what you are not and then take it easy. How much have You discovered on "your "journey"? So much, yes?

Yet at this moment, is not this discovery now revealing "new dimensions" of understanding? Thus, is it not now time to simply relax? If you do so, then the beingness for the remainder of the manifestation can still have Reality overlaid upon it.

After that happens, a Show of Love can happen, and Bliss can happen, and Joy can happen, and fun can happen, and the dance can happen. And it will all happen in a "much more wonderful" manner than ever imagined possible.

Also, is the pointer offered earlier now understood so that it is seen how I can be "here" and there" and "everywhere"? What did Maharaj offer in that regard? He said, "Non-being…it gives birth to being. It is the immovable background of motion. Once you are there you are at home everywhere."

It is that "immovable background" that has brought stability to the relative existence of this speck called "floyd." Abiding as an immovable background, then up's and down's disappear; turmoil disappears; chaos disappears; perceptions about "good vs. bad"—along with all instability that is rooted in such movable dualities—disappear. Mutatio terminus. Stabilitas. Stabilitas bellus.

Furthermore, if you review earlier pointers in light of the pointers offered today, you can also understand why there is no "loss." You will understand what Maharaj meant when he said, "Once you go beyond your self-identification with your past, you are free to create a new world of harmony and beauty. Or you just remain—beyond being and non-being."

At that point, it becomes your call: generate beauty…or harmony… or both…or neither. That is what was being pointed to when My Cherokee Grandmother modeled "The Great Whatever." Whatever. Whatever, indeed. Either way, fear not…dread not. Nothing is lost.

Now, for those who still think that Realization must surely involve the loss of something and fear that it will leave them robotic or will rob them of some of their current degrees of pleasure, know that those beliefs could not be farther removed from reality.

A visitor suggested: I hear You often in various conversations, and usually hold my tongue for obvious reasons! HA! Your last few pointers have offered the best explanation or definition of "as if" living when You speak of the overlay of Reality on relative. Worth expanding on at any opportunity and furthering the "practicality" of the teachings for "every day" life. That is what You do if keeping sane is "important." You know it's all bullshit and act as if it matters. Real Love just Is...with no irritation, not even a ripple, not even a sound. Love

The Reply: On page five of the book FROM THE I TO THE ABSOLUTE is this: "The version of the Advaita Vedanta (Non-Duality) message that I offer has been characterized by one protégé as being 'Applied Advaita.' I will present the concepts of non-duality, yes, but eventually they are to be applied in everyday situations and used to bring peace and acceptance around the issues of the day. Ultimately, the concepts can be tossed, your everyday situations will be discarded, you will have no mind capable of being disturbed, and you will have no issues-du-jour."

So, to expand the "practicality" as well as the understanding of "the way that AS IF Living happens when Reality is overlaid upon the relative," understand that Reality brings with it to each and every event the traits that are unique to Reality but which can allow a level of joy not previously known to manifest once identity ends and once the I AM THAT; I AM is understood to be advaita..."not-two"...One.

That means that when the relative becomes swathed in Reality, the consequence is that every happening which was previously strapped with cultural boundaries, with conditions and conditioning, with so many qualifications, with limitations, with a sense of incompleteness, with ambiguities, with adulterations, and with self-consciousness suddenly all happen in a manner that is the "embodiment" (so to speak) of the Absolute.

All relative happenings (once Reality has been overlaid upon them) happen Absolutely without boundaries, Absolutely without conditions, Absolutely without qualification, Absolutely without limitation, Absolutely without any sense of incompleteness, Absolutely without ambiguity, Absolutely without adulteration, and Absolutely without self-consciousness.

When happenings no longer happens in "a relative mode" but happens in "an Absolute fashion"; then, the unblocked, manifested consciousness might be heard to speak of "more colorful colors"; of "something sweeter than the sweetest sounds, namely, the sweet sound of silence"; of "tastier tastes"; of "beholding beauty at levels never before imagined"; of "lightness"; of "'Love' rather than 'love'"; of 'Showing Love' rather than 'making love' or having sex; of "feeling feelings rather than emoting"; of "being so attuned to all in nature—to all that is natural—that the You-Nature (that "not-two" paradigm) suddenly spawns delights of a previously-unimagined intensity."

Such is possible when abidance is happening as the awareness while the pure (or unblocked) consciousness is totally and completely and "unobstructedly" conscious of.

Those intensified elements of color and sound and taste and beauty and lightness and Love and feelings as well as an absolute sense of Oneness with all that is natural (nisarga) result when "living AS IF" and when happenings happen from the platform of Reality rather than from the stage of illusion. There are billions who claim that they are "alive," but they are so far removed from what that concept implies that they must be counted instead among "the living dead."

That cannot be said of any speck of unblocked, manifested consciousness that is functioning from the standpoint of total awake-ness, complete awareness, and full conscious of-ness, all manifesting in a totally unlimited manner.

After the Final Understanding manifests, then all of the five-sense-aware-nesses as well as all of the sixth-sense awarenesses that are catalogued above will be realized and the relative and the Absolute shall finally and truly be understood as not-two. Such happens when the relative is absolutely subsumed in Reality.

WHEN REALITY IS OVERLAID UPON THE RELATIVE

CHAPTER ONE

THE summative statement of the Advaita teachings - "I AM THAT; I AM" - generates much confusion. Post-Realization, am I THAT only? Does everything formerly associated with the relative end? Is the relative discounted and does abidance happen in a manner that is totally dissociated from all relative happenings?

Not according to Nisargans. Here, the point is that post-Realization, Reality will be overlaid upon the relative and the understanding that I AM THAT; I AM will continue for the entire manifestation.

The summative statement most assuredly does not imply that the AM-ness must be forfeited or abandoned. What is abandoned is identifying solely with the AM-ness.

Then, there is a return to the original simplicity that marked the relative existence of humans for millions of years ... a relative existence that was a most simple existence prior to efforts by controlling men and women to overlay supernatural concepts onto the previously all-natural existence.

It has been asked of visitors in satsang and at retreats conducted here, "Are you using your recovery program, your religious activities, your spiritual exercises, your philosophy, or your ideology not to overlay Reality on the relative but in order to try to escape reality?"

Among Nisargans, there is but one "justification" for completion of the complete "journey" to Full Realization: to overlay Reality upon the relative existence; that is, to stop trying to live in an unnatural / supernatural fashion.

The result of Realization is that the Absolute is overlaid onto the Am-ness so that the no-consciousness, no-belief, no-concept, no-duality awareness-without-awareness-of peace of the Absolute can manifest during the manifestation; thus, "I AM THAT; I AM."

Often seekers say, "You speak of overlaying Reality upon the relative. What happens differently during the relative existence after Realization is 'overlaid upon it'?"

To abide as one's true nature ...

1. is to understand that the Am-ness Is and that THAT Is;
2. is to reject the traits of the Am-ness as exist among the non-Realized;
3. is to overlay on the Am-ness the traits of the Absolute; and, as a result of that overlaying,
4. is to abide for the remainder of the manifestation in the peace of those Absolute traits, including ...

... abidance with a sense of wholeness and complete-ness rather than a sense of being broken into many pieces (that is, abiding as the One rather than as the many roles that had been assigned or adopted);

... being contaminated no longer;

... being no longer driven by the effects of conditioning;

... being influenced no more by the effects of programming;

... being unlimited rather than limited;

... being certain and sure (but with legitimate grounds at this point);

... being unadulterated;

... being awake and aware;

... being in a state where, after having been made aware of THAT, no longer being occupied with THAT, or with searching, or with seeking, or with wanting to know;

... being free of all beliefs, including belief in any concept or idea;

... being free of identity;

... being free of thoughts;

... being absorbed into the silence;

... being fully stabilized;

... being unambiguous;

... being free;

... being light;

... being in a state where AS IF living happens, living AS IF anything in the relative matters, understanding that it does not, feeling without emoting, witnessing whatever happens in order to meet the basic needs of an organism without believing that there is some do-er involved in the process;

and then:

just ... being.

Overlay Truth onto the remainder of the relative existence and You will taste the sweetness and the lightness of being that are tasted by the Realized only.

While the Realized overlay Reality upon the Is-ness, the non-Realized overlay nonsense upon the Am-ness.

How truly exhausting and consuming the relative existence is when persons do not complete the "journey"; when they do not complete "The Circle"; when they do not overlay That on "this."

Seekers that come here for retreats are always invited to consider first the noumenal shifts in understanding that precede the phenomenal evidence that Full Realization has happened.

[NOTE: While Kant is often credited with conceiving the terms "noumenon" and "phenomenon," Advaitins have been distinguishing between the two in their teachings for centuries. The term "noumenon" can be used to point to That Which Is, independent of the "mind." The term "phenomenon," then, can be used in discussions to point to (1) that which is perceived to be real by the "mind" but is not or to (2) that which is mis-perceived by the "mind" as being something that it is not. The example used here on occasion is this: a steel beam, if viewed with the aid of an electron microscope, is revealed to be something quite different from what the eye and "mind" might believe it to be.]

The "noumenal" shift (from confusion to clarity) results not only in the understanding that "It Is I that presently makes possible the typing of these words" but also in the understanding that "it is not I that is actually typing ... actually striking the keys."

Post-Realization it is understood that It Is I that presently makes possible the joy of tasting certain foods, that makes possible the registry of pain if a finger touches an excessively hot surface, that makes possible an understanding of the differentiation in "love" and Real Love, and that makes possible the ecstasy of the sex act; however, it is not I that is tasting, feeling pain, sensing Real Love, or having sex.

It should be seen why belief in either a do-er or in doer-ship ends, post-Realization: I - the manifest conscious-energy - make all of the above happenings possible, but it is not I that is "doing" any of the above.

Post-Realization, it is understood that I AM THAT and that I AM, but it is also understood that I am not "this" or "that." All sense of "WHO-ness" ends, and it is clear that

a. I am not doing anything, understanding instead that
b. being and witnessing (in a subject-object fashion) and
c. Witnessing (in a Pure Witnessing mode) and
d. understanding

are all merely happening, and happening spontaneously.

All of the elements combined as a temporary form or space allow for the functioning of any given form or space to happen in a five-sense phenomenal manner if the consciousness is manifested in association with a body-cum-consciousness; however, that does not point to Me ... to That Which makes possible smelling, hearing, tasting, touching, or seeing. I have never smelled, heard, tasted, touched, or seen anything, but nothing that was ever smelled, heard, tasted, touched, or seen was smelled, heard, tasted, touched, or seen without My manifestation making those happenings a possibility.

If you Realize Fully, then You will be able to understand how many of the happenings which you took to be embarrassing, upsetting, or disappointing involved a "you" ... a false "you" ... the "not-You."

Maharaj said that "the cause of bliss is sought in the 'not I' and thus bondage begins." Full Realization removes all sense of bondage because bliss happens spontaneously once You being to function in a fashion that is no longer blocked by a succession of "not-Yous" that had previously prevented the seeing of Reality and Truth (which, by the way, must be seen and understood if a relative existence is to unfold in a non-self-destructive manner).

It is identification with the "not-Yous" - with the "not-Self" - that drives the desire to destroy the self or the selves. The Real has no tolerance for the false. Who could possibly conclude that the understanding of Truth would suddenly make one willing to associate with the false or become tolerant of nonsense? With Realization, the previous attachment to chaos and nonsense and lies which drove the false selves to do all possible to sabotage themselves (to sabotage those false selves) ends.

And understand too that everything which drives all such destructive behavior during the relative is centered in the "mind." When Maharaj said that "selfishness is always destructive," he was referring to the selfishness that always manifests alongside "self" identification.

Further, when the pointer is offered here that the "mind" is at the center of all (relative) destructiveness, the teachings by Maharaj support that pointer as well. He said, "When the mind is engaged in serving the body, happiness is lost. To regain it, it seeks pleasure. The urge to be happy is right, but the means of securing it are misleading, unreliable and destructive of true happiness."

The joy mentioned above—whether dealing with the taste of food, with the fulfillment of knowing Real Love, or with the ecstasy of sex—can happen post-Realization without the destructive side effects of over-eating, without mistaking "love" for "Love," and without destructive sexual behaviors. Why? Because all that happens begins to happen in a mindless but not in a senseless (that is, "insane") fashion.

Chapter Two

A S noted earlier, requests have been received to explain "what Realization looks like." Some have asked for a set of "parameters" or for "a means for gauging" or for "the traits." Of course, all of those can only be addressed if the "phenomenal results" of Realization are focused on, rather than the noumenal shifts that were discussed earlier.

In fact, the only points of reference for Realization—as well as for "application of the principles even in the absence of an 'applier'"—exist during the relative manifestation of consciousness. Post-manifestation, there will be no "one" to know or not know anything ... to understand or not understand anything ... or even to be conscious or conscious of anything.

This is why those doing all of their religious and / or spiritual seeking and all of their religious and / or spiritual work will part ways with the Advaitin after the third of seven steps on the "path": the Advaitin knows that all relative-existence-misery is rooted in fear and / or desire.

The Advaitin's "journey" (which continues beyond the religious and spiritual level) results in freedom from fear and desire, but those who never transition beyond the third step will continue their involvement with dogma or with what Maharaj referred to as their "kindergarten spirituality" ... either of which will reinforce fear and desire.

The aim of such persons is to attain the fulfillment of their relative desires as well as their desires for eternal continuity and reward as well as to address their fear of punishment that they believe must be avoided at all costs (the present costs for two billion of those types being ten percent of all earnings).

With some seekers, "Applied Advaita" is discussed even though there will be no notion at all that there is some "person applying" anything. Yet the Realized Advaitin understands that whatever "effects" there might be from Realization can only manifest during the relative existence. That is quite contrary to what is anticipated by those attached to dogma and its concept of "salvation" and their belief in "eternal effects."

Begin not this Advaitin "journey" with any notion that something different shall happen post-manifestation and for eternity. What IS for eternity IS right now, already. The only "justification" for completing all of the steps on the Advaitin "path" is to be free of the belief in the concepts that result in misery and suffering now, during the manifestation.

And begin not the "journey" via the Nisargan approach if you would gain something, if you are seeking to become an expert at philosophy or spirituality, or if you are undertaking the "journey" to become a "more informed knower" rather than to be rid of the "knower" role and all other false identities.

Few will ever walk this "path," but the rub for those that do is that so many are taking the "journey" to add on new ego-states rather than to be free of all such false identities. If the intent is not to overlay Reality on the relative but to escape reality, or if there is some "goal" to become some sort of pseudo-intellectual who thinks he / she will gain more knowledge and an ability to express truth, then this "Nisargan journey" will not be for such types.

Also, before offering any considerations in this regard, understand that there is no person that is "different, post-Realization." What there is is the state or condition which manifests after the removal of the blockages that prevented the consciousness from seeing Truth and Reality.

It is clear seeing and freedom from the distortions and illusions of a "mind" which allow, post-Realization, a space or form (be it a deer or a human or a bird) to function in a natural manner rather than in an unnatural or supernatural (magically-thinking) manner.

So let this understanding remain in the forefront that post-manifestation, there is only that which is beyond the beingness and the non-beingness. At that point, there is no "one" being and there is nothing to register "having been but not being now."

The consciousness, when unmanifested, gives way to the awareness that is not aware of; therefore, embark not on this "journey" in search of anything that might remain as some sort of post-manifestation result or benefit or reward.

If that is understood, then, just as thorns can be used to remove thorns, a list of phenomenal markers can be built for the sake of discussion only.

Post-Realization, there is no mind that believes in a body identity or in any personal identity; however, the non-Realized who still believe in persons and personal behaviors might conclude that "something is now different with so-and-so" nowadays.

What can be witnessed post-Realization is:

a propensity for peace
 an ability to enjoy the silence
an end to talking in order to impress
an end to impressive talking in order to try to get persons to "love" or "respect" you
an end to needless talking entered into merely for the sake of talking and / or for the sake of being heard
an end to previous efforts to display publicly how godly or religious or spiritual or clever one is
an end to the seeking of "attagirls" or "attaboys," having realized that those can be desired only by false ego-states
an end to the belief that "something is wrong with" people when they are quiet
an end to the denial of, or dissociation from, past misery and suffering
no longer hearing anyone say, "Can you please shutup for just a few minutes?" (which may have been said or at least thought by those listening to you at work, in the home, or at your "spiritual or 'self-help' meetings")
a discarding of pride for one's "knowledge" (a.k.a., learned ignorance)
the absence of any need to insert opinions since belief in all ideas and beliefs and concepts and opinions will have disappeared
an absence of mind-chatter because once belief in the erroneous content is discarded, the "mind" automatically disappears; and,
an end to the belief in anything being "sacred," including one's "sacred cows," one's "holy book," one's "holy land," one's "holy practices," one's "holy building," and one's "holy judgments about others."

CHAPTER THREE

I^T has been noted that to assume that an understanding has manifested with any seeker can prevent the offering of an explanation that might be vital to the seeker's movement along the "path." The many obtuse perceptions received here over the years reveal the huge number of specks of consciousness that are totally blocked. The following was shared during one satsang session: "Reading realization traits, the whole thing seems boring to me. No fun."

The reply: Then obviously you are not ready. So it is. What most persons eventually find, however, is that (1) all which provides pleasure / fun eventually results in misery / not-fun and that (2) all that provides the most pleasure / most fun will eventually result in the most misery / most not-fun.

Too, many persons are addicted to chaos and noise. If so afflicted, then Realization won't appear to be "fun" at all; furthermore, there are many trying to awaken after a night of what they thought was "fun," only to find that their "fun" is taking quite the toll this morning.

And indeed some cases of seekers who have come to visit might be less fun than others. When an "Ex-Husband" revealed that he was contemplating suicide, there was hardly an opportunity for fun, but there was an opportunity for freedom and peace via Full Realization.

So there is a call to address the assumption by many that the moment Realization begins, fun ends. Some have offered the following comments or asked the following questions, shared here as evidence that the Realized do not forfeit entertainment / fun / joy.

Below are some of the exchanges that provide further evidence of the fact that Realization is totally compatible with entertainment and happiness (and which sometimes illustrate the old adage: "sardonic in ... sardonic out"):

Question: "Will I be robotic [if I Realize]?"
F.: You are already robotic, but you don't even know it.

Question: "Will I no longer feel [if I Realize]?"
F.: You will feel … You just won't be able to emote.

Question: "Will I likely find him [the Realized teacher] out in the woods
    eating nuts?"
F.: Go to the woods and look. If he's really eating nuts, take immediate
    defensive action to protect yourself.

Question: "Why do you not wear a dot on your forehead?"
F.: Why do you not keep your foot out of your mouth?

Comment: "Aha! So the teaching is not that I will tolerate everything but
    that kind of like a deer I will move away from anything that would
    be considered intolerable by the sane. It feels like some wave of light
    has swept "me" away and left behind nothing but a sense of joy. I was
    trying so hard to be "spiritual" and "super-tolerant" to fit into some
    mold of the way I thought I was supposed to act if realized. Thanx!"

Question: "What do you think is holding me back from moving forward
    along the path"?
F.: Most persons are more afraid of the light than the dark. The ostrich
    could be a universal symbol for non-Realized persons.

Comment: "I want to take you to lunch to thank you. You saved my life."
F.: I am not about to let you pin that rap of having saved you on me,
    but I will take you up on the offer of a meal.

Comment: "I just finished reading the three books I ordered ["The
    Advanced Seekers' Set"] and what you predicted has come to pass. I
    really do feel an incredible lightness now."
F.: So now, enjoy it.

Understand that entertainment and fun are at the heart of the post-Realization dance that the Realized are dancing. In that regard, the following was
offered during satsang conducted via the internet:
In the movie "Zorba the Greek," the lead character Alexis Zorba is what

some would call "a non-attached loner," described in the novel on which the movie was based as "a living heart, a large voracious mouth, a great brute soul, not yet severed from mother earth" (a.k.a., nisarga or "natural").

Zorba, with his joyous, spontaneous manner and self-abandoned happiness that finds expression through his dancing (even sans "Partner"), provides a sharp contrast to his rigid, uptight boss who knows no joy.

Exposed to Zorba's zest, elements of the boss's rigidity begin to fade even as "losses" happen. By the end, the boss's severity collapses entirely after extended exposure to Zorba's joyous nature. He finally asks Zorba, "Teach me to dance, will you?"

In the final scene, sometimes Zorba dances with a "partner" and sometimes he dances without. Either way with Zorba, the joy is there. With a "partner" or without, happiness happens. In the case of that speck called "zorba"—"not yet severed from" the natural—Wisdom Is, Joy Is, Happiness Is, Love Is.

THAT is further evidence of "the fun way" that the relative can unfold when post-Realization abidance happens in a light and joyous and entertaining manner.

CHAPTER FOUR

THE following was also shared during satsang: "After considering the pointers given, I have experienced more peace and understanding based on some of the suggestions offered therein. In particular, getting in my car and not having to listen to anything, or not having to rush home and escape into an interesting television program. Being still and being with the quiet.

"A request for 'pointers in the behavior of the realized' yielded the result I anticipated. I know you are not offering 'rules for the realized', only characteristics that are true of all things natural and uninhibited by 'ego states'. Aids seem helpful, especially if they are able to be discarded at some point, like training wheels on a bicycle.

"My new question for you is this: If one is progressing on this 'path' as not a forward motion per se but as in 'I'm drinking Advaita like coffee and it's waking me up (!)', is it a delicate situation to be nurtured or once the process begins 'it's irreversible'? The reason for the question is, I'm moving into an area where I will be immersed in different teachings ... going back to school to finish a degree in philosophy with a minor in political science.

"Can one be in the world and be a proponent of awareness through public policy, politics, law, etc.? Or is that just basing one's opinion of what is right and good for the world on an ego state? I am unsure of how to proceed."

The reply: First, know that once Realization happens, another indicator is a shift in "word impeccability" and in subject matter.

The Realized will not be heard complaining about the weather, for example. Some readers know that "floyd's" Realized Cherokee Grandmother's take on the weather was that expressed by most of the indigenous people: "When it's hot it's hot and when it's cold it's cold."

Further, when the consciousness speaks, it allows "the chips to fall where they may." The few seeking Truth will hear while the majority will hate the words and the one they take to be "the speaker of those words"; however, that will not deter the shift in topics, the offering of very direct pointers, the call to abandon old ways, or the call to reject old thoughts, old ideas, old concepts, and ancient dogma.

To see the way that such word use and subject matter determination happens, some recent examples will be cited below. Know, too, that a "shift in the degree of unblocked consciousness" becomes observable if even a modicum of enlightenment has come into play during the relative among those dealing with, as you say, "public policy, politics, law, etc."

Contrast the words spoken at a U.S. university by a U.S. politician (words that exhibit at least some "modicum of enlightenment") as opposed to the beliefs expressed by non-Realized politicians whose words are rooted in the darkness and endorse making money and gaining status and supporting torture and using bombs and military force. Here are some of those words:

"I'd like to clear the air about that little controversy everyone was talking about a few weeks back. I have to tell you, I really thought it was much ado about nothing." (Clearly an Advaitin perspective, yes?)

"In all seriousness, I come here to affirm that one's title, even a title like President, says very little about how well one's life has been led." (So much for trying to elevate the status of roles and labels and titles and other false identities, yes?)

"The economy remains in the midst of a historic recession, the result, in part, of greed and irresponsibility." (Realized Advaitins speak of the relative consequences of desires.)

"Many of you have been taught to chase after the usual brass rings: being on this "who's who" list or that top 100 list; how much money you make and how big your corner office is; whether you have a fancy enough title or a nice enough car." (Clearly pointing at that which is artificial and superficial in the culture.)

"Let me suggest that such an approach won't get you where you want to go; that, in fact, the elevation of appearance over substance … is precisely what your generation needs to help end." (A politician speaking to persons in a capitalistic country where persons are preoccupied with image-building and image sustenance, taking a swipe at appearance over sustenance? Again, when the consciousness speaks, it allows "the chips to fall where they may.")

"It's in chasing titles and status that [persons] so often lose their way." (Even a modicum of enlightenment can result in the consciousness speaking in a way that devalues the core elements of certain cultures, such as "titles" and "status." And that happens without concern for the way that some listeners will feel—that is, the way they will "emote"—and without concern for the political price that might have to be paid as a result of pointers spoken, even knowing that the words will be given national coverage.)

But the Advaita-type points did not stop there: "It is now abundantly clear that we need to start doing things a little differently … and as a nation, we'll need a fundamental change of perspective (pure Advaita) … a willingness to question conventional wisdom (pure Advaita) and rethink the old dogmas (pure Advaita)."

Look at that last pointer in particular, for something happened there that had never happened in the entire history of the U.S.: (1) a politician spoke certain words, knowing that his words were being heard in homes nationwide; (2) he also spoke those words knowing that the national audience listening to those words included a majority who believe (erroneously) that their nation was founded "by Christians with the intent to be a Christian nation"; (3) yet the consciousness, as it spoke, spoke not with "courage" but with logic and reason as it called into question the bogus beliefs of the masses (their "conventional wisdom") along with the invitation to question the teachings of their religions. (Of course that did not require courage since the religious persons listening did not know that a slap at "dogma" was really a slap at their religion's teachings.)

Is the president an Advaitin? Not likely. Could he report that "Full Realization" happened on such-and-such a day? Probably not, but possibly. So see that when even a modicum of enlightenment happens, it is not necessary to assume any "Realized stance." Indeed, that will not happen.

Whatever happens among the Realized just flows, spontaneously. There was no "mental debate" about "should I speak the same old guarded, politically-correct words that politicians have shared at graduations for centuries or should I offer pointers to the Truth that is being ignored in this culture?" The consciousness spoke … that is all.

When the unblocked consciousness speaks, it will share pointers that are based in awareness … in some sense of the Oneness … with some evidence that clarity and logic and reason are functioning. And all of that happens automatically, without pre-meditation. In the absence of a "mind," there can be no mental debate. That is the way it is post-Realization.

To utter words that denigrate status and image and style over substance and to utter words that devalue appearance, avarice, the old wisdom, and dogma in a religious, capitalistic, sleepwalking culture of arrogance is a huge shift away from the kind of "mind-speak" that flows from the mouths of the non-Realized.

So know that whatever happens with your studies and whatever follows can happen spontaneously and from a platform of Realization. Know, too (as illustrated above) these teachings can most certainly remain "applicable." And understand that none of that will be altered by whatever happens with one assigned the status of "student" by a university.

As far as "nurturing" Realization, that will become a non-issue, there being no nurturer to nurture and no "one" and no "thing" to be nurtured. Finally, see by the examples above that the teachings are certainly applicable in regards to the relative issues mentioned, issues such as "public policy, politics, law, etc."

If that seeker is involved in politics some day and if Realization has happened, then the consciousness will speak impeccably as it points toward Truth, the opinions of the non-Realized masses be damned.

CHAPTER FIVE

A S pointed out earlier by a seeker, "there is no offering of 'rules for the real-ized,' only characteristics that are true of all things natural and uninhibited by 'ego states.' Aids seem helpful, especially if they are able to be discarded at some point like training wheels on a bicycle."

Training wheels? Yes. Or thorns to remove thorns? Yes. Since some seekers have inquired about such "characteristics," they can be considered during the early part of the "journey" for the sake of facilitating the movement along the "path."

In the end, there is no "one" to have or display any traits. That said, another means for determining what Full Realization "looks like" is to review what the teachings offer and to then see if Realization has indeed happened.

One core element of the teachings is an invitation to find all of the sources of ignorance and lies and insane behavior and the sources of tales based in myths and superstitions in order to be free of all of that. Some believe that have found a single source of their problems, such as addiction to drugs or to alcohol.

They believe that if they stop drugging or drinking, then they will behave sanely, not knowing that the insanity was there first, that the insanity inspired their efforts to escape reality as well as their eventual addiction to drugs or alcohol, and that the insanity remains even if the drugging or drinking stops.

The Realized Advaitin teacher would never suggest that there is only one source of insane behavior or one source of ignorance and lies or one set of myth-ical and superstitious beliefs that are to be discarded.

The teachings, instead, invite seekers to cast aside attachment to all such sources. It matters not if ignorance and lies and mythical and superstitious beliefs are being disseminated by an individual; by a small group of persons; by a large group of persons; by a worldwide "spiritual movement" or by "self-help" groups; by political parties; by businesses; by armies; or by the 6.5 billion members of the three dominant sky cults that all evolved from the teachings of one man called

"Abraham" but that all disagree (and fight and kill) over the differences in their beliefs and concepts and dogma.

It does not matter whether a person's source of lies can be traced to (A) one ignorant parent or partner or priest or politician or to (B) the person following the lead of billions of persons who have been erroneously programmed and conditioned.

It does not matter if learned ignorance is resulting in a belief in (1) one false self, which is rare; or in a belief in (2) scores of assumed roles / ego-states, which is typical among the non-Realized.

A Realized Advaitin teacher invites persons to be free of belief in any and all nonsense and false identities and to be totally freed from being influenced by the multiple sources of nonsense and insanity in their imaginary "world." It all must go if the seeker is to be totally Realized, totally free, and totally at peace.

So, based in those elements of the teachings, if Full Realization has happened, what can be observed among what can be called, for the sake of discussion, "the Realized"?

First, associating with all persons and institutions will end if those persons and institutions claim that their teachings are expressions of truth when they are really the re-telling of ancient myths or ignorant superstitions; if stale slogans are being regurgitated by persons who are obviously just talking in their sleep; and if pseudo-psychology is being served up by amateurs who are playing the part of "experts."

Association with any source of ignorance ends, whether the source is an individual or a small group of persons or a large group of persons or a worldwide "spiritual movement" or political parties or businesses or armies or the members of the three dominant sky cults.

All such associations end, and they end spontaneously ... not as a result of judgment or intolerance but as a result of the former fondness for chaos and insanity and beliefs having come to an end.

And those associations end with conviction ... the conviction that the unblocked pure consciousness can never again prefer an environment in which ignorance and deception and distortion and magical thinking and noise and self-serving and image-building and image-sustaining talk are on display (which is the very type of environment that those playing phony roles will prefer).

It will be seen too—if Full Realization has happened—that not a trace of the effects of earlier programming and conditioning can manifest. It will also be seen that there is no longer a belief in even one false self, much less the scores of ego-states that the non-Realized assume as identities. Liberation from personality is complete.

What else can be witnessed? The manifestation of freedom from belief in any and all nonsense and freedom from being influenced either by a single source of nonsense or by multiple sources of nonsense. It all ends, and freedom and peace begin, both of which are also markers of Realization and are evidence of Reality having been overlaid on the relative.

Is there no exception? The one exception is the earnest seeker. No matter what "shape" that seeker might be in, if she / he comes to the teacher and is seeking earnestly, then the seeker's "condition" will be irrelevant if there is evidence that the seeker is ready to discard all nonsensical beliefs and is truly ready to have Reality overlaid upon the remainder of the relative existence.

If the use of ego-defense mechanisms on the part of a seeker does not end, or if the preservation of ego-states remains the driving force, or if a seeker is being controlled by insane thoughts and words and deeds, then contact with that seeker will also end.

Furthermore, once Fully Realized, if the use of ego-defense mechanisms on the part of a "partner" or "friend" are not cast aside, or if the preservation of ego-states remains the driving force, or if a "partner" or "friend" remains attached to insane thoughts and words and deeds, then contact with those persons will also end, spontaneously and automatically.

(NOTE: Skunks are 100% tolerant of other skunks, unless one of the other skunks becomes rabid and insane. Then, even skunks will stay away from that sick, insane skunk. So it is, and that is all very natural. The skunks moving to a different environment are not doing so as a result of ego, egotism, arrogance, or judgment. They are moving because it is sane and natural.)

If Realization has happened, then it is impossible to continue to accept chaos and insanity and nonsense "for the sake of this or that." There is no "one" to accept or reject anything, but what is natural will happen. (And note that chaotic, insane, and nonsensical environments are not natural).

Thus, the abandonment of unnatural and / or supernatural environments involves no judging of "others." Post-Realization, that abandonment all just happens naturally, that shift away from all unnatural thoughts and words and deeds as well as the abandonment of belief in supernatural fiction. What is really occurring is a shift toward the natural, the not-insane, the non-chaotic.

As noted earlier, insanity finds insanity appealing and talkers find talkers appealing and chaos finds chaos appealing; on the other hand, peace attracts peace and the pure consciousness attracts pure consciousness, and that also marks Reality having been overlaid on the relative.

It is the blocked consciousness that prevents an awareness of the vibrations that should normally be triggered if the innermost "center of discernment" is functioning naturally and therefore detecting the presence of pure consciousness as it speaks.

It is also the blocked consciousness that prevents a sensing of the reverberations that should be perceived when the center of discernment would typically begin resonating in the presence of a speck of consciousness that is pointing out the false.

And it is the blocked consciousness that, in fact, completely prevents that center's activation, even when a speck of consciousness speaks and points toward the Truth.

CHAPTER SIX

NOW, review this pointer: It is the blocked consciousness that prevents an awareness of the vibrations that should normally be triggered if the innermost "center of discernment" is functioning naturally and therefore detecting the presence of pure consciousness as it speaks.

It is also the blocked consciousness that prevents a sensing of the reverberations that should be perceived when the center of discernment would typically begin resonating in the presence of a speck of consciousness that is pointing out the false.

And it is the blocked consciousness that, in fact, completely prevents that center's activation, even when a speck of consciousness speaks and points toward the Truth.

If persons would be free of the obstacle of learned ignorance that blocks the "path" to Realization, then they must be able to access the "center of discernment" (also referred to as "the inner resource" or "the inner guru"); yet it is the obstacle of learned ignorance that blocks access to that center. It is that ironic "catch" which will prevent 99% of all persons from ever understanding the "Truth," from ever Realizing, and from ever comprehending the functioning of the totality.

By way of example, imagine you are traveling in a car on a fast-moving highway (be it an interstate, a motorway, the autobahn or an autostrata) when suddenly traffic slows to a standstill because a seventy-car pileup is blocking the entire roadway.

The place you wish to go on your journey lies beyond the wreckage, and the tow trucks that would clear away the wreckage are blocked behind you and thousands of other vehicles that have come to a halt.

See the "Catch-22": you need the tow trucks to assist you on your journey by removing the obstacles, but the tow trucks are blocked from removing the obstacles because so many "you's" are in the way.

As you look at the wreckage, you can only see a small part of what is really blocking the road ahead. You really have no clue about just how extensive the mass / the mess is. But the tow truck drivers have access to an overhead, overall view being sent from a helicopter's camera, and they know everything that must be moved out of the way.

The tow trucks—not unlike Realized teachers—are required to remove the obstacles because neither you, nor all of the other persons being blocked by the obstacles combined, have the wherewithal to remove that which is blocking your movement along the path.

Yet "you"—and all of the other "you's"—are ironically standing in your own way, preventing the trucks from gaining access to the obstacles and removing them so You can complete your journey.

Just as your cars are blocking the way to removing the other cars, your ideas and concepts and beliefs are blocking the way to removing the ideas and concepts and beliefs which are the obstacles that prevent most persons from ever getting themselves (their false selves) out of the way so that the True Self—and all that is beyond even that—can be accessed.

Sitting on the highway immobilized, stalled, going nowhere, you cannot possibly remove the obstacles that have formed a massive pile, just as you cannot alone remove the "mind" which has formed and which is also a massive pile … which is, in fact, one big nasty pile of beliefs.

And who can successfully cast aside beliefs when beliefs are unquestioningly … believed? Few, though it can begin to happen if the fog lifts just enough to allow the inner light of the center of discernment to shine on lies and deceptions and self-deceptions and to expose them for what they really are.

That would be no different from the barn light being turned on and allowing it to be seen that what was thought to be a snake is indeed just a rope.

One visitor recounted a case wherein just enough illumination came when the "switches" of logic and reason tripped on a light, not to expose a snake as a rope but to expose dogma as the snake that would use its venom to poison the brain so that logic and reason become atrophied and so that nonsensical, non-questioning acceptance of myths as truths will dominate the relative existence:

"I left organized religion two years ago, because it just didn't make sense to me anymore. I think once you walk away from that, you tend to want to find 'the truth', since that wasn't 'it'. And I was so deeply conditioned that I believed on some level that the basic truths I'd been taught exist in theory, but 'church people' just screw everything up. So, I decided I'd worship (my) God on my own. A lot of people I know get stuck here. And sometimes they get sucked back in by all the nagging of the conditioned ones who believe. They say you won't make it on your own. And sure enough, things you used to do 'before' start creeping in, and you run right back into the frying pan to repent and you start the whole process over again. And the urges people have are undeniable, whether it's drinking, sex, drugs, or whatever. Suppressing the urges, instead of finding out what you're trying to escape from when you do them, is prolonging the inevitable. Just like you (Floyd) said, find out why you're doing it, and I would say to them, don't expect some sanctioned 'Spirit' to suppress your need to escape. Talk about deceiving yourself! So here I am contacting you every chance I get because the pointers offered are resonating truth within me. In 'From the I to the Absolute', you speak of the 'steps' to reality so to speak, and how the religious (beliefs) experience is practically a necessary part of one stage. So now the pointer in that book makes sense, revealing why the third religious or spiritual step is usually required: once the deceptions are left behind and a vacuum manifests, then that triggers the search for Truth to fill the vacuum."

That seeker became willing to question what she was told by "them" so she "got it." Sometimes persons receive a "flash" from the light source that the center of discernment is and can then accurately see as she did, "It just didn't make sense." Yet that is rare among persons. The understanding of the false in this case evidently came not with external guidance but from internal guidance.

As another said recently: "So god put two white people in a jungle, they got it on sexually, and from that all the brown and black and yellow people also came about—all with totally different DNA and all with a surprisingly low rate of the types of deformities that result from inbreeding. Yes, that's all very plausible!"

It "hit" him, too, the awareness of nonsense when nonsense is being heard ... the awareness of the fact that something is just not making sense. But as noted in the insights shared by the woman earlier, there are those who are drinking or drugging and expecting some sanctioned 'Spirit' to suppress the need to escape.

They are so blocked from accessing the center of discernment that they are inspired to look for external guidance ... for other-world assistance. They will likely never understand that the "other world" is pure fantasy because it is just an upgrade of "this world" which is pure fantasy.

Some of those types have been much offended by remarks that the Realized will eventually vacate the presence of the non-Realized around them if those remain attached to ego, to egotism, to insane thoughts and insane words and insane behaviors, and to their destructive conduct (relatively speaking): "How dare you suggest that a partnership or marriage might end post-Realization."

But those same people joined a step-group and unquestioningly accepted it when they were offered the same pointer: "You will have to change your play-mates" and "Don't do this deal to try to save your marriage or family because that might not happen" and "Do this for yourself, because if you try to do it for others it won't work."

Yet they do not see that the ones advising them to leave their playmates will become the replacement playmates that are often as equally blind and as equally insane as the former playmates.

It does not "hit" them that both their new playmates and their old playmates might have to be forfeited as well if the entire "journey" is to be completed ... if peace and happiness are to manifest. For those who have a desire to continue to be exposed to egotism, distortion, delusional thinking, and insanity, so it is.

Follow that path rather than this one. Go to a grave feeling noble because of your "high level of acceptance" and for being tolerant of insanity and nonsense. Persons are attracted to that which is familiar, so the insane will stay in the company of the insane. But know that it is not natural, and know that, in fact, you left each other a long time ago. A shared roof does not a "relationship" make.

As for drinkers or druggies expecting some sanctioned 'Spirit' to suppress the need to escape, who believe that there is some magical power somewhere that can remove insanity upon request, they are ignoring what their own literature is telling them, namely that:

"With few exceptions our members find that they have tapped an unsus-pected inner resource which they presently identify with their own conception of a Power greater than themselves. Most of us think this awareness of a Power greater than ourselves is the essence of spiritual experience. Our more religious members call it "God-consciousness."

Yet they attack the invitation to see that there is no external god or gods, even though their very own literature offers the same pointer that "the power" is really just an "inner resource," not an outer resource.

They ignore the pointer that "most of us think that awareness [of the inner resource] is the essence." And even as they say, "This is a spiritual program, not a religious program," they are again contradicting their own teachings which say that it is their religious members who talk of "God-consciousness" rather than "awareness." So any person in that program mentioning "God" is, by their own definition, in a religious program ... not in a spiritual program.

Are you seeing how it is that so many persons are being blocked in so many ways, and even when accurate pointers are offered, they ignore them and claim to worship—as the writer above said—"my God" ... as in "my concept of god" or as in "choose your own conception of God"?

So their point becomes, "Ignore the fact that concepts got you here and come up with even more concepts" or "Cast aside your old concepts and adopt our concepts along with the new ones you dream up on your own." That is not overlaying Reality on the relative. That is overlaying insanity upon insanity.

It should be clear, therefore, that the blockages that prevent the consciousness from being aware of ItSelf, that prevent accessing that "unsuspected inner resource" or that "inner guru" or that "center of discernment," must be removed. It should also be clear why the words of a Realized teacher—not unlike the tow trucks referenced above—are almost always necessary to remove the obstacles.

The discussion will continue in the next chapter, casting light on the way that the teacher can facilitate the removal of the obstacles and thereby allowing the "journey" to continue; can assist in the happening called "Full Realization" which, in turn, allows for Reality to be overlaid on the relative existence; and can thereby set the stage for freedom and peace and joy and sanity to manifest.

Insanity cannot see insanity; warped thinking cannot see warped thinking; distortion will always mistake itself for clear insight; and persons who have been fooled have not the slight clue that they are fools.

Only if those trapped in delusion are willing to take into consideration a teacher's pointer that their words are revealing their warped thinking can they ever have any chance at all of being free of such distortion.

CHAPTER SEVEN

Apointer often shared—a pointer that many who are attached to their religion often miss—is that among the seven steps to Realization that are discussed in the book "FROM THE I TO THE ABSOLUTE (A Seven-Step Journey to Reality)" is a religious and / or spiritual step.

Humans and / or human-like types have walked the planet for over 14 million years. There was no need or opportunity for these teachings because there was no language that could be used either to point to truth or to spread lies and concepts that had been dreamed up by ignorant people.

As a result of the absence of language, there were no naive persons who could believe unbelievable claims or outlandish stories. There was neither programming nor domestication. Then, language developed and programming and conditioning and acculturation and domestication eventually followed.

Only during a very small portion of the total human experience covering millions of years have persons dreamed up myths and superstitions to try to explain what their ignorance prevented them from understanding.

Only for the last few thousand years of those millions of years have persons been programmed and conditioned to believe that everything that happens "here" in "this world" (and that is really happening naturally) is supposedly being micro-managed by supernatural beings or powers or forces that are located or residing "there" in "another world."

Now, billions of persons on the planet are living their lives according to precepts and concepts that were dreamed up thousands of years ago by astonishingly ignorant persons who assigned supernatural causes to totally natural happenings.

Now, also, billions of persons on the planet are allowing their thoughts and words and deeds (in fact, every aspect of their entire relative existence) to be controlled and manipulated by the ignorance and by the outlandishly unbelievable claims that they believe nevertheless ... claims that were dreamed up 5000 years ago by totally foolish persons.

And only fools live their lives according to the dictates and concepts of fools.

Though humans survived for millions of years without religion and without spiritual groups, such institutions and groups are now present, will not be abolished anytime soon, and must, therefore, be dealt with by seekers on the "journey."

In spite of all of the debate and fighting and separation and war and mental and emotional damage that they generate, there is no naive call for them to be abolished ... only a call to be free of belief in the misinformation that they spread.

When Reality is overlaid upon the relative, then belief in all relative concepts is discarded. It is understood at that point that all concepts are nothing more than mere figments of the human imagination. But the rationale was offered earlier as to why the seven-step "journey" now includes a religious or spiritual step:

Persons involved in either religious or spiritual groups believe that they have been filled with the knowledge of ultimate truth; have found all of the secrets of the universe that are hidden from others; have been blessed with divine guidance and protection; and have been made esteemed as a result of acquiring ideological wisdom and receiving extended exposure to theological brilliance. They feel full, which really means full of themselves and full of learned ignorance.

Yet if that sense of feeling full does not happen, then when the light from words spoken by a Realized teacher strikes their concepts and exposes them as being false, they would not otherwise feel empty and be inspired to seek Truth.

If that sense of feeling full were not experienced for a time, then when doubt manifests after even the slightest application of logic and reason makes clear that all which was taught by those groups really "makes no sense," then there would be no resulting sense of emptiness which can lead to the action described by the visitor who said, "I think once you walk away from that, you tend to want to find 'the truth', since that wasn't 'it'."

Billions of persons have been indoctrinated into the dogma of religion or the teachings of kindergarten-level spirituality (as Maharaj called it). Persons must, it seems, be made to feel fulfilled by what they think they have received from their religious or spiritual work, must eventually see it was all false, and then must be willing to continue with the search for Truth before they can possibly move beyond the third step on the "journey."

Shared with that seeker were observations set forth in I AM THAT by Advaitin Douwe Tiemersma:

"There are various religions [that all] suffer from certain inherent limitations. They couch into fine-sounding words their traditional beliefs and ideologies, theological or philosophical. Believers, however, discover the limited range of meaning and applicability of these words, sooner or later. They get disillusioned and tend to abandon the systems, in the same way as scientific theories are abandoned, when they are called in question by too much contradictory empirical data."

The reply to that seeker was this: Douwe seemed more confident about the number of "believers" who will "discover" than I. The fact that You HAVE discovered prepares You to continue the "journey" to the end. I'll be around to point if You continue to ride along. Peace and Light.

Thus, there is another indicator for those seeking signs of Realization: when Reality is overlaid on the relative, that which does not make sense is seen to not make sense. Nonsense is recognized as nonsense.

[Understand also that a way to test something to see if it is nonsense is to see if the billions of persons who make up the ignorant masses believe it to be true.]

If the masses question or debate or challenge certain pointers, then the odds are great that the pointers are indeed pointing toward truth. Sense is the marker of the minority on the planet … nonsense is the marker of the majority. If one feels aligned with the thoughts and values and beliefs and concepts of billions, that is the surest sign that he / she is out of touch with Reality … with Truth.

Next, to the observation shared by the woman that "sometimes they get sucked back in by all the nagging of the conditioned ones who believe. They say you won't make it on your own. And sure enough, things you used to do 'before' start creeping in, and you run right back into the frying pan to repent and you start the whole process over again." Related to that is the following exchange:

A visitor said: "Must be fascinating actually – witnessing the lives that are touched by the teachings."

The reply: Sometimes, yes, when the shift happens and holds, but some regress as a result of fear: "Maybe I better give a nod to some god, just to cover all bases."

A visitor asked: That is what I am doing I figure – the nod to some god. I have been examining this idea of "self" and "Self". The "self" as illusory body, mind, personality construct is clear. On reflection, it seems that "Self" in "my" construction is really just a non-religious version of "some god". I mean, you explain the there is no "Self" – this is just another view or witnessing mode. Is this line of reasoning accurate?

The reply: Yes, the "True Self" is understood at the second level of witnessing, that is, Pure Witnessing. Since even that particular speck of witnessing consciousness will not be manifested permanently, then even that shall not last and cannot be an "identity."

Since "self" and "Self" and "God" and "gods" are all man-made conceptualizations, then belief in them—and in all concepts—disappears when Reality is overlaid on the relative.

When a "state" of zero concepts is reached, it is understood that there is nothing with any "identity" at all, including "a personal god with a personal identity." Even the notion of "a god with beingness" or of "a Supreme Being" dissolves. Of course, this requires that the nothingness be understood, as explained in the book FROM THE ABSOLUTE TO THE NOTHINGNESS .

In satsang sessions and during retreats here, several pointers have been offered that "Nothing from nothing leaves ... nothing, not "SOMETHING."

Any words such as "Absolute," "THAT," "Brahman," "God," "energy," "energy-matter," "Consciousness," "Awareness," and "SOMETHING" are still man-made labels generated by persons.

In terms of the no-concept, non-dual Reality, there is no room at all for any present identity, personal identity, past identity, future identity-to-be, eternal identity, or some "other" or some "Other" with an identity.

The Traditional approach of Advaita Vedanta gives nod to "Brahman" and some even assign personal traits to whatever they take that to be. Egotism simply cannot accept the fact of no "Self-ness."

Those who are questioning the teachings of Hinduism and consider Advaita as a alternative still usually adopt a version that is more like their former religion rather than less like that religion.

Thus, they argue: "Well, even if I'm not that, I HAVE to be something." It is asked, "WHO says so? If it is seen that a mirage is not really a mirage, why must it then be re-labeled as something else? Just because it is seen that the snake is not a snake but a rope instead does not mean that the same type of conclusion must be drawn when it comes to the self / Self debate. As with the mirage, it might be that nothing really is nothing ... just a misconception ... a misperception ... a mirage."

Yet an ego-state that is still missing Advaita's pointer regarding "even beyond non-beingness" will not be able to buy into the non-somethingness nature of the original nothingness. It really all depends on how far a seeker can move to a full understanding of the original "pre-this" void.

Some stop at the third step; some go a little farther along "the path" and find the Self; some understand what is beyond "Self-Realization"; some understand "awareness"; but no more than a fraction of a fraction will grasp the void (including a void that is void of a god or gods).

What has served the cause in this instance is a study of what has been called "The Genesis Vacuum": a perfect vacuum can be produced inside a clear container in a lab. Then, a speck of "something" can suddenly manifest, even though what it appears to be is not that at all.

The next argument raised is, "But you said that matter cannot be created nor destroyed, so something must still be something." What is missed is that whatever WAS and IS has not always been "here" as this universe. Before "this" that is now "here," there was nothing ... a total void.

So before any speck of what appears to be "something" appeared here, there was nothing; however,

> if it is understood that, within a perfect vacuum containing nothing, "something" can seemingly appear, and
> if it is understood that there was no "creator" of the speck, and
> if it is clear that the speck did seemingly appear into a total vacuum (a total void),
> then moving all the way back to an understanding of the void becomes easy.

To "reverse, to go back" (not just to the Absolute but all the way back) allows the understanding of that original nothingness to manifest. Abiding as the void, seeing that it (not the Absolute and not Awareness) was really the "Original no-state State," then how could anything impact Me in any way?

Abiding as the original no-nature nature allows for perfect freedom, perfect peace, and perfect clarity to happen for the remainder of the manifestation. Then, the overlaying of Reality upon the relative will also allow for freedom from belief in any concept, be it "self" or "Self" or "a God."

CHAPTER EIGHT

RECALL the pointer offered that—once Reality is overlaid on the relative—then all relative happenings unfold spontaneously. This was shared by a seeker:

"I understand, at least today, your comment that you do not know 'what you would do if....' I used to confront you with a lot of 'ifs.' One was if your daughter was murdered. But, you said you don't know what you would do in any situation until it occurred but whatever happened would be natural and spontaneous. I suppose, what you didn't say was that neither would I or anyone else know what we would do. We think we know."

Whatever is felt around any given happening is merely witnessed, post-Realization. Feelings rise and fall but do not trigger the emotional intoxication that ego-states think they are experiencing. Feelings are natural—emoting is not; too, since the cause of all is all, no predictions can be made about what will follow a cause (or a chain of causes) not yet manifested.

The pointer was offered earlier that, since all happenings among the Realized happen spontaneously and naturally, then it is understood that nothing is happening supernaturally.

Post-Realization, desire and fear both fall away, as do all infantile things, so no "Supernatural Caretaker" or "Celestial Parent" is erroneously thought to be needed; thus, total independence happens. If not independent, one is not free; if not free, then one cannot possibly know happiness or bliss.

Because the basic personality type is usually set by age six, then persons not yet liberated from personality will behave as a child, no matter their chronological age. That freedom from the fears and desires of the internal six-year-old (which is really just the influence of personality) is never known by persons who are driven throughout an entire relative existence by personality. To understand that is to see another "trait" which evidences the fact that Reality has been overlaid on the relative:

"They" may have fooled you and thus made you into a fool, but that ends, post-Realization. Post-Realization, there is the You—that unblocked pure consciousness that witnesses Truth and witnesses foolishness and then differentiates between the two spontaneously and automatically.

Post-Realization it can also be seen clearly the way that any dependency—even on a "power-giving god"—generates misery:

A man who is tolerating near-intolerable conditions in the workplace is also a man who has been overwhelmed with childish fears all his life. He has expressed for months that he wants to quit the job … that he is now even dreaming about telling the boss that he is leaving.

The fear of searching for a job during a recession, though, has paralyzed him, as if he could not look for employment while being employed, a point shared by his wife who has said that she is sick of his being sick over the abusive conditions at work.

Yet note the supernatural (magical) thinking that has evolved from his fear of change and action. Excuse-making and justification for non-action have manifested thusly: he said he told his wife, "This discussion is over. I don't want to hear another word about a job change because I prayed about this and God told me that I was right where he wanted me to be."

So his God is one that accepts his suffering and misery and would prolong it? Yet the personality Type Eight that he disintegrates into when stressed is the power seeker, seeking both relative power in all its perceived forms and seeking supernatural power that can give him even more control over relative issues. That is how obsessed the Type Eight is with having power and Power and control.

He wants the power to change his life, but since fear is blocking the way, he employs his concept of a greater power not in order to face but in order to escape … which has always been a marker of his relative existence: avoidance … escapism … neglect … evasion.

Is it just chance that the way "his God" thinks is exactly the way that the man thinks, or is it possible that what he is claiming to be "a voice from without" is really just a "voice from within"? Is it possible that he is not hearing god but is hearing himself … his false fear-based self?

By the way: he was fired within two weeks of reporting that he was "where God wanted him to be," his god evidently having a mind that can change very quickly.

In the book SPIRITUAL SOBRIETY (Recovering What Religions Lost) Dr. Jeffrey A. Schaler's quoted explanation of what is really happening in the instance above is shared: "Hearing voices in one's head is normal. We generally call it "our conscience."

[Other times, it is just our self-will, our ego, granting itself what it wants in the guise of God. Most often, it is just a self-generated thought, not an "other-worldly message" picked up by some internal, supernatural receiver. f.h.]

Schaler continued: "Psychosis is the belief that the voices in one's head belong to another person. The denial of voices-as-self is an attempt to deny the truth. It is a way of saying 'this is not me.' Pretending that the self is split or dissociated is a way of avoiding responsibility."

The person with accurate perception can clearly differentiate the symbolic from the real and the metaphorical from the literal.

Claims that auditory, mental locution is happening between two entities living in two different worlds is not evidence of "spiritual development" but is evidence of schizophrenia and many other disorders; additionally, the desire to claim that one knows exactly why everything is happening the way it is happening as a result of a special relationship with a god that is communicating regularly with so special a person is evidence of egotism and dissociation from Reality.

For persons to claim that they want to break their old dependencies and that the way to do that is to create a new dependency is a peculiar machination that could only be thought to make sense by use of the always-warped and always-fiction-filled "mind."

This was also shared by a seeker and is relevant here: "I liked the analogy of the backed up traffic and the tow trucks. Still, there is this futile attempt to understand with the mind. Instead, what has seemed most successful here is simply read the pointers – again and again – within an environment that is stress-free and quiet; to allow the direct communication between You and Me without throwing up distracting obstacles."

The reply: Exactly. And how does the "God-you" differ from the You-Me? The difference deals with duality vs. the unicity, with consciousness speaking to ItSelf. When Floyd the speck of consciousness speaks and that resonates simultaneously with Ginny in the northeast, with Raja in India, with Louise in South Africa, with Jean in France, and with Peter in England, it is not "Them" hearing "Floyd's voice" from afar. There is merely a speck that is speaking and triggering an internal center of discernment that is not different from, that is not separate from, the center of discernment wherein the pointers originate.

There is no claim that there is an "I" in one place that is speaking to some

"You" in another place. The understanding is that when consciousness speaks, it is sensed via the inner resource or the inner guru, but there is no suggestion at all that there is "an entity in one place" and "an entity in another place" that are communicating.

To the contrary, the teaching is that there are most definitely not two ... that there is only the advaita ... the "not two." All else is "mind stuff" ... a "mind" thinking it is hearing the voice of a Power that resides in some other sky world.

Furthermore, freedom and peace cannot come when the "mind" is engaged. Peace of mind is a pipe dream, an impossibility, because that which is the source of the lack of peace cannot also be the source of peace.

Additionally, freedom and peace cannot come when God is sought because that which is being sought can never be found. Freedom and peace can come when the Self is sought because that which is being sought can be found.

Are you seeking a god or gods? Is your search a result of fear and desire, including relative fears that are without basis and relative desires for both relative things and "eternal things" as well, such as continuity of the body and mind and personality?

Have occasional glimpses happened which allowed the opportunity to see nonsense as nonsense? Did you ignore that and then begin again to give a nod to god, just to cover all bases? WHO is playing such a game?

Are you proud of giving up dependencies while unconsciously forming new dependencies? When Reality is overlaid on the relative, nothing is sought. All has been found, and no dependencies remain.

With all having been found and with nothing being sought or desired, then boundaries become set for the first time ever. Later, the discussion will reveal how those playing the role of "The Spiritual Giant" will claim that "living in a mode of total acceptance" is the key to their happiness.

An alternate consideration will be offered and discussed, namely that the ennobling of the concept of "acceptance" will lead to the senseless acceptance of anything. Meanwhile, the reminder is that these discussions are never offered publicly to try to "reform" or "educate" anyone. The public at large, hearing these pointers, will either kill you or at least want to.

CHAPTER NINE

CONSIDER: I AM THAT; I AM is not a contradiction, but it does have an element that seems paradoxical at first glance, yes? Similarly, being and abiding as that which is limitless—even as the limited relative existence continues—is not a contradiction but it does have an element that also seems paradoxical.

And for that which is boundless to set boundaries during the remainder of the relative manifestation is not contradictory, but the pointer does seem to have an element that is paradoxical, if not outright ambiguous, to some seekers.

Thus, many seekers who reach the third step—along with most persons who take themselves to be religious or spiritual—believe that "acceptance" becomes a hallmark of their newly-elevated status and a barometer that can be used to gauge just how "spiritually-fit" they are.

That belief is just further evidence of deception of the type revealed by certain statements from visitors, including one who asked, "How can you claim that Maharaj was realized and at peace when he got mad and ran people out of his house?"

Remember the belief that if one is Realized, he can and will tolerate loud noise? And the implication that Realization has obviously not happened if one does not accept whatever is happening in life and all around her / him?

The fact is that once Reality is overlaid on the relative, then spontaneously there is a shift away from nonsense, insanity, and chaos. Persons are not only tolerant of nonsense and insanity and chaos but actually think they are thriving on all three, are willing to contribute to the perpetuation of all three, and are, in fact, quite attached to all three.

They set no boundaries and tolerate all three. And all of that non-nisarga, unnatural behavior is rooted in fears and desires, such as the fear that you will not be "loved" and the desire that you will be loved ... forever. That really just sets the stage for you to tolerate the most intolerable nonsense—relatively speaking—that is imaginable.

Do your actions reveal you believe that fifteen minutes of sex is worth tolerating the most outrageous conduct from a partner for the remainder of your 24-7 existence? Then your failure to set boundaries and your ennobling of the concept of "acceptance" will cast you into prison.

Do your actions show that a certain elevated lifestyle is worth accepting misery and tolerating suffering? Then your failure to set boundaries and your ennobling of the concept of "tolerance" will lock you into a maximum insecurity jail.

You will believe, "Better to be incarcerated with company than to be free but 'alone'." And nothing will lock persons into tolerating a continuing state of misery and suffering more than when they desire others to believe that they have reached some superior state of spiritual rank and use "acceptance" to provide evidence of that rank and to perpetuate their bogus image.

It is not blind acceptance of anything that the sane would see is intolerable that marks the post-Realization existence. What is accepted is anything that cannot be changed during the relative, so the indigenous people of America did not complain about weather but knew that "when it's hot it's hot, and when it's cold it's cold." That is sensible acceptance.

It is also a freeing perspective. But it is not a freeing perspective to conclude, "When he's nice he's really nice but when he's mean he's really mean, and I accept that" or to conclude, "When she's here it's really good but when she's out running the streets and doing drugs it's really bad, but I accept that."

It is not a freeing perspective to conclude, "When he's showing me attention, even if it's just to use me for his personal gratification, it still feels pretty nice, but when he ignores me completely, it feels pretty bad, but I accept both."

It is not a freeing perspective to conclude, "When she's not stealing money from me and the children and our families, it's really nice, but when she is doing that, it really feels bad, but I love her and I took a vow so I will practice acceptance and will continue to sleep with my greatest enemy whom I blindly take to be my greatest friend."

It is not a freeing perspective to conclude, "Life in our home is nothing more than continuous chaos and going and doing and zooming, but at least it's not boring so I not only accept that ... I welcome it."

And it is neither a sane perspective nor a freeing perspective to conclude, "If people are spiritual or Fully Realized, they can and will put up with anything." To the contrary, when Reality is overlaid on the relative, de-accumulation happens.

And along with all else that is discarded is a tolerance of nonsense, insanity, chaos, and the acceptance of being used and abused.

There is an end to accumulating lovers to treat an absence of Self-Love and esteem; less seeking of anything occurs—not more. There is an end to accumulating sources of noise and seeking opportunities for chaos; suddenly, less of both follows Realization and the quiet result is enjoyed.

There is an end to seeking to accumulate status and respect and glory for being "so religious" or "so spiritual" and "so tolerant of anything and everything" and "so accepting of whatever comes my way."

Rather than tolerating more and accepting more and accumulating more, there is de-accumulation which happens automatically and spontaneously in every aspect of one's relative existence since peace cannot be compartmentalized and neither can BS.

Thus, one might conclude that Maharaj was not realized and at peace as evidenced by that fact that he did not accept and tolerate the behavior of everyone who walked into his loft; in fact, the occurrence of that automatic and spontaneous and natural act of "discrimination" during the relative existence is precisely the evidence which proves that Full Realization has happened and that the peace and the quiet have automatically become the norm rather than the exception.

Therefore, for that which is boundless to set boundaries consistently during the relative manifestation is not a sign of any lack of Realization but is confirmation that Realization has happened fully.

Realization is marked by an end to the acceptance of BS, not by the development of a blind tolerance for, and acceptance of, BS. So, yes, Maharaj did cast out of the loft any that would attempt to introduce BS.

CHAPTER TEN

A GAIN, Realization is marked by an end to the acceptance of BS, not by the development of a blind tolerance for, and acceptance of, BS.

Blind tolerance for BS and proud acceptance of BS are not markers of being either Realized or "highly spiritual"; they are markers of either insanity or serious personality disorders.

When the center of discernment does not reverberate or activate because of the blocks set in place by programming, conditioning, adulteration, domestication, and acculturation, then among the non-Realized ...

fact is thought to be fiction

fiction is thought to be fact

an accurate pointer toward the truth is taken to be BS

BS is assigned value, and

concepts and beliefs deactivate an ability to use logic and reason.

The end result of such distortion is not unlike this scenario involving an aunt: bedridden with bone cancer for eight years before the manifestation ended, she was told by her doctors that the best she could hope for was to find some effective means of pain management.

When living under the influence of programming, conditioning, adulteration, domestication, and acculturation, the best that most persons (the non-Realized) can hope for is to find some effective means of misery management and suffering management.

Most, however, turn to ineffective means of misery and suffering management: drugs, alcohol, shopping, gambling, sex, food, nicotine, religion, spirituality, accumulation, ad infinitum.

Moreover, the non-Realized are seldom ever in touch with their misery and suffering. They are in total denial, their egotism and their dual-minded condition driving them to claim that "their lives are good," that "their marriages are good," and that "they are really happy"; yet 99.9% are addicted to something and are using their addictive practices to try to escape the suffocating conditions of their relative existence, even as their dissociation and their denial and their reframing of falsehoods as truth combine to influence them to upgrade the actual status of their lives and to ignore the facts surrounding a relative existence that is pockmarked with illusions.

The result is a global population of persons who are walking about in their sleep while thinking they are awake; who are thinking that their dreams are real; who are mistaking images for the actual; and who have not only normalized misery but have also subjected their suffering to a process of "spin doctoring" whereby they believe the lies that they tell themselves ... that misery is happiness, that suffering is bliss, that their lives and relationships are "good," and that "this is just the way it is and just the way it has to stay."

Realization brings to an end the self-deception that otherwise prevents the non-Realized from seeking that which could end misery and suffering once and for all, convinced as they are that "everything's good ... really ... it's all good."

Post-Realization, when Reality is overlaid upon the remainder of the relative existence, then fact is never thought to be fiction, and fiction is never thought to be fact; accurate pointers toward the truth are accepted and understood; nonsense is no longer valued; and logic and reason displace all beliefs and concepts.

In short, those persons who were made into fools as a result of warped programming, perverted conditioning, stifling adulteration, oppressive domestication and twisted acculturation—and who have continued to fool themselves via denial and dissociation and reframing and dual-mindedness and egotism—will never again be fooled, post-Realization.

All of the ego-defense mechanisms that ego-states used to sustain their false image are discarded; all of the effects of having been misled by cultures that teach nonsense fall away; all dual-mindedness ends with the end of belief in the content of the "mind"; the ability to differentiate true from false manifests and happens ... always and automatically; the conscious efforts to manipulate and to control (along with the unconscious agendas that drive personal thoughts and personal words and personal actions) all come to end; then, the remainder of the manifestation—at least for Realized Nisargans—happens in a natural, spontaneous, agenda-less fashion. That is further evidence of the way the relative unfolds when Reality is overlaid upon it.

CHAPTER ELEVEN

A couple shared this: "My husband and I left organized religion several years ago and have been searching for something to fill "the void." Then Tom heard about a connection between Christ and Advaita so we googled "jesus advaita" and found you. Thank goodness! My husband and I have wondered why a few of your words have had more impact than years of sermons, then your explanation of praying to a god versus hearing your words explained it. Tell us more! Thank you. Katherine and Tom."

Louise in South Africa wrote: "Your writings are so much a part of me now, and I enjoy the relaxation of being able to just trust what is written – to be able to let go of the hypervigilant bullshit detector that operates so strongly here. I am glad there was the momentum to continue. I find it hard to believe sometimes that it was through the relatively recent accidental stumbling onto your writings that I first heard the words "advaita" and "Nisargadatta" ... and "floyd henderson". You must be aware of the effect on visitors. This comment by you had a resounding impact, although I don't know why: And how does the "God-you" differ from the You-Me? The difference deals with duality vs. the unicity, with consciousness speaking to ItSelf. When Floyd the speck of consciousness speaks and that resonates simultaneously with Ginny in the northeast, with Raja in India, with Louise in South Africa, with Jean in France, and with Peter in England, it is not "Them" hearing "Floyd's voice" from afar. There is merely a speck that is speaking and triggering an internal center of discernment that is not different from, that is not separate from, the center of discernment wherein the pointers originate."

As for the passage, that pointer was originally offered years ago during satsang when an accusation was leveled by a religious attendee who said that Advaita's claims and my claims were not different at all from his claims about prayer except that Advaitins and I were so arrogant that we were placing ourselves in the god role. The passage you referenced is close to the response offered to him in the late 1990's or so.

As for the impact, a part of that is likely the result of understanding a pointer that was not stated but that can be inferred by awakened specks: there are no persons, so there are no persons talking and there are no persons listening. That is really the essence of what is Realized when Realization happens and is overlaid on the relative: all belief in anything personal ends, and it is realized that there is no personal petitioner, no personal hearer, no personal god speaking, no personal god listening.

There are simply waves of energy that ride along streams of consciousness, and at times the waves are diverted from their boundless, undirected path ... drawn to an inner source, and allowed to surge on occasion into the quiet cove called "the inner resource" and settle in that place.

(At least that is what can happen in the case of a cove that has not been blocked in the fashion that most specks of consciousness are blocked because of the dams of programming, conditioning, and acculturation which prevent the flow of those waves from reaching that peaceful bay known as "the inner guru.")

The other difference is, with that "You-Me," there is an energy transmission that travels directly from one center of discernment to one center of discernment with no stopover in a "mind." With this Advaitin, nisarga approach, such stop-overs are not required since "both" centers are understood in the end to be the same center. In Reality, there is no "from here to there," no "from this center to that center" going on; there is only the "here."

I am not talking to you or to You. I am talking to My Self, which is You. Thus, there is really no message "going" anywhere—only the triggering of a message that is already within. Consciousness speaks ... that is all that happens.

That is far different from the claims based in the magical thinking that dominates religious persons and (kindergarten level) spiritual persons. They adhere to a concept—to a dualistic belief—that there is an "A" talking to a "B" and a "B" answering an "A."

The truly Realized understand that the notion that one is "hearing god speak" is really just a case of the "self" talking, not of a god talking. The Realized understand that the belief that "a personal god in another world is talking specifically and personally to me in this world" is just an erroneous belief held by an ego-state that is being driven by a sense of "special-ness" which is a result of the influence of massive egotism.

The Realized understand that a schizoid-style "hearing of voices in the head" is nothing more than nonsensical "mind stuff" ... pure nonsense ... total "BS" as Louise said.

So understand that there is no "floyd" and there was not a "maharaj." Again, I am not talking to anyone. Understand too that whatever you might think either did or has done is insignificant. Understand, too, that what either might know is meaningless.

The question is always, "What do You know? What is it that You can come to understand via the inner guru ... the inner resource? What is it that is blocking You from tapping into that which the inner guru is aware of but that you cannot bring into consciousness because the pure consciousness which You Are (and which can know ItSelf) is blocked from 'being aware of' by all of the bogus content of the 'mind'?"

When Realization happens, when the blocks are cast aside, and then when pointers to the truth resonate via that inner center of discernment, then the Truth rushes into consciousness and peace and freedom finally begin.

CHAPTER TWELVE

ONE seeker protested: "Dear Sir: everything happens for a reason."
The reply: If that is a counterpoint to the pointer explaining that there is no personal god (and therefore no personal god that is directing anything), the fact is that you have reached three erroneous conclusions which can all be discarded thusly:

1. I am not "dear" (but you don't really think that anyway, do you?)
2. There is no justification for an appellation of respect such as "sir," (but you don't really feel that anyway, do you?)
3. Everything happens not for "a" reason but is caused by all causes.

When you claim "Everything happens for a reason," the closest thing to fact that can be said is that, yes, there are reasons for everything, but no one who has ever said that truly knows what the reasons are. In every case, the speaker of that line goes on to reveal that "the reason" is some god-conceived "divine plan."

More accurately, though, there are trillions and trillions of causes that preceded (and set the stage for) any given happening, but not even one of those reasons is a god who is micromanaging every event in the universe.

[Since all is energy and matter and since neither can be created, then there cannot possibly be a "creator."]

Moreover, such a belief always ends up being used to justify suffering, misery, pain, and an assortment of other afflictions or agonies that would drive logical persons away from that god—not closer to any god—if that god were really employing such methods and working in what is called "mysterious ways."

Furthermore, the use of such a phrase so minimizes and normalizes suffering, misery, pain, afflictions and agonies that no effort at all is made to alleviate suffering, misery, pain, afflictions and agonies. Why?

The non-Realized who believe such a concept always conclude that their suffering and misery and pain and affliction and agony will eventually be revealed to have been "beneficial in the long run" by the god who is believed to keep such implements in his celestial toolkit and who is believed to use them with such ease and abandon.

How insane can persons be when they believe such nonsense? One woman said, "I think that there was a reason I was assaulted. God is using that attack to make me better in some way." A man said, "I am about to lose my family because of continuous sexual misconduct over the years, but so far god has kept me from drinking or drugging around that."

[If it sometimes seems that an Advaitin site or an Advaitin teacher is a clearinghouse for insanity, that might be the case.]

When Reality is overlaid on the relative, such nonsensical beliefs end. The functioning of the totality is understood, and the cause of all is understood, so no single cause is assigned blame for any particular happening. The result is an elimination of the use of reasoning fallacies (a practice that dominates and perverts the relative existence of the non-Realized).

Other evidence of what the relative is "like" when a Nisarga-style Realization is overlaid upon it is revealed via an exchange several decades ago with a U.S. expatriate who had been living in Venice, Italy for years. During one of many visits there, she asked during a conversation about Nisarga yoga if the word sprezzartura might capture the essence of "the natural life."

After a discussion of what she understood the word to mean, the reply was "Not quite." Sprezzartura, she said, is about "making the difficult look easy." Nisarga-style living, by contrast, results in an actual ease that suddenly characterizes the post-Realization, simplistic existence that had previously been perceived to be "difficult."

Understanding the difference in sprezzartura and in AS IF natural living might, nevertheless, facilitate an understanding of the post-Realization existence. Sprezzartura refers more to a "rehearsed spontaneity" which means it is about image and appearance (as typifies the pre-Realization relative existence and the notion among persons that it is better to do whatever is required to "look good" than to take the steps required to "feel good").

Whereas sprezzartura refers to a "well-practiced naturalness," the post-Realization understanding is that there is no "one" to practice anything; then, natural functioning happens without any beliefs at all, including the belief that there is a "functioner" involved when such natural functioning occurs.

When the word sprezzartura points to a "studied carelessness" or to a "studied absence of attachment or assurance," then it misses the mark as well when trying to describe the post-Realization manifestation. Recall the comment make earlier by the woman that said, "I can 'train myself' to live in the moment, and not grasp, or reflect, or obsess, etc. But how do I know that's not my mind conforming to a new pattern?"

She understood that such "training" of a "self" would not be an indicator of true and Full Realization. When Reality is overlaid on the relative, then there is no "one" to train a "self" and no one to work at being one way or another. Neither would happen during a naturally-spontaneous, post-Realization existence.

Post-Realization, all simply happens ... simply. All simply happens automatically and spontaneously. When the deer arise this morning and begin moving about this area, there is no "plan." There is no "Great Planner and Director in the Sky" who will be "guiding them throughout their day," either.

Where they go and do not go will not be planned. Their day will be marked by "an actual ease," human interference notwithstanding. They will perceive nothing as being "difficult." They will not rehearse a "posture" of spontaneity that they will then display for others to see.

They will not "practice" being natural ... natural living will just happen. There will be nothing displayed that is "rehearsed" or "studied." They will, instead, move through the hours of the day without attachment, without a need to feel guided by "A Great Guider from Another World."

They will function without playing the role of "The Spin Doctor," so if another fawn is stillborn outside the window of this office, as happened once before, they will not dream up some supernatural, other-worldly explanation for something that occasionally happens during the manifestation.

If a deer can go through the day in so free and easy a manner, why could any person not do the same? The many causes might include the fact that Realization has not been overlaid on the relative.

If Realization via the Nisarga understanding has happened, then the deer's manner will also be the exact manner in which your day will unfold today and every day ... naturally, spontaneously, and automatically without a need to try to "put a spin" on anything ... without the need to try to work at being content ... in fact, without, period.

CHAPTER THIRTEEN

THE actual peripetia—that "flash moment" when ALL that is false is finally seen to have been false—does not come in a flash for most seekers but happens at the end of a long search that led to the Advaita teachings which led, in turn, to questioning past beliefs rather than these present teachings.

One seeker responded to the pointer offered earlier by saying: "I have to work for a living. I HAVE to plan my day to accomplish what I have to accomplish."

The response: WHO is that "I"? As with marriage, it has been explained that "wifing" or "husbanding" can happen even while there is no belief at all in the person / persona of "The Wife" or "The Husband" (roles which are always soon upgraded to the status of "The Super Wife" or "The Super Husband," leading to divorce when one becomes convinced that he / she is "super" but the partner is not).

If planning happens without a belief in "The Planner" or "The Super Employee" or "The Super Boss," then so it is. More to the point was the invitation to abandon the belief that there is some "Great Planner in the Sky" that is subjecting you to anything and everything that happens in the relative, including that which generates misery and suffering and pain.

Further, the invitation was to stop assigning supernatural cause to entirely natural happenings.

In contrast to those questioning the teachings rather than their own bogus belief systems, the following was shared by Dan in the U.K. The comments will show what can happen if the opposite approach is taken, namely, questioning beliefs instead of pointers:

"I've been reading your book 'Finding Real Love' and thoroughly enjoying it. Thanks again for another great one. For me this is one of your best books yet. I feel the reader is given more of a window into what the realised life looks like in the life of 'Floyd' and as a result I have found the understanding to deepen.

"For me your books have been a great help. Since coming to the recognition of ego states and roles and how destructive they are in one's life, I have not been

410   FLOYD HENDERSON

pulled around or emotionally intoxicated as much by them (although, I don't think I'm anywhere near Realised yet).

"Realizing that 'teacher' is merely a role I'm playing in the theatre of the lie means my days flow by much more peacefully. I could not handle criticism or failure before and now they have really lost a lot of their sting, and if they do 'bite', I can observe more and the feelings subside very quickly.

"Also, I'm in a relationship where I don't need my partner to agree with everything I say. It's freedom, and it's very nice indeed. As you can probably tell I am still not really devoid of concepts, but have come a long way since I started reading your works and for this I thank you again. Dan."

The paradox of the Realization process is this: seekers formerly never questioned anything; then, the teacher that invites seekers to question must also be willing to accept questioning from seekers.

At some point, though, a willingness on the part of the seeker to accept pointers as a viable possibility worth considering objectively—rather than debating continuously—becomes a requirement for Full Realization to happen.

As Dan admits, though the "Final Shift" may not have happened yet—though the moment of peripetia may not have yet struck—there are shifts (or "gauges," as one seeker called them) that are indicating movement away from the trappings and traps of programming and toward the peace and freedom.

Even if the entire relative existence has not yet been wrapped completely in the cloak of Realization, the warmth of covering many parts of it—as is the case so far with Dan—provides a palatable shift away from angst and toward comfort.

CHAPTER FOURTEEN

ANOTHER seeker said: "You made a very key point regarding Realization earlier. It's not a matter of acting stoical, rational, calm, or non-emotional. It's simply that is the byproduct of being Realized (so you say)."

The reply: Yes. As the non-Realized wander or ricochet through the relative, they take their "world" to be a stage (to use a Realized poet's words). Their imagined "world," then, is conceived to be a stage and "all the men and women, merely players." Each plays a role in the Theater of the Lie, in the Drama of Fiction, and eventually they all become convinced that they are the roles being played.

When Reality is overlaid on the relative, then the acting ends. There is no one to "act stoical, rational, calm, or non-emotional." There is no one left to continue living in the mirror as happened before. Realization is about not acting and about seeing that the stage is a stage and that persons are all actors; about seeing that so many are merely putting on an act; about walking off the imaginary stage; about no longer accepting roles that inspire depression, anger or fear; and about moving through the remainder of the manifestation fully awake, aware, and conscious.

[Add "in a totally spontaneous and natural fashion" if the Realization happened via Nisarga yoga.]

The "Night of the Living Dead"-type of robotic-like, trance-like walking about as if asleep ends. The way the relative unfolds post-Realization was also addressed in this exchange after a comment about the ways in which "the humours" fluctuate:

By the way, to consider the sanguine and phlegmatic and choleric and melancholic humour states to be a part of what is natural is not outside the nisarga understanding—back to the biorhythms and the body's cycles—as long as it is clear that all of that involves a body and nothing more.

Consider this exchange with Louise in Cape Town:

Louise: "A couple of years back, I had the sense that a feeling (joy, sadness, love, pain) blows through consciousness like a wave. Then human beings caught in that wave, personalize it. We say "I am sad because ... blah blah blah").

F.:   Or that could be said to be "mind-alizing" it as well as personalizing it. If Fully Realized, then there can be no thought following a witnessed feeling.

L.:   Is this true – the idea of a feeling wave? With personality in place, the humours or even the fundamental feeling tone of the enneatype must play its tune. How is that natural? Or is it only unnatural when we personalize rather than just witness the feeling?

F.:   It is natural in that the efficiency level of the brain's operations—as well as the fluctuations in the body's levels of energy—continually fluctuate in all humans, animals, birds, etc. You infer accurately when noting that it becomes unnatural when the "mind" personalizes that which is not a "feeling" but is an "emotion." Only ego-states can generate emotions ... the emoting that leads to emotional intoxication, acting out, etc. It is the unblocked, post-Realization consciousness that can Witness feelings rise or fall without emotional intoxication. Consider: Maharaj noted that the body pain from his throat cancer had nothing to do with "Him" (the witnessing consciousness). Just as "He" pointed out that "He" was merely the witness of the body and the pain, You and I could as easily say, "Ah, the space has some of that black bile stuff going on - the stuff Shakespeare mentioned." The body has certain imbalances in its chemistry today, so the consciousness is registering or noting some sense of "melancholia," but that has nothing to do with the witnessing agent. To watch a train plowing through a truck that stalled on a railroad track is not to be plowed through Your Self. Maharaj explained that Westerners usually display tamas (darkness, melancholia, passivity) and rajas (motion, restlessness, the going-doing-zooming syndrome) rather than sattva (being as opposed to doing). Tamas and rajas can indicate a lack of Realization if involved with "personalizing" sadness or if rooted in fears or desires that trap persons in their continuous efforts to accumulate and escape. When that is the case, there is no going into or out of harmony and disharmony. The disharmony dominates the existence. Yet fluctuations in what were once called "the humours" can also manifest as a result of the body's physical condition. As is the case when a mix of water and gasoline are introduced into the tank of a car and the engine misfires, such is also the case when a food plan is being followed that is not the plan for a particular body type—three different types being in existence. Maharaj addressed that very effect, making note of the way that the body's chemistry can be out of balance, (the body being nothing more than a plant food body, chemical at its core.) Either an absence of Full Realization or a body's chemical imbalance can result in one exhibiting similar behaviors, but the causes are obviously quite different and require quite different approaches in addressing the real issue. No matter what, however, the body has nothing to do with What You Are or with What I Am.

L.: Okay – that is clear. So there may be effects that arise from the body (pain from illness; biorhythms, hormones, effects of diet or poor quality of food, etc) – but since I am not the body, these can simply be witnessed.

F.: Exactly. Sickness and health can be associated with the body and are aspects of the consciousness, yet I am not the consciousness—neither are You. How is that known? Sickness and health are dualities and dualities have nothing to do with You or Me. That Which You Are and That Which I Am is beyond the consciousness, beyond the beingness and even beyond the non-beingness. The body needs so many things, but neither You nor I need anything. As for consciousness, it too is restless in that it is always in motion. Stability can only come via first abiding as the original nature, as that original state. Then, unwavering peace and resolute freedom come when abiding as the Void.

CHAPTER FIFTEEN

THE next "gauge" for seeing that Reality has been overlaid on the relative is seeing that all delusions about (false) "love" have ended and that <u>REAL LOVE</u> is understood because the Oneness is understood.

During the "journey," this can be seen: just as THAT can be overlaid on the AM-ness, a phenomenal manifestation of Love and a noumenal manifestation of Love can also happen concurrently and be demonstrated concurrently.

When Full Realization happens, it becomes understood (more specifically than the initial understanding above) that "two things" are not happening in a concurrent fashion at all; instead, all is realized to be One.

Thus, the current Reality is that—just as this speck lost any and all ability to believe in even one single concept—so this speck has lost any ability to differentiate ItSelf (its present beingness) from the manifestation of all beingness. The illusory belief in a multiplicity has dissolved and given way to an understanding of the Reality of the Unicity.

Once <u>Reality</u> is overlaid on the relative, it is understood that those various locations and the variety of physical appearances have nothing to do with what is Real.

To those not yet Fully Realized, you are invited to understand this: to think that one is witnessing another person is to be in delusion. That which is real is "not two"; that which is real is One … without "differentiation."

No two persons (the non-Realized) will ever be the same in terms of thinking or speaking or in terms of behavior or physical looks. All of that supposed variety erroneously supports the false belief in differentiation. Understanding that should make it possible to see, therefore, that persons cannot meet the criteria for being That Which Is Real.

Furthermore, when persons judge the Realized, trying to overlay their relative, personal concepts onto what they erroneously perceive to be what is real, they fail to understand that "nothing personal which they try to assign to the Realized" will be true.

My teacher taught that, while all pancakes are actually the same substance, no two pancakes will ever have the same appearance. Some will take one shape, some will take another. Some will bubble in this fashion, and some will bubble in that fashion. Some will be thin and some will be thick. Yet they are all the one, same thing (supposed differentiations in appearance notwithstanding).

Revel in that understanding. Join in and dance the dance of joy, the dance of knowing the Oneness, the dance of being the unicity, the dance of overlaying Reality upon the relative, and the dance of being <u>free of belief in any duality</u> or separation or aloneness ... knowing the all-one-ness instead.

CHAPTER SIXTEEN

WHEN Reality is overlaid on the relative, the irony is that nothing changes even as everything changes. What is Real was always Real; What You Are post-Realization is That Which You Were prior to Realization; that which You sought is What You Already Were; and where You would Be, You have always been. Nothing that is real can change.

Everything in the relative will seem to change simply because the former, faulty perceptions about things relative will end. Whatever You witness post-Realization will be witnessed accurately, so that is the only "change," really, a change from seeing in error to seeing clearly. The steel beam is understood not to be a steel beam at all but is seen to be a swirling mass of energy.

A man came into the house to begin the second session of a one-on-one retreat. He set his copy of a book he had bought the previous day on the table between the two chairs where sessions occur.

He turned on the lamp, and then began reading pointers about being liberated from personality, a liberation that is required to move to the fourth of seven steps on the "journey" to Reality. Then, he set the book down and said, "I'm not convinced I'll ever really understand the Oneness at all."

It was explained that he cannot even imagine now what he will see post-Realization, "but it will include looking at this table and that lamp and at Me and seeing ONE thing only because You will understand: that everything in this universe began as a single hydrogen atom; that the only reason that there appears to be a difference in the table and the chair and Me is because of the variance in vibrational rates of energy; and that the table is a table-cum-conscious-energy, that the lamp is a lamp-cum-conscious-energy, and that what he takes to be "body-floyd" is just a body-cum-conscious-energy ... all three vibrating at different rates."

When his expression revealed a lack of understanding, this pointer was offered: "Try not to see with eyes that have only looked at things through a mask of darkness the things that can only be seen in the unmasked light."

That is another of the post-Realization "changes": the uninterrupted light (which is cast forth when the consciousness is no longer blocked) allows for perceiving all as it truly Is.

All that was formerly thought to be a certain way is no longer thought to be that way at all because all thoughts will end. How could thoughts possibly occur after it is seen that the content of the "mind" was all false and after all that is false has been discarded?

The post-Realization, AS IF relative existence happens for humans as spontaneously as it does for all else that exists in nature … birds, squirrels, plants, deer … whatever. The brain that is rooted in the elements, as well as the consciousness that is rooted in the Absolute, begin to manage all of the operations that had occurred in the past under the auspices of the "mind" which was rooted in faulty programming and bizarre conditioning.

After completing all seven steps on the "journey" to Reality, the sixth sense is tapped into once more; the intuition becomes a driving force, replacing the body-mind-personality set of motivators that drove all thoughts and words and deeds before; and the inner guru—that inner resource, that center of discernment—become the compass that points out the way by which the remainder of the relative existence can unfold spontaneously.

The relative "changes," then, include a shift from what you thought (false) "love" to be to an understanding of what Real Love is. What was thought to be "special" and "precious" will no longer be perceived in that manner—all ego-generated and all egotism-based differentiating having ceased.

There will no longer be the belief—held by 87% of the non-Realized persons in the United States—that "making babies" involves three parties (a female, a male, and a creator god). No elemental body (that resulted from what was merely an act of friction involving two plant-eating bodies) will be thought to be "god-given" and "unique" and "exceptionally distinctive."

Yes, Real Love might be witnessed, but what will not be believed in is the notion that a particular impregnation is a result of two very special individuals having accomplished something that is very special and having "made" something that is also very special.

Dance the dance of joy if you choose, but be not deceived that the elemental body (which results some nine months after conception) is a result of a ménage-à-trois with you and a mate and a god. Dance the dance of happiness, but do not believe that you are dancing to music that is being provided by a celestial choir.

Such deception cannot happen post-Realization, and that is another change that can happen: because all beliefs are cast aside, then belief in myths and super-stitions and tales and nonsense also fall away.

[Has Real Love manifested in regards to that which is labeled "floyd's daughter"? Of course. What is absent is the love of self ... the pride in self ... the notion that some "Super Father" really exists who has "created" a "Super Child." What is also absent, therefore, is any "Super Parent" making perfec-tionist demands that someone must play flawlessly the role of "Super Daughter" in order to sustain the phony role of a flawless   Moreover, with the post-Realization absence of a <u>"mind,"</u> "The Thinker" will vanish, as will all of the chatter that rattles about in the heads of the non-Realized. That head-noise will necessarily end (as will a seeking out of loud, ambient noises) since there will no longer be a device by which that former process of "thinking" took place and since there will no longer be a need to try to escape the unbearable sounds of insanity.

Furthermore, what was thought to be an unshakable source of peace and strength will be seen to have been an illusion. The evidence was there before because the "supposedly unshakable" was thoroughly shaken when put to an actual test.

Those testifying to sufferers that they need but put their faith in what the testifiers describe as an "unshakable power" were able to talk with conviction until it came time for them to face their own misery and suffering and relative challenges.

Then, more often than not, the whines began as the sufferers asked why the power had forsaken them (even as they continued to testify from a position of dissociation that they were "doing fine ... hanging tough—tapping into some external, other-world power for comfort").

That which can provide fixation in a state of unshakable peace is that which allows abidance to happen as the original state. It is the tapping into an internal resource which can sustain the unshakable peace. When abidance as that original state manifests, even as the manifestation of consciousness continues for a time, then nothing changes even as everything (relative) changes.

That Which cannot change is That Which You Are ... That Which Is Real. That which can change is the way the relative was formerly perceived to be (when it was not actually that way at all.) With that shift in perception, then the remainder of the manifestation can be—and most certainly will be—enjoyed, post-Realization.

CHAPTER SEVENTEEN

WHEN Reality is not overlaid upon the relative, then the entire existence of the non-Realized will be driven by both conscious and subconscious desires and fears. Personality will rule, and since personas are mirages, then the lives of the non-Realized will always be ruled by delusion.

How did that speck called "maharaj" describe the post-Realization existence? He noted that, when <u>pure awareness</u> happens, then neither needs nor desires exist any longer. Even the attachment to, and glorification of, the "Am-ness" ends. Rather than the "life is precious" argument being one's core belief, the Am-ness is seen as nothing more than "a useful pointer, a direction-indicator" to the Absolute.

Some who believe in concepts will say, "It is only if you are willing to die that you become able to live fully." While their point is understood, the Advaitin's take is that it is by understanding the simplicity of the unmanifestation process and the simplicity of re-absorption into the peace of non-aware awareness which allows the manifestation to pass in peace and to happen spontaneously.

To "identify with" the awareness even as the manifestation continues will make clear that the unmanifestation process is nothing more than "crossing over" into a state that You are abiding as already; therefore, there can be no fear of "change" or "loss" and no effort exerted to try to assure "eternal reward" over "eternal punishment."

For those who erroneously believe that they were born and who therefore fear "dying," Realization offers a "try before you buy" method of understanding which can alleviate all of the mystery and the fear and the desires that trap the non-Realized in their anxiety-producing false beliefs.

Those who are justifying and minimizing their present suffering because they are convinced that they shall receive "a reward of eternal life and eternal bliss later" could be relieved of that misconception and could know the bliss at the only time it can be known … now, during the manifestation, if only they completed <u>all seven steps on the "journey" to Reality.</u>

Once Reality is overlaid on the relative existence Post-Realization, then even awareness of the I AM ends as awareness ItSelf displaces even that by-product of consciousness manifest (specifically, undue concern with the Am-ness). Whatever happens with the Am-ness at that point excites no more interest than standing outside in the sun and having someone step on your shadow.

When Truth is seen, then an always-clear perspective marks the relative. Of course sensible care is provided for the body for whatever period the manifestation continues, but concern for all of those shadows (for all of those shadow-selves) comes to an end.

What prevails is that which cannot be described, that which is beyond words. The pointer is offered here often that the Truth can be understood but cannot be stated. Post-Realization, it is the non-stated Truth—not the formerly-cherished lies—that prevails.

It is then during the period which is post-Realization / post-identification-with-the-Is-ness that the Real is finally seen. It becomes understood that this temporary manifestation of consciousness is nothing more than a fleeting "relocation" from that former state of pure potentiality. It is that state that was prior to manifestation … that was prior to conception.

[It will only be the "most advanced" seekers that grasp what was <u>prior to the Absolute</u>.]

Maharaj taught that an understanding of the Absolute (of the pure awareness) guarantees the further understanding that the Am-ness—and all that is perceived as "this world" or "this universe"—are mere reflections of That. "It is this reality which a jnani has realised," he said.

The state that Maharaj discussed is the state that came into being after an atom entered into what can be called "The Void." Understand that abidance as the Absolute / the unmanifested awareness certainly provides peace during the remainder of the manifestation; however, it is only the "most advanced" who will abide as the pre-Absolute Nothingness state. Imagine the level of non-attached freedom and peace that can mark the relative if identification with some Infinite (Absolute) Self gives way to abiding as … nothing … as The original Nothingness. Nothing can ever be bothered by anything.

Consider the degree to which the relative will unfold in a natural and spontaneous manner when there is no attachment to any identity, which also means that there can be no attachment to outcome involving any relative happening.

Only those attached to Am-ness control and to Is-ness power will find such a pointer to be an abomination, refusing to forfeit their delusional notions about a self that is able to dominate others and about a self that can have "power now."

[Witness there the slaughtering of another very popular sacred cow with the debunking of that concept of "power now." WHO wants power? To what end?]

Alongside the invitation to consider the pointer above regarding non-attachment is an additional understanding offered by Maharaj: understand that no person is addressing seekers and understand that questions happen and that answers happen … that is all that is going on. Only persons believe they can attach to anything and that they are talking to persons. It is consciousness that speaks when Reality is overlaid on the relative.

That is not unlike the pointer offered here that "husbanding can happen without an assumption of the ego-state of 'The Husband'." Only then is there no attachment to the player of the co-dependent counterpart to that illusory role, a co-dependent counterpart that is always required for the belief in any role to continue.

After understanding that no persons are involved, then "husbanding" or "wifing" can happen … or not. In a conversation with a couple that had enrolled in the enneagram classes offered here, it was shown that both had been driven blindly throughout their entire existence; that he had not the slightest clue about Who / What He Is, that she had not the slightest clue about Who / What She Is, and that neither had the slightest clue about the bogus nature of "love" or the true nature of Real Love.

As both considered whether or not they had even the slightest desire to remain married, the suggestion was that—before they race off to find a lawyer and a divorce court—they might try one alternate approach.

It was explained, "Before trying to settle such issues as child custody, disposition of jointly-owned property, etc., you might both try something different first. See, you've been married to the not-Him; you've been married to the not-Her; and you've both been attached to not-Love.

"If a marriage were to evolve in which a Real Self and a Real Self and Real Love are all manifested, You might find the resulting relationship to be rather pleasant, relatively speaking. Of course, that's just a suggestion."

If such Reality is overlaid upon the relative, then that which persons call "a healthy relationship" can have a far greater chance of happening.

Chapter Eighteen

ALSO, when the Reality is overlaid on the relative, the Realized can most certainly feel but can no longer emote.

One definition of "emote" is "to display strong emotions, especially when acting." Another is "to express emotion, especially in an excessive or theatrical or histrionic manner." A third is "to become emotional and enter into a state of mental agitation or disturbance."

Post-Realization, all acting ends, all histrionics end, and mental agitation and disturbance end because the fiction-and-nonsense-filled "mind" that was the seat of all mental agitation and disturbance has dissolved.

Feeling without such emoting happen only when the fifth of seven steps on the "journey" to Realization is reached. Emotions happen only among (a) the non-Realized who are identified with ego-states or among (b) seekers that are earnestly on the "path" but have not moved beyond the first, second, or third steps.

After reaching the witnessing step, then it is still possible to "feel"—the Realized do not become "robotic" or "cold" or "unfeeling" as some believe. At that point on the "path," feelings are watched as they rise and as they fall, but they do not trigger emotional intoxication.

Emotional intoxication can only happen when an ego-state is supported by egotism (as well as a host of other ego-defense mechanisms) and when an ego-state believes that it has been interfered with or threatened or challenged.

For example, when one believes that he is "The Husband" and is therefore co-dependent on "The Spouse" for his very "existence," then emotional intoxication can result when words such as "I'm leaving" or "I don't love you anymore" are heard.

Though what is ending is just a false role—a role dreamed up by a culture—the person / persona will think that it is dying; that thought will trigger a reaction—an emotion—that will lead to a series of actions and reactions that trap the person in a state of misery and suffering which often leads to suicide or murder or both.

Even those seeking earnestly but who are not yet free of the belief in false identities can experience considerable angst on the "path."

Thousands over the years have enrolled in the <u>Understanding Personality Via the Enneagram Sessions</u> and hundreds more during Advaita Retreats have completed the enneagram test and have been guided to freedom from attachment to false identification with personality.

But during the process, ego-states will "fight to the finish" even as persons begin to drop their beliefs in certain false identities but continue to cling to the ones that they believe have best served them throughout their existence. They refuse to see the toll paid even when such identities drove thoughts and words and deeds and produced (relative) harm and / or self-destructive behaviors.

While there are no stereotypical patterns—seekers of either sex being capable of exposing the same behaviors when trapped in ego and egotism—some males over the years have appeared to be in shock when invited to abandon the role of "The Boss" or "The One in Control" or "The Aggressive Macho One." (Yes, the same has happened with females.)

As they actually face the prospect of casting aside <u>a false state-of-being-whatever–they-yet-cling-to</u> as an identity, some have been witnessed to perspire profusely; some have been driven to stand up and walk about; some have had to leave the room or the retreat; some experience a panic-attack, so convinced they are that they cannot survive without continuing to play a macho role, a take-charge role, or a role intent on controlling things and "the world" and the people that they want to dominate.

Some, especially those who have been sexually-abused as children, balk at the suggestion to abandon the role of "The Super Lover," "The Super Stud," or "The Super Seductress."

They have become convinced (as a result of the long-term influence of an "instinctual variant" to their primary personality type) that their very "self-preservation" is dependent upon the continued use of sex to manipulate and to gain housing, food, clothing, money, attention, respect, power, control, and other things imagined to be "necessities" or "the finer things in life."

Their sense of entitlement often reinforces the "positive" view they hold of their past "success" of using the body to get what they want, so they are often trapped in that role and will play it to the end of the manifestation. They will never know the Reality or the joy of overlaying Real Love on the sex act. Nor will they know the pure pleasure of such love/Love activity because they will only be engaged in it for manipulation and "gain."

To invite them to break the attachment to their body identification as well as to the personas that they subconsciously and consciously believe "have gotten them through life so far" is tantamount to inviting them to commit suicide, at least in their "minds."

Some in this group have also been seen to perspire, to feel knots tighten in the stomach, to feel a shortness of breath, and even to cry in many cases. When Reality is overlaid on the relative, even the causes of crying undergoes a shift.

Those people described above are crying over the "death of a mirage" ... over the death of an image ... over the potential loss of what they take to be the source of their greatest relative power. Their crying is ego-based. Their crying is based in self-absorption.

Their crying is based in total self-ishness, in the delusion that they are really losing something which was actually nothing more than a mirage to begin with but which was a mirage that had the ability to control their thoughts and words and actions and the thoughts and words and actions of "others." In using "others," they simultaneously used and abused themselves and allowed others to use them, but few will ever awake to that reality.

They are mourning an imaginary "loss" that nevertheless seems real because certain roles have been played for so long (and have garnered selfish, relative "results" and have allowed them to gain what they desire and to evade what they fear) that the abandonment of the use of what their egos take to be their most-effective tool triggers a sense of vulnerability, powerlessness, interference, hurt, and even death.

Can the feelings among the Realized trigger tears? Of course, but the Realized cry over nothing that is self-based. The Realized might cry over what is based in an awareness of the Oneness, feeling what the abused feel, feeling what the oppressed feel, feeling what the molested or injured or battered feel.

What can register via the unblocked consciousness among the Realized is not "another's pain" (which is about the physical body) but is a registration of the "mind"-based and emotion-based misery and suffering of the masses.

When seekers read the book" FROM THE I TO THE ABSOLUTE (A Seven-Step Journey to Reality"), or when they attend an Advaita retreat, the very last ego-state to go might be those mentioned above ("The Lover," "The

Controller," or "The Seductress"). More often than not, however, the last false identities to go are "The Religious Person" or "The Spiritual Giant" and then "The Seeker" as well.

When duality drives persons to replace their former "bad" roles with either or both of those two "good" roles, then the invitation to cast aside belief in any and all roles has a hollow ring. As much arrogance and self-deception and sense of "separation" will be engendered by those two "good" roles as by any of their former "bad" roles, yet they will cling to those identities and will be driven by them.

Only if those roles are transitioned can a shift to the fourth step on "the journey" happen. Only if all seven steps are completed can the "journey" to Full Realization be completed, and only then can Reality be overlaid on the relative.

CHAPTER NINETEEN

IT has been said that when Reality is overlaid on the relative, then freedom happens. Why, then, do so few seek that freedom? Because most are dreaming that they are free and will never awaken from the dream and know the degree to which they are imprisoned.

The masses are absorbed in denial, are playing "spin doctor," are minimizing their misery, and are constantly upgrading or downgrading their illusions, so nothing can follow except entrapment in delusion and distortion.

What else could follow all of that except living an existence that is dominated by "The Dilemma That the Relative Is"? What exactly is a "dilemma" and why does that characterize the relative existence so accurately?

From the Greek "di" meaning two combined with "lemma"—referring in this case to "an ambiguous assumption or proposition or problem"—the association of the relative with duality and ambiguity and problems and conceptualized assumptions is clear.

By referring to "a state of uncertainty or perplexity, especially as requiring a choice between equally unfavorable options," then the concept-based dilemma of the relative existence become clear. It should also be clear why there can be no peace or freedom or sanity when persons are attached to an existence that is marked by "dualistic problems":

Are late-term abortions to be considered acceptable, or should doctors offering the service be assassinated?

Are Christians to be allowed to "go to the four corners of the planet and convert all to Christianity," or is the world to be one giant theocracy where everyone either converts to Islam or dies?

Should everyone live according to the dictates of right-wing fundamentalists or according to the beliefs of those attached to left-wing beliefs?

Should spouses or partners bring to their relationship the unconscious repetition of parental patterns and beliefs, or should they abandon those patterns and beliefs and adopt the ones being brought to the relationship by their mates in order to "keep the peace and sustain the relationship?"

Thus, the relative existence can be seen by definition to be nothing more than a "problem of duality," fitting the definitions of "dilemma" exactly:

Dilemmas are "'problems rooted in doubles' where two possibilities are presented though neither is practical nor acceptable"; or a dilemma is "a situation in which persons are called on to make a choice between two disagreeable, undesirable or unfavorable alternatives"; or "a situation that requires a choice between options that are or seem equally unfavorable or mutually exclusive"; or "a fallacy of oversimplification that offers a limited number of options (usually two) when in reality more options should be available for consideration," as in this actual quote:

"Either you become a good Christian and forget that Advaita crap or we're getting a divorce." The basic "Dilemma That the Relative Is" is that it is based in dualistic concepts and is plagued by one dilemma after another. The problems come when persons (trapped as they always are in their dualistic beliefs and concepts) try to fit the square peg of the relative into the round hole of the Absolute.

It cannot fit. For persons (i.e., the non-Realized) to try to overlay their relative, dualistic concepts onto the Absolute results in the lunacy of their claiming that "I know what is always right and I know what is always wrong and I can explain it to you in an inerrant and unequivocal manner ... in no uncertain terms."

The further result is that the non-Realized live out a life marked with the mental and emotional illness that is referred to here as "The Goldilocks Syndrome"; therefore, the non-Realized move through the relative existence with the belief that absolutes can apply and can produce perfect results and can provide perfect fulfillment of all relative desires:

"That woman is too hot but that other one is too cold. I want one that is just right."

"That Christian denomination is too liberal and that Christian denomination is too fundamental. We need to find one that is a perfect balance in between."

"Either this Muslim sect or that Muslim sect is right about who the true descendants of Muhammad really are, and all of the members of the opposite sect must be destroyed to make a perfect world."

"Either you follow our dictates exactly or you go to hell … we are the only ones who know the perfect way to live."

What are some of the dilemmas you have faced that are nothing more than conceptualized, dualistic "problems?" What experiences have you had where you were trapped in the "too-this and too-that and just-right" mentality that was displayed by the child Goldilocks who could only be pleased if everything was "just right"?

CHAPTER TWENTY

WHEN Reality is not overlaid on the relative, then the most fundamental aspects of the relative existence will guarantee (a) belief in nonsensical dualities; (b) instability rather than steadiness; (c) the restlessness of doingness rather than the freedom of beingness; and (d) dilemmas to deal with rather than detachment.

Furthermore, look not to the consciousness to provide a respite. So many Advaitin seekers overvalue the consciousness, missing out on the bliss of <u>pure awareness</u> and ignoring the fact that the consciousness will be ever-in-motion as long as it is manifested.

It is no accident that "motion" and "emotion" are akin, both of which lead to the kind of going-doing-zooming existence that sets the stage for entrapment in a state of emotional intoxication. Yes, the unblocked consciousness is the vehicle that can be used to reach that state of pure awareness even as the manifestation of consciousness continues, but it cannot be the actual basis of peace and freedom from chaos.

Peace and freedom and joy and bliss lie beyond the relative and beyond the consciousness and, most assuredly, beyond the "mind." The "mind" is nothing more than a repository of falsehoods and operates in tandem with the consciousness that is ever in motion (and therefore ever in an emotional state as well).

Even that Self, which so many also overrate, is impacted when the consciousness becomes nothing more than the programmed or conditioned facet of the True Self. So many seekers have been misled to believe that they can take the steps required to free the "mind" of the effects of conditioning and thereafter be at peace.

But there is no such thing as <u>"peace of mind"</u>. That which is at the root of angst and misery and suffering cannot possibly be the antidote for angst and misery and suffering. To know joy and bliss, the "mind" must go while the unblocked consciousness remains. You are invited to understand that even the

FLOYD HENDERSON

unconditioned "mind" is a facet of consciousness, but the bliss of pure awareness is far beyond that.

Here is an additional pointer that few seekers will ever grasp: the True Nature of Reality lies beyond Self-Realisation, and peace every day manifests not when identified with the consciousness but when abiding as THAT and then eventually abiding as That Which Is even beyond THAT.

(A pointer for seekers far along "the path": The ultimate bliss and unassailable peace awaits only beyond THAT, beyond that which many still use as an assumed identity. That "new" identification slings them right back into the trap of personality, even as they claim to have found a "non-personal identity."

It is only when abiding as <u>the no-concept, no-identity Nothingness</u> that the dilemma-less peace and unwavering stability can happen during the period of the manifestation of consciousness. For more on those topics, see the books CONSCIOUSNESS / AWARENESS and FROM THE ABSOLUTE TO THE NOTHINGNESS.)

Maharaj explained it thusly: "I am not the entity that imagines itself." That includes any imagining (which still involves a "mind" and consciousness in motion). While the True Self is that which is engaged in Pure Witnessing, the point was made that if one were to stand motionless, as during the witnessing process, what is finally seen is that "the Self" is even beyond the witness and that peace is even beyond the Self.

Regarding the Nothingness mentioned above as well as regarding that which is required to guarantee a "motionless" existence, Maharaj said:

"The three states rotate as usual - there is waking and sleeping and waking again, but they do not happen to Me. They just happen. To Me nothing ever happens. There is something changeless, motionless, immovable, rocklike, unassailable; a solid mass of pure being-consciousness-bliss. I am never out of it. Nothing can take Me out of it, no torture, no calamity."

In other words, not a thing associated with the relative existence nor anything associated with the manifested consciousness will provide access to the stability and peace and freedom that all seek (though most never even know that stability and peace and freedom are missing).

And that is what it is like to walk about in a dream, thinking one is awake, and that walking about in a dream while thinking one is awake is what assures a never-ending stream of dualistic dilemmas when Reality is not overlaid on the relative.

CHAPTER TWENTY-ONE

WHEN Reality is overlaid on the relative, then acceptance of the limited identification with the body ends. That does not mean that caring for the body ends during the remainder of the manifestation. Nor does it mean that no pleasures can happen via the body.

It simply means that there is no longer the notion that "this is what I am … this physical body." Identification with the "mind" ends also, as does any further belief in the concepts that have been stored in the "mind." As noted here on many occasions, there is no such thing as "your mind."

You have not come up with one single thought, belief, idea, or concept that is unique to you. Every concept stored in the "mind" was acquired in a home, in a school, in a culture, and—for the majority of persons on the planet—in a church or temple or mosque or synagogue.

So you have no mind of your own. It is "their mind." Anything in it was put there by "them." Now, you are walking about with "their mind" thinking that it is your mind and believing that the beliefs and values and ideas stored therein are yours and that they help define "who you are."

In fact, it defines who you are not, but thinking that it defines who you are, you will be blocked from any possibility of Realizing Self, much less understanding that which is beyond self and Self. To live under "their" influence leaves persons as powerless (and ultimately as hopeless) as living under the influence of anything else.

Next, when Reality is overlaid on the relative, then there are no more personas that are unrealistically assumed as identities. Furthermore, the effects of the basic personality type or types that blindly and unconsciously drive all persons (all of the non-Realized) dissolve.

If the effects of personality are not understood, then Reality will never be overlaid upon the relative.

Until persons complete the personality inventory which is used here to identify the personality type(s) which have been controlling them and driving them all of their lives, then they will continue to be clueless about why they—and others—do what they do, especially when what they do is self-destructive and self-defeating, relatively speaking.

Persons will have no freedom or peace or happiness unless they understand the way that personality has controlled them and unless they see that every thought and word and deed throughout their entire relative existence has matched exactly the thought patterns, speaking patterns and behavior patterns of every other person with whom they share that personality type (or those types) in common.

Those who egotistically disagree, believing that they have been making conscious decisions and being convinced that they have always had the power to choose, will never have the slightest clue of how powerless their personality leaves them.

Persons can spend thousands of hours in self-help endeavors, in group encounters, in counseling that ignores the effects of personality, and / or in any of the other avenues that persons use to try to find freedom and peace and happiness, but it will all be for naught.

Furthermore, those who have studied personality and "personality traits" will assert that at least 1/3 of those traits are "assets" though 2/3 might be liabilities. Their assertion would only be true among persons who have "integrated," who are not stressed, and who are not arrogant—all three of which leave persons trapped in "the liability side" of personality.

Yet the masses on the planet are not "integrated," are stressed, and are arrogant—trapped in ego-states and subconsciously using ego-defense mechanisms to defend their false personas / personalities.

To understand personality and the way that it drives persons can open the door for them to understand for the first time ever how their personality has always driven them and always controlled their thoughts and words and deeds. That awareness reveals the extent to which personality mars the relative existence and can inspire one to begin to seek freedom from personality.

For example: it is only if persons living under the influence of the Type Three personality can understand why they unconsciously think and talk and behave as they do that they can stop their habit of putting a delusional "spin" on events and thereafter stop the self-deception that follows. Type Threes have been heard recently saying the following, all of which are typical Type Three statements:

"That was the third job I lost because of sexual misconduct, but to hell with 'em. There's only God's will and this is just His way of closing one door so he can open another door for me and move me to something even better."

"Actually, when that man mugged me and beat me, he was doing me a favor. It has made me a stronger person."

"The loss of life and property from these tornadoes is a gift … God is trying to tell us something, and we better accept His gift and listen."

The Three's self-deception is often misclassified by listeners as evidence of "optimism." Be not deceived. It is not optimism but it is the delusional distortion of facts, and distortion and delusion and denial of self-destructive behavior patterns (or the actual continuing effects of certain events) will block all opportunity to see what is driving a person, will block any chance of abandoning behavior patterns that are (relatively) harmful, and will guarantee a relative existence that is being driven by subconscious nonsense.

Such subconscious nonsense will insure that destructive patterns of thoughts and words and actions will continue when this type minimizes the facts by use of the dualistic expression "it's all good"; therefore, the untreated residual effects of trauma will also continue to impact every aspect of their lives because they are denying that the impact even exists.

Is it any wonder that Advaitins for centuries have invited persons to be free of the influence of personality? The inspiration that can manifest from being aware of the way that personality has been the driving force throughout an entire relative existence can motivate persons to take the necessary steps to be free of personality and its effects. Afterwards, the "journey" to Full Realization can be completed.

Only then can Reality be overlaid on the relative, and only if Reality is overlaid on the relative can an end come to being driven by personality disorders, by false identities, and by hidden agendas that prevent peace and happiness.

Please visit
FloydHenderson.com
&
advaitavedantameditations.blogspot.com
Other of the author's books are available through
Amazon
in the U.S.
and
in the U.K.
and
in Germany

CPSIA information can be obtained at www.ICGtesting.com
Printed in the USA
LVOW121717090312

272172LV00007B/4/P